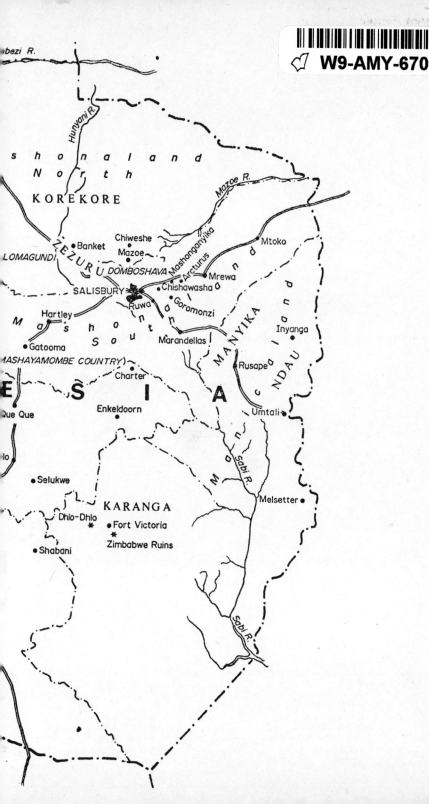

An Ill-Fated People

AN ILL-FATED PEOPLE

Zimbabwe before and after Rhodes

by
Lawrence Vambe

With a Foreword by Doris Lessing

UNIVERSITY OF PITTSBURGH PRESS

First published in England in 1972 by
William Heinemann Ltd
15 Queen St. Mayfair, London W1X 8BE

Library of Congress Catalog Card Number 72–87477

ISBN 0–8229–3256–3

Endpaper map supplied by G. Hartfield Ltd.

The photograph on the jacket is used by kind permission of the
Rhodesian Mission of the Society of Jesus

Printed in Great Britain by
Redwood Press Limited
Trowbridge, Wiltshire

To all my oppressed people
in Zimbabwe

Contents

Acknowledgements

This book expresses my personal point of view of the Rhodesian situation and I accept full responsibility for all its contents. But in writing it I have had considerable inspiration and encouragement from several people. My first draft was read and commented upon by two members of my own family, my daughter, Elizabeth, and son-in-law the Hon. Stephen Pollock. Their reactions were that I had a story worth telling and that I should persevere with it. Their corrections and suggestions were extremely useful.

The next person was Mrs Doris Lessing. I met Mrs Lessing in Salisbury shortly after the Second World War and through the now defunct Rhodesian Labour Party, of which we were both members, I became aquainted with her views on the black and white problem in my country. Her writings need no pen of mine to commend them to anyone. But for me she is, and always has been, one of the most admirable and highly regarded people to have been nurtured in the otherwise poisoned atmosphere of my fatherland. It was therefore something of a moment of personal triumph when I managed to place my manuscript in her hands. She in turn not only gave me all the professional advice I needed, but also found the publishers for this book. It was most appropriate and a real privilege for me that she should agree to write the foreword to this book. My debt of gratitude to her is beyond any words that I could find to express it.

Last, but by no means least, is Dr Richard Gray, of the School of Oriental and African Studies, London University. Dr Gray has been a friend of many years standing. His appraisal of the manuscript, based on his deep knowledge of this part of Africa, was of great value. I am deeply indebted to him.

I have dedicated this book to all my people in Zimbabwe. But I particularly wish to mention one man as a tribute to his contribution to the cause of freedom for which he died. He is the late Mr Leopold Takawira who died in 1970 in Mr Smith's prison, reportedly from diabetes. We went to school and grew up to manhood together. His death was as much a personal loss to me as it was to all my oppressed fellow men. I am convinced that he did not die for nothing.

Lawrence C. Vambe

London, 1971.

THE NEW RHODESIA

Events in Africa change swiftly. Since this book was written, the British Government and the Smith regime have reached a 'settlement'. Like all the other previous decisions about Rhodesia, this agreement is between white men. The black majority was ignored. As one of these people, I will need a great deal more than just glib phrases and promises to convince me that this 'settlement' is not a licence, granted by Her Majesty's Government, to white Rhodesia to entrench white supremacy and perpetuate its system of racial discrimination. What an appalling colonial legacy for Britain to leave to the peoples of Africa!

I hope history can prove me wrong.

Lawrence Vambe

26th November 1971

Foreword

It was painful reading this book. I hope it will be painful for other white people to read. I hope particularly that it will be read by the white-skinned British, who are responsible for the double-dealing, the negligence, the cruelty, the atrocities described here. Africans in Rhodesia think of us as the victims of Nazi oppression thought of the Nazis, and so will we be remembered by them, so will we figure in their history. The indictment is being made now—*An Ill-Fated People* is part of it.

We see history as events described in print. This is an attitude so ingrained in us that few Europeans seem able to step outside it. To us a verbal tradition is not 'history'. A book written by a professor who has got his facts from the custodian of a verbal tradition is history, and is treated with respect. Only last week I heard a literary man say dismissingly of verbal records that 'they contradict each other', just as if 'historians'—that is, people who write books—don't contradict each other. 'History' is what is written, breeding other books, textbooks, essays; it is taught in universities and schools, and becomes part of a country's view of itself and the world. It only becomes verbal again in the catchphrases and commonplaces of the street and the home. These are most often expressions of national pride and prejudice. 'An Englishman's word is his bond.' 'Britons never shall be slaves.' 'The British make the fairest administrators.' European nations have no verbal tradition in the sense that an African would understand it. Up and down Africa, history is kept carefully in the minds of black men and women chosen by their heredity, or because of their suitability, for this task. This is how history has always been kept by them, as record, story, legend, in traditions of healing, good government, the life of the tribe in nature. Some of these traditional custodians of oral history are writing down those parts of it which they have decided white people may know, but we, the white people, should remember that the history of the professors and the universities is often quite different from what Africans are recording, memorizing, cherishing, and which they will allow us to know only when we have shed our prejudices and our white man's feeling of superiority.

Lawrence Vambe is the grandson of the Chief of his tribe, and has had access all his life to the records and the knowledge of his people. He is a Mashona, and his accounts of Shona history are not what is generally taught.

The Mashona are the main tribe of Rhodesia. Unlike the Matabele, descendants of the Zulus, they were not organized for war, but for agriculture and the arts of peace. The white people in Rhodesia teach their children (and the Africans in the schools) that the Mashona people were helpless victims of Ndebele aggression, and that therefore the white people were in the right to take Rhodesia, which act protected the Mashona from the Matabele. This view is not shared by Mr Vambe, and the Shona historians.

I was brought up in Rhodesia, from the age of five to nearly thirty—1924 to 1949. I am roughly the same age as Lawrence Vambe. I was the daughter of a white settler, member of an oppressing minority then numbering a hundred thousand. My parents bought from the Government for a few shillings an acre, land off which the Africans had been moved to free it for 'white development'. That is, the Africans whose land it was were forcibly moved off it—by physical violence.

This is not how the white people who 'settled' the country saw the process. They saw themselves as 'civilized', being white; while the black people were savage, and indeed benefitting from contact with these superior beings.

The Africans were put into Native Reserves. The Native Reserves of Rhodesia, like those of South Africa, had, and have, the poorest soil, the least water, the worst of everything, from roads to shops. It is almost impossible to convey to people in Britain what a Native Reserve is like. The nearest to it is perhaps Dartmoor, imagined hot and arid. On it are scattered groups of mud and grass huts, and a store, which is a brick room selling cloth goods and the cheapest of groceries. There are no good roads, telephones, cinemas, facilities for sport or recreation. Into these deserts, completely cut off from modern life, are forcibly herded people whose way of life before the white man came was as wide, variegated, full of potential, as Africa itself. The white people began to steal the land as soon as they arrived in the country. They now have taken more than half of it, are always taking more and more and more.

It happened that Lawrence Vambe's people, the VaShawasha, were close to Salisbury, the capital city, and they suffered an early dislocation by contact with the white man. Mr Vambe is particularly well-equipped to describe at first hand the drastic effects of 'white civilization' on tribal life. A black man once said to me : 'We Africans have never seen the white man's face, we have only seen his backside.' Mr Vambe is also qualified to write of an experience shared by nearly all the present leaders and administrators of independent Africa—he had a Mission education. In his case, it was the famous Rhodesian mission, the Chishawasha Mission, run by the Roman Catholics. I remember visiting it one Sunday afternoon. It was a pleasant excursion for white people who wanted a focal point for a drive out of the city. The white Fathers of the Mission always welcomed white visitors, since they were trying to influence the white citizens (who were the ones with the vote) into approving of education for the blacks. For there was no education in the early days of Southern Rhodesia, except what the Missions provided. The whites believed that an educated 'munt' or 'kaffir' or 'nigger' or 'Jim Fish' was 'spoiled' because 'he got ideas into his head' and 'always got above himself'.

A white person visiting that Mission was like someone visiting a game reserve. For one thing, for most white people it would be the first time they had ever met a black person who was not a servant or in some way in their employ. I remember troops of well-drilled obedient boys and girls, who stood to attention, sat down, stood up, curtsied, filed off, at the orders of the Fathers.

I remember, too, how beautiful a landscape it was, fresh, well-watered, scattered with the homes of the VaShawasha people—as lovely a place as Lawrence Vambe's description of it.

Being so rich and fertile, it was inevitable that it would be taken away from the Africans—I hear that Smith and his bullyboys are engaged in dismembering what remains of Lawrence Vambe's people, and forcing them into the Reserves, or into the African ghettoes of the white towns.

Reading this book has made all sorts of memories and thoughts breed together in my mind.

One is this.

I visited East Germany in 1952, and spoke to Germans who had been exiled in America during the war, and who had returned. A woman said to me: 'All through the war we were told about the atrocities and the camps, and we saw every German as a monster, like cartoons of wickedness. Then I came home and they were all just people, like the Americans I had left. They saw themselves as victims. They talked about their sufferings, and when I asked about the extermination camps they either said it was all propaganda, or that they had known nothing about them.'

Another thought is that every one of the public butchers of our time, from Eichmann up and down, has seen himself or herself as a good citizen, equipped with civic virtues. Murderers and exterminators may be good husbands and fathers, may love Beethoven and poetry, may be cultured and educated people. They give to charity and pay their taxes—and obey orders.

The white men and women of the district of Banket, Lomagundi, of Southern Rhodesia, now Rhodesia, among whom I was brought up, were all good people. That is, they were no better nor worse than any handful of white people you could pick out of a crowd. Rather better in many ways, since every one had left a safe and narrow rut of a life out of a sense of adventure and a need to widen horizons, for a country to them wild and often dangerous. It cannot be said that they were a cultivated or wide-minded people, for most fitted Olive Schreiner's definition of the South Africans of her time as 'a nation of petty bourgeois philistines'. They still do. But to each other, they were kind, generous, hospitable. Nearly all were religious, that is to say, church-goers. To their black servants, labourers, the African population they ruled, they used the behaviour for which the world calls people Fascist and Nazi. At their best, they were (are) not as kind to a black man or a woman as one might be to a dog or a cat.

Just before I left Rhodesia, I remember how something struck me—forcibly and for the first time. It was this. That I had spent fifteen years arguing, day in, day out, with my family and almost all the white people I knew, about the monstrousness of the society we lived in. All that argument had not changed anybody's mind by a fraction. People's minds are not changed by argument. What does change attitudes? Recent research shows that in any group of people, one third are impervious to reason —that is, once they have made up their minds, nothing will change them. In places like Rhodesia, where opinion is continually reinforced by strong self-interest, the percentage must be ninety-nine. What can sometimes (not often) change the opinions of white racists, is not argument, fact, statistics, but taking him out of his environment and exposing him, or her, to different ideas. But some people believe all their lives what they were taught as children. A white Rhodesian or South African has sucked in with his bottle-milk that he is better than a black man, and has the right to order him about. He has never been able to treat a person with a dark skin as human. The indoctrination starts from childhood. A white child may see his parents accelerate a car along a road just behind a group of Africans travelling on foot, to scare them, 'just for the hell of it'. A white child is taught to shout orders at a black man or woman who may well be old enough to be his grandparent, to call him 'boy', or 'hey there!' A white person treats any black person in sight as there to serve him, whether personally employed by him or not.

The customs, taboos, conventions were (still are) irrational and silly, and no wonder that the black people conclude the white man is mad as well as wicked. For instance, the precious white children are cradled, nursed and loved by black women, but once at school age, may not touch black flesh. A black man or woman may wait upon white people in the most intimate and personal ways, but if one was to sit down in a chair in a white house, the society would rock. To detail the sheer irrational perversity of 'white civilization' is a task best left to—the black writers. There have been, there are, many white writers recording disagreement and criticism of what they were brought up in, but not one has written with as sharp a dislike, as vivid a criticism, as Lawrence Vambe.

It is possible for a white person to have disliked 'white civilization' ever since one came to see it at all—and still to miss, not only detail, but basics. For instance, the Mashona Rebellion, whose suppression is the most painful part of this book. That war was the parent of modern Rhodesia. It crushed, humiliated, degraded the Africans—degraded and corrupted the whites. It was so shameful that the truth about it was suppressed. I don't remember it being mentioned in my childhood, except as a thing of long ago, of 'history'. Yet that war was yesterday, in the eighteen-nineties, only thirty years before my childhood. It was not until I read Olive Schreiner (revered as a writer by white South Africans who admire her fame, but would be shocked if they actually took the trouble to read her) that I learned the truth about that most ruthless of wars of conquest. 'The Rebellion', to the whites of Rhodesia, was and is an incident during which 'we' fought with bravery against treacherous savages—an incident in an imaginary epic story called 'The White Occupation of Rhodesia', concocted by the whites to flatter the whites.

I shall tell again an incident which I have written down before, but which I have brooded about for forty years and still think about. It seems to me to hold in a small space the essence of the split mind, the double standards, which make it possible for people who believe themselves to be decent and principled to lose all humanity, to behave with savagery towards those different from themselves.

It was when I was ten or so. A white woman who was religious, charitable and kindly had sat up every night for a week to nurse a small black child, a servant's son. He had pneumonia, due to the cold damp hut he lived in, and he was in any case suffering from malnutrition. She did not see this poverty as her responsibility, for the white people of Rhodesia, like the rich Victorians with the poor, or slave-owners with their slaves, hate and despise the black people for the degradation they—the whites—have created and maintain them in. But she nursed the child with devotion. He died, and the white woman was miserable about it.

The same week, on a nearby farm which belonged to a white farmer known to everyone as particularly 'tough with his workers', this happened. The white man was missing some soap, and he decided that his cook had stolen it. The cook said that he had not. The white man, after the usual sermons about honesty, tied the black man to a tree and ordered his (black) bossboy, or overseer, to beat him with a hide whip. But the cook would not 'confess'. The white farmer untied him from a tree, tied him to his horse, and made him run in the dust several miles. But the cook still refused to give in. He was again tied to the tree, until sunset, without food or water. He was then released from the tree and sent back to the compound for the night. Now, he could easily have run away to the Portuguese border, which was quite close, as many dissatisfied workers did, or those in trouble with authority, staying there until things had cooled down. Or he could have run away from the farm. But next morning he presented himself to the farmer, saying that he had not stolen the soap. Whereupon the farmer tied him to the tree, had him beaten, and again left him there all day ... but the man never 'confessed'. The farmer, defeated, at last said: 'I've taught you a lesson, I've taught you to be honest.' The man continued to work for the farmer, who told this tale all around the district, as a boast of his skill in 'handling kaffirs'. The woman who had sat up for a week of nights with the sick black child and who had wept at its death, heard the tale with approval, and quoted it to everybody she met with, 'That's the right way to treat them.'

We all know this by now: that it is possible, indeed, common, for groups and nations to behave like monsters while preserving a flattering image of themselves. This knowledge is what our horrible epoch teaches us most often and relentlessly. Good kind white Americans wipe out red indians, lynch negroes, commit genocide in Vietnam. Delightful Australians wipe out aborigines. Good kind decent British, our kith and kin, run one of the world's nastiest police states, in Rhodesia. In South America civilized governments deliberately exterminate Indian tribes to get their land. A great European nation massacres five million Jews . . . and so it goes on. We 'know' it; it could almost be described as a cliché—since we describe as clichés things heard often, not things necessarily understood or digested. Perhaps we shouldn't say that we 'know' a thing until we behave as if we know it—until we are able at least to wonder in what ways our blindness is working now? Where is our myopia operating as we read yet another record of stupid brutality—like this one, of British behaviour in Rhodesia, from our conquest of that country until now?

Various points to remember:

One. Britain, that is, *we,* are responsible for the state of affairs in Rhodesia. We could have stopped what was happening at any time—we had the full legal right to do so. The Africans were always expecting us to do so. At every private gathering of black people, every public meeting, always, everywhere, you would hear : 'When the white people in Britain know how we are being treated, they will help us.' But the white people in Britain were not interested, were indifferent, would not listen. Rhodesia is one of the most beautiful, the richest, countries in the world. It is being ruled by an arrogant mediocrity, Ian Smith—because we allowed this to happen.

Two. The white ruling minority in Rhodesia still numbers two hundred thousand. There are five million Africans. Rhodesia is the size of Spain. The white people who speak for Rhodesia and Rhodesians in print, on the air, on television, have spent their entire lives being waited on by black people, who they believe are inferior, whose languages they do not speak, whose culture and history they do not know, and whose feelings they have always ignored, or insulted.

Three. The fact that black people, in groups or as nations, are likely to behave as badly as white people is not something we are in a position to criticize. No modern black nation has approached the savagery of Germany's recent history, or even the horrors of Vorster's South Africa, or Smith's Rhodesia.

Four. White people visiting Southern Africa will no doubt continue to return praising the hospitality, the kindness, the charm, the habits of the white people. It ought to be taught in school, as Civic Lesson Number One, that the way people treat those like themselves, to whom they are bound by obligation, is no measure of how they treat people outside their kind.

Just before the Kenyan war broke out, I met a man who had returned from several weeks of visiting among the white farmers of the Kenyan Highlands. He was preaching, like an article of religion, that it was not possible for there to be 'trouble' in Kenya, because the same farmers were so delightful, so pleasant with their houseboys, and such good hosts. I have no doubt at all it was so. Why not? He repeated these things until the Kikuyu Rebellion, and then, devastated, couldn't understand it. But the point is, it has all happened so often in our time that there isn't any excuse for not understanding it.

Doris Lessing

February 1971

Author's Note

SHONA: This name describes the various tribes living in what is called Mashonaland in modern Rhodesia, who speak dialects which are practically identical. Before the occupation it related to the group of people who belonged to the Monomotapa and Rozwi dynasties in Zimbabwe and parts of Portuguese East Africa. They were divided into six main groups, each with its own dialect: Zezuru (to which the VaShawasha people belonged), Korekore, Manyika, Ndau, Kalanga and Karanga. My guess is that the terms SHONA and MASHONA are a European distortion of MASWINA, which is what my people call themselves to indicate that they belong to the CHISWINA culture and civilization. Thus a single person was MuSwina and many MaSwina, distorted to Mashona.

Except for the Kalanga who have been absorbed by the Ndebeles, the Shona people have changed little in language or customs since the time of the occupation. They are geographically situated as follows: Zezuru, Central Mashonaland; Korekore, Northern Mashonaland; Karanga, Southern Mashonaland; Manyika and Ndau, Eastern Mashonaland or Manicaland.

There are various tribes and clans within each bigger group which are distinguished by *Mutupo,* totem. The VaShawasha people, for instance, have always been known by the totems *Murewha* and *Soko** and it was very important to know a person's totem, essential if marriage was to be permitted. Examples of other tribe names are the VaBudja of the Korekore;

Murewha is an abstract totem. *Soko* is derived from '*Tsoko*' meaning 'monkey'.

the VaMbire of the Zezuru; the VaUngwe of the Manyika, but the whole linguistic and cultural pattern is too complex to analyse fully here.

In all Shona dialects, as in all Bantu languages, unlike European languages such as English, the singular or plural forms of nouns are commonly indicated by the use of specific prefixes. Thus a single person in the Shawasha tribe is a MuShawasha and many are VaShawasha. At the same time 'Va' is used as a mark of respect to an older man or woman or one in authority. Among ourselves our chiefs would always be referred to as 'VaMashonganyika'. Whether 'Mu' and 'Va' should start with a capital letter is a debatable point. Shona language experts do not appear to have reached any agreement on this point. If one wished to be strictly formal in addressing a person, one would use the term 'Changamire' which means 'Mr', 'Sir' etc. But in the majority of cases 'Mu' and 'Va' convey these distinctions. Hence the capital letter in each case would seem to be the proper form.

NDEBELE: I have used the form 'Ndebele' throughout to describe the inhabitants of Matabeleland. 'Matabele' and 'Ndebele' are used interchangeably by the people themselves, though I prefer 'Ndebele'.

I

Early memories of Mashonganyika village, Chishawasha, its dogs and cattle; the pregnant condition of Mandinema causes a family crisis and a quick marriage.

Almost as soon as you began to be able to absorb facts and to recognize human and animal forms you saw dogs everywhere. There was an infinity of dogs, little, big, tame or vicious, dogs whose physical condition largely depended on what they could sniff and scavenge out of the village garbage heap rather than on the generosity and animal-loving nature of their masters. You learnt to talk to them and to know each dog by name, the majority of which were given with some mischievous intent. It was the custom that if you disliked a neighbour you gave your dog a name descriptive of him and his peculiarities, and in that way you provided yourself with a constant outlet for expressing your petty hates, prejudices, even oaths against that person by means of the mute, if innocent dog. Soon enough you got to know that the sole purpose of a dog's life was to hunt and scare away dangerous animals and possibly men in the hours of darkness; beyond this utilitarian function they might as well have been as inanimate as blocks of wood or rocks, noticed only if they were in the way. If they misbehaved, that is if they snatched food from humans, a temptation to which, with a diet as meagre as this, they frequently succumbed, or if they shamelessly performed the sexual act in the presence of their extremely unpermissive owners, they were thrashed with any weapon to hand. In short, they had no rights whatever, except only to serve their masters well.

However, the number of dogs round and about was insignificant compared with the number of cattle owned by the tribe,

1

cattle of all kinds, humped, horned, hornless, pure black, spotted, pure brown, or grey, tame as well as pugnacious. Their condition was seasonal. They were fattest in the rainy season when grazing was plenty and lush, and leanest when the seemingly endless sun of the Rhodesian dry season reduced the entire countryside to a dreary prospect of parched, brittle, yellowy grass and leaves. At these times the merest spark could turn whole areas into a conflagration that burned for days and nights on end. Sometimes, the dry season went beyond the normal nine months, stretching to twelve months or even longer, so that the rivers and ponds dried out and drinking water for both man and beast was scarce. Then the condition of the cattle became really pathetic, that is if they did not perish altogether by the lingering death of thirst and starvation. My people, though accomplished food-growers and agriculturists in the most general sense of the word, knew nothing about water-conservation and hay-making for their animals. Luckily, misfortunes of this kind were rare, but when they did happen they were regarded as total disasters brought about by the displeased spirits of the avenging ancestors, who required immediate appeasement in the form of tribal prayers and spirit dances—often, at least in my experience, with dramatically positive results.

Cattle were as important to my people as the white man's bank account. All day the drama of the inextricable relationship between men and cattle was constantly being played out in one form or another, so that one soon learned that cattle represented a man's or a woman's security, livelihood and almost their entire purpose for living. The whole social, psychological and tribal standing of a man depended on the number of cattle he possessed. They bought him a wife or wives; they earned him respect and admiration, and since the arrival of the white man, cattle, like maize and rukweza,* had considerable cash value with which one could buy clothes, food and in a way power as well. The drive to possess cattle, like money in white societies, seemed to be the root of all good and all evil in the tribe. Cattle caused men to be good, generous and kind toward their fellow men, if they considered they had enough of them, or to be hard and vicious, if their interests were at risk. In short,

*Rukweza or rapoko, finger millet or eleusine coracana.

they constituted one of the most powerful motivating forces in the individual members of the tribe; they were at the bottom of most tribal disputes, rituals and almost every form of friendly or hostile communication between men and men, women and men, or women and women.

Mashonganyika, particularly our section of the village, was situated on sloping ground, and although there was no view on the eastern side behind our huts where the land rose sharply to a ridge, it was possible to see far into the distant west, south and north, which offered beautiful views of numerous hills, valleys, streams and any number of trees, rocks and plains. When the rains were good, the whole countryside was clothed in lush green grass and thick foliage. It was enchantingly beautiful, to my mind even more so than the rest of Chishawasha which has an almost picture-book beauty, with its many hills, valleys, meandering rivers and brooks, wide sweeping plains and balancing rocks that seem to have been fashioned by a bizarrely imaginative sculptor. The VaShawasha people had chosen well in coming to the country that they called Chishawasha.

For some reason the doors of all the huts and houses looked west, where the ground first descended to the plain and the main river, and then rose gradually to higher terrain. Between the village and the western horizon where the forest began, the country was so bare of trees that it was possible to pick out any human being or animal coming or going for a good mile or so.

Among my earliest recollections of Mashonganyika was an event which established in my mind one of the most important facts of our tribal society, one that had not occurred to me before. It was in the early 'twenties and the incident concerned my aunt Josephine Mandinema. The latter name, translated, meant 'you speak ill of me'. It was customary for parents, particularly the mothers, to give their offspring a name that defined their own philosophy of life or attitude to their neighbours. When my grandmother, Madzidza, was carrying Josephine in her womb she learned that some of her female neighbours, true to character, were making sniggering remarks about her, saying that the expected baby would no doubt be another girl, just as the first three were girls and that, 'it serves her right',

3

she would never have a boy. The fact was that female offspring were of less value in the tribe, except in so far as they brought in cattle or money in the form of *lobola** from those who wished to marry them. As indeed these busy-bodies had predicted, the baby proved to be yet another girl, and grandmother, just to remind everybody that she had not been unaware of their pettiness and ill-will, called her Mandinema and Mandinema she remained.

One Sunday afternoon Josephine returned from Church in a particularly black mood and did not show her usual interest in people or food, but instead sat apart on the stoep of the family granary, where she soon started to cry with audible sobs and visibly flowing tears. She was very tense and seemed to have something to say but could not find words to say it. Before that moment I had never seen her cry; she had always struck me as one of those rare individuals who felt that life was too short and precious to waste in inane tears and pointless complaints. Until now, her contentment and chatty gregariousness had been unbounded, even to the point of being tiresome to her two surviving sisters, who were more introverted than she was. Realizing that something serious had happened, I informed grandmother, whereupon the whole family was summoned. They gathered round Josephine, plying her with sympathetic questions and gazing at her with eyes which said many things that could not be expressed in words.

When Josephine had recovered her composure, the news that poured from her mouth affected everybody who heard her like a flash of lightning, stunning them into a complete, menacing silence. It lasted several minutes, and then was broken by the tears and groans of her sisters, Catherine and Maria. Later there were harsh recriminations.

What Josephine said was simply that she was expecting a baby.

In the verbal scuffle that ensued, the family was sharply divided. On the one hand grandfather Mizha, Catherine and Maria ganged up together against Josephine and minced no words in reminding her of the consequences of her irresponsible disregard for the rules of Christian conduct which the Church imposed

*Bride price paid by the bridegroom to the family of the bride.

on its tenants in Chishawasha. She might have exercised a little self-control, they said, wise after the event. She was selfish, thinking only of herself, when duty, common decency and the good upbringing she had had might have reminded her that in these matters the interests of the whole family were at stake. Why had she been so precipitous? Was she so weak that she could not have resisted the wild demands of Martin, her fiancé? Look now, what a mess the whole family was in!

On the other hand, grandmother Madzidza took a completely opposite point of view, and was supported by several other women closely related to our family, who had by now joined our internecine group.

Stating her own case, Madzidza, whose prejudices against anything alien were always strongly expressed, spoke as if this was the best news she had had for a long time. She said she recognized no law outside that of the tribe. She was nauseated, repeat nauseated, by the views held by Mizha, her husband, and her two sin-fearing daughters, who took too much account of the peculiar opinions of the interfering white clerics at Chishawasha Mission. This matter was African, she said, and strictly domestic. Why should a white man be permitted to thrust his red nose into it? She asked this question again and again, ramming her clenched right fist into the open palm of her left hand, dramatizing each word, each phrase and looking contemptuously at her husband and the two daughters in league with him as if they were the guilty ones. For just this once, she emphasized, the Father Superior at the Mission might be told to mind his own business while the Africans, especially her family, minded theirs. As far as she was concerned, her daughter and husband Martin, for husband he now was, had done no wrong whatever. God bless them, they had shown courage and true African independence of mind in these critical times when all sorts of white men were charging about the country, expecting and demanding blind obedience from black people who asked for nothing more than to be left alone to live their own lives and follow their God-given customs in peace.

Mizha, Catherine and Maria were visibly pained by this approach. But Madzidza ignored their mild protests and went on heaping abuse on the 'silly' religious regime at Chishawasha

5

Mission, together with its priests, lay-brothers and nuns, its teachers and agents of Christianity. Giving what she considered to be good, common-sense advice, grandmother said that instead of recriminating over what the missionary might have to say— 'and he will have a lot to say, given half a chance'—the family should rejoice in the expectation of a happy event, for what greater gift was there to any man and woman, to any family and any tribe than the gift of a living, breathing, crying human being like any one of us! If the white man's God was going to be offended by the conception of a human being then she could only conclude that He was against black people. In that case, He could not be much good, Madzidza stated.

Turning to Josephine, Madzidza spoke reassuringly, saying that she rejoiced that she was a real woman, a fruitful woman, who had proved to her husband her ability to bear him as many daughters and sons as his heart desired. Just think for a moment, she warned, what could and might have happened if Josephine and Martin had contracted the unbending Church marriage first before they had proof that both were capable of producing children?

The dramatic effect of Madzidza's last statement was heightened by the other older women, who showed they shared her line of thinking with their chorus of 'Yes, yes . . .'

What grandmother was saying was simply this: among our people the birth of a child was the only binding factor in a marriage, almost the only reason for getting married at all. If no child was born of a marriage, a man was entitled either to give up his wife and demand the return of his *lobola* payments, or to have her sister as his second wife in the hope that she would fulfil his desire for children. By conceiving now, Josephine had therefore taken a worrying load off the family shoulder. There was no doubt about that, just as there was no doubt that every family in Mashonganyika village giving away a daughter in wedlock passed through this psychologically excruciating crisis until it was proved groundless. But it took Madzidza, steeped in tribal conservatism, to accept this fact without worrying about the reaction in the complicated minds of the white missionaries. More than that, Madzidza, rebellious by nature, saw something of herself in Josephine, whose pregnant

6

condition she regarded as an act of defiance against the alien religious system that she detested and felt it her duty to denounce day by day. So strong were her anti-Church views that she resisted being baptized to the very end.

However, grandfather Mizha, being practical and an old man who wished to spend the rest of his fast-diminishing days in peace, chided his wife for using brave words to minimize the seriousness of the situation which threatened the very peace and security of the family. 'What good can brave words do? We are a subject people. Your daughter has broken the white man's law. . . . What does the white man care about our customs? He has power to punish,' said Mizha calmly, but firmly.

Mizha frequently used the word '*muchena*', 'the white one', who, of course, was the Father Superior of Chishawasha Mission at the time, whom the entire African population nick-named '*Mataramanga*', 'the stern one'. He was a tall, strong man, with a firm face, set jaws and blue eyes that were capable of seeing into the hearts and minds of men and telling accurately what was inside them. Again, they occasionally referred to him as *Mupuranga*, 'the gum tree', because of his tall, erect figure; when he walked his foot-steps were so solid that his boots squeaked and sounded from a distance, like horseshoes striking the ground. All these characteristics stamped him as a man whose authority was in no doubt whatever in the mind of the tribe.

Although at this stage I had not met this renowned priest, I had formed an image of him—and it wasn't a very flattering one; for all the members of my family and the neighbours conveyed the impression that, though a man of God, he was cold and ready to punish on the slightest pretext without fear or favour or compassion. But he had the ability to make his sermons alive and dramatic and therefore attractive to a predominantly black audience which relished as much emotion and imagination as possible in teaching the gospel. When he preached about Hell, his congregation could almost see and feel the huge, leaping, lapping flames of the all-consuming fires in this cruel abode of the wicked. He was fluent in Shona, but for his German accent, and his stentorian voice spoke in rushing angry cascades,

7

striking the ears of his enthralled listeners like the blows of a hammer. But for the fact that the Catholic Church did not allow congregational shouts of 'Amen' and 'Hallelujah' and other such emotional displays, the people liked his style of preaching and found it not dissimilar to their own tribal forms of worship.

However, Father *Mataramanga* was at no time a light-hearted man. He was as grim as he was passionate in delivering the word of God. His frequently recurring text in the Sunday pulpit was about sin, particularly the sins of fornication and adultery, which he had reasons to believe were the common indulgence of his Mission people. If he picked up the slightest smell of a scandal about any of his Christians, he did not hesitate to denounce him or her and, if circumstances warranted it, ordered the unfortunate person to stand up for all to see.

Understandably, this puritanical atmosphere that Father *Mataramanga* and his predecessors had built up in the Mission, the village of Mashonganyika, and all the other villages in Chishawasha, produced its own crop of informers—appointed as well as self-appointed—who wished to curry favour with the Church, or, in their own peculiar understanding of things, considered the exposure of sinners a vital part of their Christian duty. Father *Mataramanga* was unlikely, therefore, to remain uninformed for long about most things. Some critics, though, said that he was grossly misinformed about a great deal of what actually happened in the African villages, which he did not visit except to give the Sacrament of Extreme Unction when someone was on the point of death. Amply supplied with tit-bits of salacious information, real or imaginary, his sermons were full of denunciations of fornicators, adulterers and other wicked men and women, who, he imagined, were still dabbling in heathenism and witchcraft. Of course, as everyone admitted, there was no evidence that he enjoyed this recitation of sins, for, on the contrary, he spoke with visible fury and hatred for the sins of the flesh.

It was this priestly wrath, more perhaps than the sense of wrong, which terrified Josephine, who would inevitably be publicly rebuked and humiliated, denied Nuptial Mass and possibly become the cause of her whole family being expelled from

Chishawasha, particularly if her proud, stubborn husband Martin refused to do a public penance.

Yet from the African point of view, no tribal law had been broken. Everything Josephine and Martin had done was perfectly honourable and consistent with the tradition of the tribe. Far from being a dissipated delinquent young man, Martin, whose family lived two or three hundred yards away from us, had gone through the complicated tribal custom of *lobola* very conscientiously and paid in full the cattle and other fees that went with the transaction. The moment that grandfather and grandmother had finally expressed themselves satisfied that their prospective son-in-law had fulfilled his part of the *lobola* bargain, our law stipulated that Josephine was his; and he had proceeded to take her as his wife both in spirit and in flesh, deciding to cross the Church bridge when he came to it.

But Josephine, being a woman, and the women in Chishawasha took Christianity infinitely more to heart than the men, had lost her nerve. The impromptu family conference lasted the entire afternoon and well into the evening and was extremely painful, generating heat and bitterness as tempers flared and harsh words flew and scattered like sparks of fire from burning wood. Never before in my experience had the family been so divided and so free in the expression of their highly charged emotions—emotions which suggested a basic feeling of psychological insecurity. Indeed, for me it marked a definite stage in the development of my consciousness: I became aware of one of the ugly realities of the world into which I had been born. As the fierce conflict led my family deeper and deeper into their quarrel, it became clear that the point at issue had little to do with the question of right and wrong. The family was at loggerheads because Josephine had flouted the authority of the Church, an alien institution which, together with the autocracy of the white rulers of Southern Rhodesia, was superimposed on all our customs, traditions, tribal will and values. Mizha repeatedly emphasized this unpleasant fact of our existence. We were no longer a free people, but since 1890, that year of national tragedy, we had been subject to the whims and foibles of the white man, whether he was in or outside the Church. What mattered was not what we judged to be right, but what the white man ordained we should or should not do. The Church was now the Chishawasha landlord and when its regulations were broken, as in Josephine's case, its methods of gentle persuasion were transformed into those of coercion and dictatorship. No amount of wishful-thinking could alter the course of white justice, if the *muchena* at the Mission decided to enforce the spirit and the letter of his laws with full rigour.

Each word Mizha uttered about our place in the Southern Rhodesian sunshine was forced into my receptive mind like unwanted food down my throat. It was deeply humiliating to know that in the eyes of the ruling white race in the country we were in a position little different from that into which we put our dogs, cats, goats and cattle. And yet, I said to myself, animals were different from us in physique, intelligence and habits of living, whereas, apart from the difference of colour, we were of the same human species as the white man, except that he was the bully and we were the bullied.

Needless to say, having failed to unravel this human equation, I simply cast my people into good angels and white men into wicked devils, including those who preached the word of God.

Finally, however, the family exhausted its passions, and faced the question of how to prevent the worst that could happen from taking its course. The worst was expulsion from Chishawasha. That had happened before, Mizha warned, and all recent evidence went to show that the Church was acting with much less compassion in these matters than it had done in the past. He feared, therefore, that this was almost a certainty and could not reconcile himself to the horrible possibility of having to leave his tribe and go into exile. In Chishawasha lay buried many of our forefathers, whose spirits protected and influenced our lives in every way. The familiar beautiful countryside of Chishawasha had been his entire world since birth; it was his life and his spirit and freedom and to be banished from it permanently would be worse than imprisonment; and he couldn't face it. Neither could he face the other possibility: of having his family made the subject of a public scandal by the scandal-loving Christian community of Chishawasha, he said. Mizha, like many of his generation in the village, had gone through the suffering of the 1896 rebellion and of the unexplained nemesis of the *'Furuwenza'*,* with its by-products of sorrow, hunger and death. But he had hoped that his remaining years on earth would be spent in Chishawasha in relative peace, with what happiness and contentment a defeated people could enjoy in this world. Now this! What had he done to deserve this new misfortune?

At this stage, grandmother Madzidza, who had maintained her optimistic belligerence throughout, made a number of suggestions for a solution. All but one of these were described by Mizha as 'wild' and 'impractical'. Madzidza's final idea was that Father *Mataramanga* need never know if everyone treated Josephine's condition as a family secret and made speedy preparations to get the couple married before her pregnancy was too noticeable. Mizha agreed that this was their only hope, although he was not very confident that the secret would be kept. He might well have been right, for although our village world was completely without newspapers or any of the modern means of communication, everyone, particularly the Christians, kept their ears close to the ground for anything with which to spice their neighbourly chit-chat or to use as proof of their concern for the moral tone of the Mission.

Late that evening, Martin was fetched from his part of the village and seriously advised to get married as speedily as possible. But far from being sorry or defensive, Martin's attitude approached arrogant indifference. He scoffed at the very idea of the Church having any say in the pursuit of his natural rights. This was great news to grandmother. She couldn't conceal her pride and excited delight at the discovery that her prospective son-in-law shared the revolutionary spirit that was such a pronounced trait in her own outlook on matters of Church and State. With Martin on her side, she might have steered the discussion right back to where it had started, had not grandfather Mizha firmly and angrily spelled out once more the consequences of negligence and self-deception in this matter.

However, finally Martin consented to get himself married as quickly as possible, adding, all the same, that he was going to do so only because he loved his wife and wished to put his

*Influenza epidemic of 1918.

11

father-in-law's mind at rest and not because he was bowing to the new laws of the land.

Strange as it may seem, Martin was baptized and occasionally a church-goer. But he was immensely cynical and rebellious, though like many of the young his rebelliousness, unlike that of Madzidza, was against both tribal authority and its white counterpart. He was intolerant of the slow, inhibiting ways of the tribe as well as those of the Church, which he did not particularly care to understand. If he had only himself and his wife to think of, a Church marriage would have been the furthest thing from his restless, untamed mind. In a way he was typical of the young generation in Mashonganyika and Chishawasha as a whole. Men of his age group, while gladly coming to terms with the materialism of white civilization, were both angry and confused. The reason was that they could not reconcile their way of thinking with that of the tribal system whose inglorious past, inadequate present and uncertain future held few attractions for them. Neither could they find psychological satisfaction in the Church whose mysticism, compromising position, obsession against wealth and ill-defined moral strictures were not related to their youthful dreams. In short, both institutions seemed irrelevant in the rough-and-tumble existence that the not-very-Christian, but obviously aggressive and unashamedly acquisitive white society was shaping in Southern Rhodesia.

The last thing Martin said was that he was going to the Mission the following day to ask the priest to announce the banns of his marriage so that in about three weeks' time the whole tiresome business would be over. About informers, he said, he would take the necessary precautions; but if they told the priest about his wife's pregnancy, he would thrash them to within an inch of their lives.

Martin was endowed with considerable muscular strength and everybody in the village was well aware of his quick temper and, more important, his superior, hard-hitting punches. Whether or not this reputation had anything to do with it, I do not know, but the fact remains that he and his pregnant bride created no scandal. He had a white wedding, which proved beyond any shadow of doubt that their secret was not divulged

12

to the missionary superior, who would otherwise most certainly have taken a wrathful view of such wicked indulgence.

In years to come, it became evident to me that most young couples resorted to 'white lies' of this kind to avoid similar unpleasantness and to have white weddings, with their enormous social prestige. From time to time, though, some of these subterfuges backfired, so that a few of the guilty were punished, while others, refusing to accept the penalties imposed, left the Church and Chishawasha Mission altogether.

2

The VaShawasha people and the Church;
a white policeman arrives and
grandmother orders that all dogs should
be locked up. Grandfather Mizha is
arrested; a defeated people relive
their past.

The incident I have just related was no trivial matter, not something to be easily thrown out of my memory. It has stuck in my mind like a permanent scar all these years and I can remember every detail of it, including the moods of the various individuals who argued so fiercely. It was important because it made one fundamental issue clear to me. This was the relationship between my tribe and the Church, and, of course, the political overtones of that relationship. Now I knew that the Church, both temporal and spiritual, held the whiphand in all the tribal affairs of the VaShawasha people in the Mission; it could, if it so wished, toss out of its lands any man, woman or family at any time and for any reason at all. There was no right of appeal to anyone in any case of ejection or others of a similar kind. It could therefore be said, putting it in crude, practical terms, that the Church owned the VaShawasha people; its influence over everyone was overpowering. Like the air we breathed, the Church was everywhere, as much in the loud peals of its bell which rang out continually each day and was heard for miles around, as in the authority of its dogmatic but largely mystifying teaching. In due course, this obviously master-and-servant relationship was to grow into a source of constant friction between the tribal elders and the Church, not only on the important question of land and the power which it had to expel anyone who broke its rules, but more particularly on the psychologically shattering doctrine it put forward, that the

14

Catholic Church was the only means by which one could be saved from eternal damnation.

The family wrangle over the pregnancy of Josephine brought to the surface one of the most unfortunate features of white domination in Southern Rhodesia. Because they were not in a position to have an honest dialogue with the Church, because they were not given a chance to explain their religious system and prove how positively superior some of it was compared with much of the Christian religion, the VaShawasha people understandably developed an attitude by which questions of right and wrong outside the tribal code of ethics were judged strictly according to the Church's likely reaction and not on their merits. In short, they began to observe the moral code adopted generally by European races. This was that most things were wrong only if they were discovered or were likely to invite legal penalties. Put differently, the tribe gradually realized that the best way to get along with missionaries and white people generally was by cultivating the 'virtue' of cunning; lying and dishonesty seemed to be the foundations of white religion and culture and as the white man asserted his authority, the tribe increasingly geared its thinking to this philosophy, whenever it suited its interests.

We had hardly got over this crisis when another unpleasant fact of our existence in Rhodesia was impressed upon me.

That Monday, the day began as most days, with nothing particular to look forward to and no special task to be done urgently. As all field work had been completed and we were now waiting for the maize and other crops to ripen, most people were at home and at ease. The large number of dogs that my family owned were barking, frisking, scavenging and running about aimlessly.

Sometime in the early afternoon, grandmother Madzidza, who kept a sharp eye all around and was probably more aware than most of us that in these days the tribe's freedom was liable to be illusory, suddenly announced that a white police trooper was approaching on horseback from the west. In the next second she remembered that we had not paid tax on all our dogs. We were all thrown off balance—except, of course, Madzidza. While everybody else was trying to digest this disturbing piece

15

of news, Madzidza, like a quick-thinking army commander in a tricky military situation, ordered us to assist in rounding up all the dogs and locking them in one hut. 'Otherwise we will be in real trouble from the white man,' she reminded us.

In awkward moments such as this one, grandmother always seemed to find her true personality and to triumph over everyone else in courage, imagination and cool-headedness. In the event, no one dared to disobey her orders or to doubt the wisdom of her action. And so, as if we were a squad of well-drilled, disciplined soldiers in a field of battle, we rushed to carry out her instructions and rounded up every dog in sight, so that by the time the white man galloped into our yard we were secretly congratulating ourselves on the brilliance of the whole smartly executed operation. Grandmother, to cap her mastery of the situation as well as to add a touch of humour and innocence, coolly walked forward to greet the imposing representative of the law, bowing and curtseying in the traditional manner, which all seemed to disarm the trooper.

However, any idea that the dogs might have been in tune with our way of thinking was soon shattered. The constable finished checking up on the poll-tax receipts of all the adult males, which I thought he did quickly and politely, and was just about to take leave of our company when the dogs, enraged by the claustrophobic atmosphere of the small, windowless, dark and nearly airless hut, suddenly and simultaneously began to howl. They shrieked and snarled like a pack of irate, hungry hyenas and loudly proclaimed their illegal imprisonment and Madzidza's little plot. The white man turned beetroot red. Grandmother almost collapsed in shame and terror. Grandfather Mizha, who, as usual, had not been consulted by his wife, but had not expressed any objections to the scheme, was obviously also shaken. All he could say was that he had known all along that the whole idea was as crazy as most of Madzidza's impulsive notions were. I was terrified, to say the least, wondering what the haughty-looking copper was going to do next.

He soon made his intentions clear and they were not for our comfort. He called Mizha a 'skellum'* and cursed several times. My vocabulary of foreign words was by now large enough

*Scoundrel (Afrikaans).

for me to recognize that he was calling us 'kaffirs, bastards, bobojaans'* and several other names. When he had vented his feelings, he got down from his horse, walked to the hut that imprisoned the protesting dogs and gave the door an angry kick with his brown-polished right boot; it flew open and the dogs rushed out, some still biting and fighting one another and others attacking him as if he had been responsible for their confinement.

Just as he must have guessed, he noticed that every one of these canine animals was a 'bandit', in other words, untaxed for that year. They were not wearing the Government collar and tax disc. Perhaps because he felt that he had been made a fool of, perhaps because he was appalled by the very idea of black people robbing the government of its much-needed tax revenue or because he felt sorry for the dogs or for all these reasons, the trooper cursed us again angrily and loudly with another fair mixture of 'kaffirs, niggers, bobojaans' and similar, typically Rhodesian-South African expletives.

I experienced here for the first time what I think has been and still is a strong factor in the reactions of colonial Africans to white people, particularly those in authority. There is fear in all of us, fear that either drives us to irrational aggression or makes us merely stand still in paralytic helplessness. In my experience, the fear that we Africans had for the Europeans was of the latter kind and, I venture to suggest, perhaps largely accounts for the prolonged state of subjection of the Southern Rhodesian Africans. To say that this is a sad reflection on the black people of the country, as most people outside Rhodesia tend to do, would be an over-simplification of this issue. This total, helpless fear did not exist in the Africans of my country before 1896. But after being utterly defeated on the field of battle, and subjected to every form of control, subtle and violent, the entire African population lapsed into a state in which the passive instinct of self-preservation became predominant: this contributed as much to UDI as the arrogance and dementia of the Rhodesian Front Party. What I find dangerous and abhorrent now is the attitude of the autocratic white minority, who after so many years of silent obedience from the Africans,

*Baboons (Afrikaans).

17

are so sure of themselves that they think they can hold power indefinitely.

On that memorable Monday afternoon in the village of Mashonganyika I witnessed a situation which, more than anything else, convinced me that we were not only a conquered people, but a people that the conqueror did not even respect. The white policeman, though alone, behaved as if he owned us and the very ground he trod on. He did not even pretend to hold his revolver at the ready as a warning to any would-be attacker. Indeed, I was certain that if he had wanted he could have marched us all anywhere without any trouble at all. However, he did not go that far; instead he proceeded to handcuff Mizha, old and frail as he was, without the slightest compassion or regard for his age. Nor did it worry him that his prisoner might need food and other personal comforts on the way. On the contrary, he rudely pushed Mizha in front of the snorting horse and took him away to face whatever punishment might be in store for his crime. Nobody, man or woman, raised a finger in protest. We were all reduced to a state of sheepishness and timidity. Such was the fear the lone officer and the forces he represented had instilled into the hearts and minds of my people. All grandmother's verbal courage and quick, biting tongue had melted and vanished into thin air. Even Jakobo, Mizha's eldest son by his first wife, who normally never stopped boasting of his bravery and expressing his contempt for the rest of his fellow tribesmen, suddenly seemed to have become a coward like everyone else and merely stared into space. There was his father, being removed from our presence as if he were a dangerous criminal and Jakobo had absolutely nothing to say or do in his defence.

For many days and nights after, I tried without success to fathom the peculiar relationship between my people and white men, between justice and injustice, between right and wrong, the value of the dogs against the rights of men and asked myself again and again why a tax had to be paid for possessing a mere dog and not for a chicken or a cat. Anyway, why had it to be paid to some impersonal white government, whose usefulness to my people was non-existent as far as I could see? It was all sheer robbery, criminal plunder of the weak by the strong. If there was any justification for taxation, the least this alien authority could do was to ask for it politely instead of extorting it by arrogance, threats and use of force. I could see no reason why we should not be left in peace, as Madzidza always said, minding our own business while white men minded theirs. We were a free, happy people, peaceful and law-abiding after our own fashion, but suddenly a white constable, complete with khaki uniform, shiny boots and leather leggings, pith helmet and a revolver, descended on us from the blue and decided that Mizha should answer for his misdemeanour at once instead of allowing him to do so at a more convenient time. The white man did not even ask whose idea it was that the dogs should be hidden away. Nor did he politely ask Mizha why he had not paid their taxes at the right time. Surely, I said, it would have been more humane to fine him on the spot and leave the poor old man in the peace, security and comfort of his home? Anyone with compassion could see that my grandfather was hardly in a condition to stand up to a twelve-mile walk, let alone serve fourteen days in gaol with hard labour, all for the paltry offence of overlooking his tax obligations. I saw no point in any white-made laws, least of all in our duty to obey them. We had our own and they were good enough for us. They were sensible, humane and democratic, but not a single one of them involved extorting money, grain, cattle or labour for the benefit of some self-appointed clique in the tribe.

With this kind of reasoning, strongly reinforced by my general tribal education, I simply saw the whole incident as a piece of deliberate provocation, an act of monstrous injustice.

By the very nature of things and because of my age, it was, of course, a fruitless exercise at this stage to try and puzzle out the Southern Rhodesian racial equation. Certainly, in this case grandmother did nothing to lessen my confusion. She seemed to have been too shocked to explain anything in rational terms. Until Mizha returned from his imprisonment at Goromonzi—and he was haggard and looked older than when he was taken away—Madzidza had very little to say, except from time to time to remind anyone willing to listen that these were rotten times, unlike the good old days when there were no policemen, no money-hungry governments and therefore no taxes to pay to

19

anyone. It was a fair point, but hardly one to give comfort to anybody. Nor did it alter anything, save only to increase the sense of bewilderment and defeatism which overtook every member of the family circle as well as most of the adult population in Mashonganyika village, who took Mizha's peremptory arrest as a gruesome reminder of our conquered status. The most painful aspect of this event as well as our general position in the Rhodesian scheme of things was that there was nothing we could do either as individuals or as a tribe. The ugly facts of our history were overwhelmingly painful enough for the elders not to forget in a hurry that the white man could not be disobeyed or challenged with impunity. That realization was a sufficient reason for them to swallow most of the humiliations, provocations and insults from their rulers in seeming spinelessness.

When Mizha came back there was much rejoicing, but of a muted sort, for everyone knew that ours was a position little different from permanent imprisonment; we were under permanent supervision, in no way capable of deciding our own future, and we could not put a foot wrong without the Government or the Church using punitive powers against us. We were painfully aware that policemen could come in and out of our village as they wished, and for all sorts of reasons, and upset our way of life. For this reason we could not lull ourselves into a sense of security.

This was the general theme of Jakobo when he made a speech of thanksgiving at a beer party held in honour of Mizha's safe return to the comfort and freedom of his home and family. Speaking in a very solemn tone of voice befitting the occasion, Jakobo thanked the spirits of our ancestors who alone had preserved the life of his father during his period of incarceration and called on them, through their love and tenderness for the living, to continue to give this protection to every member of our family and the tribe. The white man, he reminded the ancestors, was like a porcupine, covered with erectile spines for the infliction of pain and sorrow on the African people. 'For reasons we have never been able to understand, you permitted this *ngozi** to fall upon us. . . . You allowed victory to go to them rather than to us. . . . You must know better than we do that we

*Bad luck, curse, catastrophe.

shall always need care, succour and safeguards against the machinations and knavishness of the white men who say they are our masters and come into our homes as it pleases them to make criminals of us. . .' Jakobo spoke to this effect.

The ancestors were always brought into matters of this nature and were spoken to as if they were alive and physically present and could hear what was being said. Thus they were treated with all decorum and a deep feeling of affection and reverence. When they were invited by the living they could hear, feel, taste and participate in everything. Therefore, you spoke to them directly.

This belief, so strongly embedded in the consciousness of my people, acted as a potent spiritual tranquillizer, generating a real, often instant and effective, sense of well-being and optimism, even in a crisis of the most serious kind. If the world had turned topsy-turvy and life become sour for any individual of my grandparents' or Jakobo's generation, the ancestors were always there as the last hope and source of physical and spiritual assistance. In all my village upbringing I never came across a case of an individual who cracked under the weight of social pressures and personal problems. I have no doubt whatever that this faith in the power of the ancestral spirits had much to do with the extraordinary perpetual sanity of my people.

While Jakobo was communing with the ancestors no one uttered a word or as much as coughed. But once this touching ritual was over, the large body of male well-wishers present broke into an impressive rhythmic clapping of hands, while the womenfolk sent sharp ululating shouts of joy into the air. For a few minutes then one could appreciate, not only the happiness of everybody at Mizha's safe return, but also how the lives of the living were interwoven with those of the dead. They then drank a toast to grandfather and later, at a given signal, all and sundry sat in solemn and respectful silence while grandfather gave a brief and restrained account of his experiences as a prisoner of white men. Always a man of few words and given to understatements rather than to an emotional and highly coloured expression of his opinions, he said that on the whole he had been treated as well as a black man could expect of a white

21

man. However, he did not like the food and most certainly hated the sight of most black policemen and messengers, especially the Chief Messenger, Pitiri, whom the tribe accused of having been a quisling in the 1896 rebellion. But above all else he hated the whole system which enabled a foreign race to make laws and to imprison black men who broke them. But it was unnecessary for him to exhaust his feelings on that point because they were no different from those of everyone in the tribe, he said, and concluded his account.

At the end of this undramatic report, all the men and women in the gathering settled down to steady beer-drinking.

When men and women came together for beer, they never lost the opportunity to unlock their hearts and minds to one another and go through the full range of common family, tribal and national problems. As they used to say, a social meeting of this sort should make honest individuals share their thoughts and wisdom with their fellow human beings. In this way, information of every kind was exchanged, tribal public opinion on any crucial issue was assessed and often important decisions were reached, which would be confirmed or rubber-stamped later at formal tribal council sessions.

On this special occasion, however, the complicated politics of Southern Rhodesia took precedence over the usual tribal, family and agricultural topics. The arrest, imprisonment and, thanks to the good graces of the ancestors, the home-coming of Mizha provided an excuse for everyone to discuss the past and the present of the tribe—with great relish and considerable passion. Understandably, the conversation concentrated on a broad recapitulation of some of the highlights of the 1896 rebellion, its causes, effects and aftermath. As time went on during my tribal upbringing, I was to learn that this was easily the most popular topic of discussion at informal tribal gatherings. It cropped up at all sorts of occasions and for all kinds of reasons, particularly when people were involved in religious controversies or airing their strong views on current political issues and the burdens which were imposed on them by white rule. Listening to these reminiscences, as I did on numerous occasions, I formed the clear impression that the VaShawasha looked at white people and their ways as a perpetual pestilence.

22

As in this instance, the starting-point for damning the white race in Southern Rhodesia, its system of government and its civilization was invariably the rebellion. And as most people of Mizha's and Jakobo's generations claimed to have had personal experience of this bloody confrontation between black power and white power which so decisively changed the fortunes of the Shona and the Ndebele people in my country, the amount of firsthand information available on the subject in the village was immense and colourful. Each man claimed to be a war veteran, each prided himself in possessing some special knowledge of the fighting and suffering of this war, which no one else had. They did not need much encouragement to tell what they knew and did so with candour as to the weaknesses of their forces and the strength of the enemy, the Europeans. Each time I listened to this account, a whole world of human savagery, misery, injustice, blood and death was revealed to my mind. And, of course, I never tired of hearing the exciting details and in the process developed a compulsive urge to remember as much as I could of my tribe's contribution to the struggle for their freedom, as well as their interpretation of Rhodesian history.

If I had been born in a healthy, just society, where the accidents of birth and colour were of no importance, I should probably have treated this oft-repeated story with no more than romantic interest. But after the family crisis caused by Josephine's pregnancy, the arrest of Mizha and subsequent incidents, which loudly spoke against the white man's system of government in Rhodesia, my curiosity about the 1896 rebellion became very much stronger than it might otherwise have been. What the two events did was to make it painfully obvious that our society found itself in hostile circumstances; and so I developed a hankering to discover what had brought them about. Luckily, when I was young the great events which led to the usurpation of Zimbabwe from its indigenous people were still too recent to be forgotten or treated lightly; and ever since I have had the privilege of an education I have longed to recreate in writing the life of the VaShawasha tribe of this period, to tell how they viewed their past and reacted to the humiliation of defeat and the savage destruction of their culture that followed.

I am going to do so now, basing my writing on the evidence of the people I knew, particularly members of my family and other relations. They were a simple, honest, straightforward people and I firmly believe that they had a much greater sense of truth about their history than most advocates of European rule in Southern Rhodesia.

But first I must return to my family scene.

Grandmother took some time to live down her impetuosity. Although it was obvious that Mizha would have been arrested in any case for not paying the tax for the family dogs, whether they had been hidden or not, she suffered from a chastening sense of guilt because she felt that she had been entirely responsible for what he went through. While this feeling lasted, she was humbler and more submissive to his authority than she had been before: To say that Mizha welcomed this transformation in his wife's attitude would be to state the obvious. For once, he was able to assert his manly authority as head of the family. But, unfortunately for him, Madzidza's new character proved too good to last, and in time she became her usual self once more.

The two were complete opposites in character and temperament. Mizha was extraordinarily gentle, kind and saintly. Self-effacing, patient and tolerant, he always put others first where there was any question of advantage such as over food or other domestic comforts. In most other households, the male head of the family, as Shona was and still is a patriarchal society, demanded and was entitled to the biggest and choicest portion of meat and other items of food. But even if Madzidza was generous, which she was from time to time and gave him a liberal helping, Mizha would either protest and ask her to lessen his share or himself give some of it to me. More than that he preferred to take the blame for anything that went wrong if he thought it was going to cause unpleasantness, especially when outsiders were involved. Unlike most Africans, he was unemotional, did not indulge in flattery or talk too much. Neither did he raise his voice unless he was driven to it and felt it was in the interests of all concerned. Otherwise he expressed

24

all his ideas and emotions and his reactions to happy or unhappy events in a cool, calm, almost detached manner. I think
he would have made a good magistrate or judge in a court of
law, for he was so fair and just and always tried to think the
best and not the worst of people, unless of course, they proved
him wrong. But even so he would search to the bottom of his
kind, generous heart to find some redeeming feature in their
favour. As they used to say in Mashonganyika village, a man
condemned by Mizha was a man beyond redemption.

On the other hand, grandmother Madzidza was impulsive,
flighty, imaginative and as tough and outspoken as it is possible
to imagine any tribal woman of that period to be. Thrusting,
witty and reckless, Madzidza was more often than not the boss
of our household, if not the whole neighbourhood. Her eyes
missed little and her sharp, quick tongue lacked no appropriate
word or phrase for the praise or abuse of other people and
systems that set her vivid imagination into action. Mostly, however, it was abuse rather than praise of people she indulged in,
for Madzidza did not rate human beings very highly, except, of
course, her only son, Marimo. In her eyes there always seemed
to be something wrong with other men and women; the more
distantly related to us the more freakish or unattractive they
were. Men, for instance, were all mad, selfish, unreliable, in fact
anything but normal sensible human beings. But her feminine
neighbours were not much better. Grandmother would not find
it difficult to pick out some characteristic or blemish and use
it as a weapon against whoever happened to be within the
range at that particular moment. Thus old Mrs So-and-So would
suddenly turn out to be abnormal because Madzidza detected
something sinister in the look of her eyes. Mrs A could not have
been up to anything good, grandmother would say and find all
the reasons in the world to justify this shrewd piece of observa-
tion. Next time it would be Mrs B who was certainly a witch,
liable to dig up human bodies from their graves in the dead of
night. If not, Madzidza would ask seriously, why then did
she have those owlish eyes, long teeth and that silly grin? In
short, from her rich vocabulary and picturesque phraseology,
grandmother would pour scorn all around, sticking evil squint-
eyes, bow legs, thieving fingers and other ugly features and

traits onto anyone she disliked at any particular time. Under her devastating verbal assaults, a handsome person became most repulsive, and a reasonable man or woman was turned into a ridiculous figure of fun. It never occurred to her that she was being uncharitable or wrong in making hasty conclusions about other people.

Given this forthright, if often virulent, nature and a simple, unashamed pride in her African heritage, my grandmother found it easy to justify her antagonism to European rule, religion and anything else that she suspected of being unAfrican. As it was, the arrest and imprisonment of her husband only made her harden her attitude to foreign interference even more.

In this case I was entirely on her side. Until the white trooper had removed my grandfather from our home so abruptly and jolted me out of my youthful innocence, I had been brought up in the time-honoured tribal tradition that the elderly should be treated with great reverence. I had taken my grandfather to be inviolate, above ill-treatment or abuse from any man or woman, white or black. That day, however, when his hallowed image was violated by a policeman young enough to have been his son this false notion was shattered. The constable's manners, authority and lack of humanity so clearly showed that white people regarded us black human beings, irrespective of age, as inferior. In that single act, legitimate though it was as far as the policeman was concerned, I had some appreciation of what white rule meant and why my people complained so bitterly against it. It was a rude awakening to the fate that Cecil Rhodes had designed for Africans when he translated his empire-building dream into reality and took over the country in 1890.

3

White rule is an imposition, resented by a
people who know they are self-sufficient
and value their independence;
Shona history distorted to justify
colonial rule in Rhodesia; Patrick
Gordon Walker and the Chiefs.

White rule in Southern Rhodesia, then as now, justified itself
by declaring that this was essential for the well-being of the
Africans. But to the VaShawasha people, as well as to their
compatriots, of this and any other time, this claim was wholly
false, and had they been granted the right to say what they
preferred they would have rejected it outright. As far as they
were concerned, they owed the white man nothing except a
deep animosity; they wished only to be left alone. We were a
self-reliant and independent entity. As far as good government,
peace and individual freedom went, the white man could have
learnt many valuable lessons from the tribe. In our tribal
community everyone was guided by simple, clear-cut rules of
social discipline, common-sense decency, a strong sense of duty
and of belonging, as well as respect for truthfulness and honesty.
Ours, therefore, could be said to have been a more civilized
society than that to be found anywhere in the white-controlled
towns and mining compounds in the Southern Rhodesia of the
early 'twenties. Life could be and often was very satisfactory,
if not idyllic, until it was disturbed by external interference, in
most cases from the Church, prying police or individual white
men. We always felt then that as a people, with our own spiritual
and cultural heritage, our own country, language, paramount
chief, tribal council and other indigenous institutions, we were
quite capable of charting our own course. We did not need
favours or guidance from the white man.

Left entirely to ourselves, the white world tended to be at best something to be despised and sneered at because it seemed false and artificial, and at worst something to be resented and fiercely attacked as an intolerable imposition. We were convinced, at least the elders were, that the white man had nothing of spiritual value to teach us. Our religious beliefs seemed stronger and more satisfying than those of the Europeans. This was no idle boast, for most of the VaShawasha people, as yet uncorrupted by Western materialism, still tried to live by the tenets of their religious system. But they observed that the European was guided by power and wealth rather than by his Christianity. As they frequently pointed out, the manner in which the white man cheated his way into Zimbabwe, subjected Africans by trickery and force and imposed a political, economic and social order in which the value of a human being was measured by the colour of his skin, contradicted every one of the ten commandments that formed the very basis of his religion. They were also highly amused, and in consequence became even more sceptical of Christianity, by the fact that it required many conflicting tongues and warring Churches to interpret its teaching. At this stage, the Roman Catholic, Anglican, Methodist, Salvation Army, Presbyterian and other religious denominations in the country were fiercely antagonistic to one another in their battle for the allegiance of the African. No such conflicting institutions existed to propagate Shona religious beliefs. Neither did our religion threaten with the appalling prospect of hell fire to ensure its acceptance and obedience by men.

Furthermore, the tribe detested the white government which ruled by force, and naturally preferred its own government which ruled by consent and therefore enjoyed popular loyalty, born of genuine patriotism and not fear. Having gone through the appalling experience of the 1896 rebellion and now the harsh and colour-conscious system of white control in the country, it seemed to all the VaShawasha people that the government was a system of abominations: taxes, the police, magistrates, judges and that horror of horrors—the gaol. Without these instruments of terror, they said, and quite rightly, it could not even commend itself to the majority of the settlers themselves, a lot of whom struck us as being reckless and lawless savages.

Our own simple form of government did not have these built-in fortifications. It relied mostly on the quality of its civilized standards. Not only were food, fuel, shelter and other necessities of life amply supplied from our own resources, but the individual was also given full physical, psychological and spiritual security by the tribe from the cradle to the grave and beyond.

It was within this general philosophical framework that the elders of the tribe—parents, uncles, grandparents and other responsible people—strove to educate and bring up their young in the to them not unrealistic, but of course vain, hope that the VaShawasha concept of nationhood would be perpetuated and our people would eventually recapture their glorious past.

In this kind of environment, no one, young or old, needed special instruction or indoctrination to grasp the broad questions of politics, justice, right and wrong. Then as today, the Rhodesian white society loudly spoke against itself, the more so when a policeman visited our village to enforce laws which emphasized our conquered status rather than making us feel proud to be identified with white civilization. In these circumstances, our tribal past became more relevant and important than it would otherwise have been, and my tribal history was presented in a light which was later to conflict with most Rhodesian 'history', written by those who have ignored the African point of view. Without wishing to make too great a distinction between the African peoples of Southern Rhodesia, this is especially true in the case of the story of the Shona people, which has been treated with little more than cursory interest by most historians. Indeed, much of the history that has been told in textbooks about the Shona of the periods both before and after white settlement is, like the history of the Zimbabwe Ruins,* a compound of mystery, myths, fantasy and distortion, mostly tailored to suit the racial prejudices of white Rhodesia. We perhaps more than any other group of people in Africa with an interesting past are something of an historical enigma. Our past and present have been so grotesquely misrepresented that we appear to be the most politically backward people on the African continent, a people without guts or political acumen, whose future should depend entirely on the pride and prejudices

*The ruins of a number of stone fortresses of Shona origin in Fort Victoria.

29

of the ruling white minority. And what a blind, intransigent minority it has shown itself to be! Written history provides only scanty evidence of the thriving Shona culture, that was so ill-equipped to withstand nineteenth-century white colonialism, but if we had been able to write our own history, the rest of the world would have known the kind of people we really were and the extent of the destruction of our culture and achievements committed by white colonialism. This task has had to be done by others who have given us very little credit; an outsider has to be exceptionally unprejudiced and analytical to be able to see through the smoke-screen of the Southern Rhodesian official propaganda and slanted newspaper coverage in Western countries, to discover the true position of the people of Zimbabwe and their real aspirations.

To illustrate this point, I must describe a scene I witnessed when I was an adult and more aware of the deviousness of the Southern Rhodesian white politicians. This was in the early 1950s.

Although no British colony in Africa was as yet independent, the winds of change were blowing strong enough for white political bigwigs in Southern Rhodesia to be able to predict what might happen in the African territories near their empire of white privilege. What they predicted, realistically as it turned out, was simply the coming of black governments. They were afraid and with good reason their fear became an obsession. Again with good reason in so far as they were, unhappily, incapable of coming to terms with history, they felt it a matter of duty to forestall this ominous course of events in the only way they knew.

Confident of the magic influence they had usually had on the Parliament at Westminster in the past, they demanded a federation of Southern Rhodesia, Northern Rhodesia and Nyasaland. This brought Mr Patrick Gordon Walker, the then Secretary of State for Commonwealth Relations, down to Salisbury in 1951 for the purpose of 'consulting' African and European opinion on the matter. A colleague and I, both employed on a paper called *African Weekly*, happened to be the only African political reporters in the country at the time. Because of the critical line we took on all aspects of the Southern Rhodesian native policy, we could not very well be kept out of this tricky question. And so we were grudgingly admitted to most of the conferences which were arranged for Mr Gordon Walker.

I remember one conference particularly well. The British Minister was to meet most of the leading chiefs of Mashonaland. So far as I knew this was going to be the first time that Shona Chiefs had ever met a British Government Minister and expressed their views. They nursed many grievances against white rule in Rhodesia and the inaccessibility of the British Government, supposedly the protector of African rights. They would certainly have a lot to say and they would say it without reservations, I told myself.

Eventually we reached the conference rendezvous, a country home. If the Southern Rhodesian Government had had any respect for Shona customs and traditions, the proper place for a meeting of such importance would have been at the headquarters of one of the Chiefs in the area. But following the policy that had evolved since the 1896 rebellion, the Government did not think African traditional rulers that important. They were being 'consulted' on the Federation question only at the insistence of the British Government. Naturally, I expected we were going to meet inside this building. But we did not. We assembled instead in the open air, under a clump of eucalyptus trees. This struck me as odd, especially as I knew that when the morning sun moved on, so would the shade and thus ourselves, unless we did not mind roasting in glaring heat as the day wore on. But I soon realized that this arrangement was intended to give the proceedings an air of Shona traditional consultative dignity and a democratic character. The Native Affairs Department, which administers the policy of segregation, had omitted no detail in stage-managing the occasion. I should also add that the conference had to be in the country rather than in Salisbury to emphasize to the Chiefs the principles of separate development enshrined in the Land Apportionment Act. That part I knew all along. But I would never have dreamed that we would meet under trees.

Neither was I prepared for the decision to use white men as interpreters. However, they spoke Shona well, at least well enough to be able to provide a word-for-word translation in both languages, I said to myself, remembering the few occasions that I had heard them converse with Africans. The fact that this task had not been allotted to Africans, who would do the job much better, I put down to the usual practice of the Native Affairs Department of keeping black men well in the background in most things. The real reason for this arrangement went deeper, as I was to discover when the talks were really under way.

The Chiefs, not looking particularly attractive in their gaudy official uniform, consisting of bright red and blue gowns, white helmets and brass discs chained round their necks, needed no encouragement to express themselves and to pillory the Rhodesian Government. This was exactly the sort of talking that the Native Affairs Department had anticipated; it was to render it harmless that they appointed these interpreters. It must be said that many of the views coming from the aged and ignorant sycophants were not only irrelevant, but also on the whole gibberish. It was obvious that they hardly knew what the issue of the Federation was about, nor why suddenly the Government of Great Britain had become aware of the existence of Shona Chiefs. But the more enlightened of them went straight to the point and tore the country's segregation policy and its injustices into shreds. They tried to prove to Mr Gordon Walker that the white rulers of Southern Rhodesia were too committed to their policy of race separation to be entrusted with the fate of the inhabitants of Northern Rhodesia and Nyasaland. With an incisive mind and frank approach one of the Chiefs summarized the case of his fellow countrymen in what I thought was a logical and reasonable statement. He said that before Africans could seriously consider the merits of Federation, the white man in Southern Rhodesia should put his own house in order. All the white man had to do was to scrap his oppressive native policy and create conditions in which all the citizens of the country were on an equal footing legally, politically, economically and educationally. Unless this were done, it was logical to suppose that a Federation inspired by an unreformed white-ruled Southern Rhodesia would be used to introduce the same pattern of racial segregation into the northern territories and thereby

32

put an end to the prospect of eventual African majority rule in the protectorates of Northern Rhodesia and Nyasaland.

I recall feeling utterly stupefied and disgusted, and unable to take any notes, as one of the official interpreters put into English what the Chiefs were supposed to be saying. His translation, if translation it could be called, so differed from the meaning and intention of most of the Chiefs as to have been quite something else. He was censoring their views. I remember hearing the assertion again and again that the Chiefs thought the Federation was a good idea, but that they needed more time to think about it. This, of course, was the point of view that the Native Affairs Department wished the British Minister to hear. But as for the Chiefs' strong and relevant criticism of the Rhodesian Government's misdeeds, to that no reference was made whatever, as far as I can remember. I understood now why it had been decided not to employ the services of an African interpreter. An African translator, and there were several very good ones in the country who worked in the courts, would have dutifully put into clear, unequivocal English what the Chiefs were saying. That wouldn't do.

I had been a journalist for nearly six years, and while conditions had been generally difficult for me, as for any other African writer, I had managed to maintain an impartial attitude at Press conferences. But that day my patience and professional standing were put to the supreme test. Feeling angry and outraged at what was a deliberate distortion of African views on such a vital matter, I decided to make a protest there and then. But before I did so, I thought it wise to tell my colleague what I felt I should do as a matter of duty. He was just as angry, but pointed out that if I said what I felt I would create a crisis which would result in my losing my job; and I certainly would not be employed in a similar capacity by anyone anywhere in the country. 'I am afraid you would be starting a war you would never win in the end,' he said.

I took his advice and said nothing; I sat in mortified silence, but raged inwardly throughout the proceedings which I dismissed as a piece of blatant trickery from start to finish.

Having, at that time, confidence in Britain, I believed that the real views of the African Chiefs would influence the course of the negotiations on Federation and would be conveyed, word for word, to a British Minister. After all he represented a government and a party which had given convincing proof both at home and abroad that it stood for equal rights for all men everywhere. Since the end of the Second World War I had read any amount of literature on the British Labour Party. My imagination had been fired by its record of service to humanity, especially in alleviating the lot of the British working classes and in speaking out against colonialism everywhere. I knew that they had freed India. I knew the views on African questions of some of the Labour Members of Parliament, the Fabians and the Movement for Colonial Freedom and I believed these people to be against class and colour privilege. And so I was pleased to think that, given a few more years of power, the Labour Government would live up to its principles by sorting out the accumulated mess left through neglect by previous British Governments in Southern Rhodesia and set the country on an even political and racial course.

Of course, the outward appearance of Mr Gordon Walker did not encourage these hopes. He did not say much at any of his conferences, nor did he get worked up about anything so that you could assess his feelings one way or the other. Apart from fondling, lighting and from time to time smoking his pipe, he seemed to be somewhat indifferent and bored. But this mattered little to me, and even less to the Chiefs reciting their tale of oppression and repression by the Government of the Rhodesian white minority. In their eyes he was the Super Chief of white Rhodesia and he had to be told of all the settlers' misdeeds and lack of conscience in their treatment of the black man. In their African simplicity, the Chiefs expected that this man, who was the British Empire, the British nation, Monarchy and Government all rolled into one, would have all the power in the world to discipline the white settlers and so lighten the white burden on the Africans' shoulders. And even to me, the way Mr Gordon Walker sat on his chair or looked, with his strangely serene, contented face, was unimportant. Like the Chiefs, I was too wrapped up in my illusory dreams to take account of such trivial details. I had put the Labour Government and the Labour Movement on a pedestal. Therefore I was indescribably furious that this Minister was not being properly informed of what the African Chiefs thought, not only about the Federation, but more important still, about the whole train of events which had turned Southern Rhodesia into a pocket edition of South Africa without the mighty British Government raising a finger. Apart from this, I wanted a correct record of the feelings of our representatives, so that historians would know that the Africans of Southern Rhodesia were totally against race segregation and its possible extension to the protectorates north of the Zambezi.

One of the suggestions made on this occasion needs repeating here. The Chief spoke to this effect:

In one of your laws of international conduct, you stipulate that a conquered nation should pay an agreed sum of money to the conqueror over a period of years, say twenty-five years. When this and other conditions have been fulfilled, you forgive each other and live as friends afterwards. You did this to the Germans after the First World War. And even after the recent war you do not seem to bear a grudge against the Germans. You certainly do not segregate or discriminate against any German. But you have not shown this human and Christian attitude to us black people. We fought you in the 1896 rebellion and that is a very long time ago. Yet you have not forgiven us. On the contrary, the more progress we make the more you harden your attitude and enact harsh laws against us. . . . Why don't you exact some punishment on us as you imposed on the Germans? We are prepared to pay whatever fine you choose to state as long as we know that this will buy back our freedom in the only country that God gave us.

It was a peculiarly African piece of logic, but only understood by Africans, and as I remember only too well, none of it reached Mr Gordon Walker's ears.

The experience I have just recounted is most important to the theme of this book. This and the less obviously Machiavellian tactics used by the white Rhodesians and their friends in Britain to achieve UDI show that the facts about Rhodesia and her indigenous people have been cleverly, but sadly, twisted and made to suit the interests of those who control the country. In most cases they are totally unreliable. The country has gone from bad to worse and will continue to do so, as long as white Rhodesians and their friends go on evading the truth. This truth is embodied in the unalterable solid fact of our existence, five million of us, who want to decide our own present and future in our own country, just as the British, Americans and any other group of people do in theirs.

4

*Oral tribal history: the origin of the
VaShawasha people; their arrival in
Zimbabwe and their identification with Shona
civilization; prosperity under the
Monomotapa dynasty; contact with the
Portuguese; eventual break-up of the
Monomotapa empire.*

Even in Mashonganyika village, with its voluble oral historians,
the past of the VaShawasha people and their Shona kith and
kin was largely lost in antiquity, especially the history of the
period before the arrival of the Ndebele from South Africa.
However, in telling what they knew, the elders of the tribe gave
their history lustre and romantic glory which should be put
on record. Predictably, their accounts conflicted with many of
the negative representations of Shona society that have been
put forward to the outside world by ill-informed European
historians. Unfortunately, because of the inferior education of
my people and other imposed handicaps, we have not as yet
produced our own scholars who could do some thorough research
into the full history of the Shona and put it into its proper
perspective. Consequently, this kind of work has mostly been left
to Europeans. The result is that for the most part the Shona
have been portrayed as a primitive, cowardly people.

In the opinion of my tribe, however, the facts were very
different. As was natural, in their general enthusiasm to impress
and inspire the young, the VaShawasha historians talked a great
deal of the era before white occupation, recalling freedom and
peace, and emphasizing the achievement of an African civilization which was unique. That civilization put the dignity and
equality of the individual first and foremost. Race, colour, wealth
and creed, which were now the most important considerations

C

under white rule, had no place in the Shona empires that flourished in old Zimbabwe.

Of course, one was in no position to tell what was strictly true, what was half-true, what was embellishment and what was sheer patriotic fantasy. But I still count myself fortunate in having heard firsthand certain facts and facets of the chequered story of my tribe which I would not have known, had I been born in an urban environment. From these facts I was able to form a fair knowledge and understanding of my tribal background and the part that the VaShawasha people played in the defence of freedom in Zimbabwe, both when the Ndebele threatened it, and, much more important, when the Europeans arrived with their philosophy of total and permanent subjection of the black man.

From what is known so far, there is little doubt that the VaShawasha, a Shona people, are a branch of the Bantu. Like all the other African tribes belonging to this polyglot group of people, they once moved constantly over the vast areas of northeastern, central, south central and southern Africa, if not parts of west and equatorial Africa. Some of the more assertive village historians claimed that the original VaShawasha came from Ethiopia or near its borders. During this period, which lasted several centuries, whole tribes, mainly of the Bantu stock, moved southwards reaching as far down as parts of what is today the Cape Province of South Africa. That these tribes were possessed of extraordinary energy can be judged by the example of the Zulus, Xhosas, Sotho and other Bantu people who reached southern Africa several centuries before the white man, and established tribal kingdoms that took the Europeans the best part of the last century to subdue.

However, it would seem that once they had reached Zimbabwe, the VaShawasha decided, as did the other Shona peoples, to stake their future permanently in this beautiful country, so richly endowed with a good climate, rainfall, grazing pasture and other natural assets. There is no evidence that they moved any farther south. Why they came all this way from Ethiopia is one of the great mysteries of these strange times. It was probably a combination of collective tribal adventure, lust for power and the search for a more congenial environment and richer sources of food supplies. As it happened, their choice of Zimbabwe could not have been improved upon. The country offered every advantage and lent itself to a stable and creative human existence. Being a virile, war-like and well-organized people, they were destined to make a strong impact on the development of human societies in this part of Africa. For some considerable time, they established themselves in what is today the Fort Victoria area, in Southern Mashonaland.

Nevertheless, in due course, they left this part of the country and indulging, as of old, in a nomadic existence and a certain amount of blood-letting, they made their way to Central Mashonaland. In fact a section of the tribe remained in the Fort Victoria part of the country where to this day there are many people of Shawasha origin, who are no doubt the descendants of those who refused to join the general exodus of the main tribe to what is now the Salisbury district. However, those who left never returned.

Under various paramountcies, particularly that of Tingini, who gave them strong and aggressive leadership, they appear to have attained a position of unmatched power. They became the leading tribe and held sway over all or most of the other Shona tribes, who, in the manner of those days, attributed the invincibility of the VaShawasha to some secret medicine. But their power was tempered with good sense and humanity. The VaShawasha avoided a policy of senseless destruction and permanent subjection of other people. The evidence I got from Chishawasha shows that they could easily have subjugated many of their fellowmen in the Zimbabwe of that period, if they had chosen to do so. But they did not, and revealed their military prowess only if one or other of the neighbouring tribes threatened the peace of their country. In other words, they mostly played the role of policemen. They are perhaps one of the very few peoples in history who were not corrupted absolutely by absolute power.

They eventually settled down in that part of the country which they called Chishawasha. Chishawasha in ChiZezuru simply means 'a country of the VaShawasha people'. The name is also given to a small, lonely hill that stands out like a watchtower between the present Mission establishment to the south and the range of hills behind Mutimumwe village to the north.

39

The people they found there were Rozwi Shonas. These, not unnaturally, resisted the invaders, but lost the ensuing battle and were forced to move elsewhere, allegedly to what is now called Enkeldoorn. Those who did not go were absorbed into the VaShawasha society.

Because of their military, numerical and organizational supremacy, the VaShawasha were widely feared and respected. The memory of this reputation was alive even in my young days. By then every tribe in Southern Rhodesia had been effectively levelled down and tribal aristocracy was a thing of the past. Yet a great many of our neighbours, both as families and as individuals, wished to attach themselves to my tribe, to inter-marry with the VaShawasha and even to claim our totems. It was very much like the height of the British Empire when many Europeans wished to be Englishmen. Indeed, our past splendour was so strongly imprinted on the memories of some of our Shona countrymen that they were still saluting us as 'the brave', 'tamers but generous conquerors' and various other compliments when I was a child. Behind these expressions of admiration were a recognition of the courage of the VaShawasha people and the positive contribution they had made to the security, peace and prosperity of the Shona societies of free Zimbabwe. From some of these admirers I gathered that the VaShawasha were the main pillar of Shona civilization. They feared no one, had never lost a single battle or bowed down to the authority of anyone until the coming of the Europeans from South Africa. These accounts merely confirmed what the VaShawasha said them-selves.

Among ourselves we addressed each other as '*Mukanya*', '*Soko*', '*Matarira*' and '*Murewha*', salutations which are hard to translate, but which invoked the deepest feelings of tribal pride, identity and kinship. Thus in a moment of crisis, such as aggression from outside, these names would be spelled out as a clarion call to battle and no able-bodied MuShawasha worth his salt would flinch from losing his life in the cause of the freedom of his tribe or ally. In every case these names reminded any true MuShawasha that only the very best was expected of him, the very best in physical and moral courage, truth, justice, mercy and compassion. A member of the tribe was there-

40

fore not only expected to be the vehicle of the best of human virtues, but also to feel that he was inferior to no one, except to God and the dead ancestors. In the 1920s, the white man was most certainly not the equal of a true MuShawasha.

One of the obvious advantages of this military, but magnanimous reputation was that the VaShawasha could always pick and choose the most beautiful women from their admirers and, in consequence, the bulk of the men and women in the village of Mashonganyika were strikingly handsome, intelligent and physically strong. The then Chief Mashonganyika himself was an extraordinarily handsome man.

In Chishawasha they had found a piece of country which was very much to their liking. From then on, rather than concentrate on maintaining their military superiority, they decided to pursue the arts of peace and friendly co-existence with their Zezuru, Manyika and other Shona-speaking neighbours. They played a decisive role in building up the Shona democratic societies and maintaining the peaceful conditions that prevailed in central Africa for almost as long as this area remained untouched by external aggression. In the absence of written records, it is, unfortunately, impossible to guess exactly when the VaShawasha arrived in Central Mashonaland. At this stage, however, this is not important. But it is interesting to note that in this part of Zimbabwe, the VaShawasha people took their place among Shona societies that were very much akin to those they had left in the south. Apart from language similarities, they were organized into a confederation with well-established democratic institutions and a long tradition of national consciousness and progress.

The salient features of these societies included a strong awareness of their ethnical, religious and political ties. Under this system, these people were not only able to defend their corporate freedom, but also prospered and became highly accomplished in iron craft, trade and diplomacy. In the long period of peace that followed, they were able to devote plenty of time to the study and knowledge of the weather and the development of what was for those days a very high degree of agricultural production. The results were so satisfactory that the need for maintaining a military organization, such as the one that the VaShawasha had built up in the past, was no longer considered necessary. And so they, like the Romans, lost their military arts and developed a love of peace and its material and spiritual rewards.

It would be wrong, however, to suppose that there were no conflicts between the Shona paramountcies during this epoch. There were, but I was assured that they were on a minor scale and were quickly sorted out, thanks to the good sense of these people, who put first the ultimate interests of their common culture and welfare. When tribal differences occurred, the VaShawasha were, more often than not, called upon to settle them, either by mediation or by punishing those who were in the wrong. But on the whole, they enjoyed a long period of peace and prosperity.

In recounting our history, my grandparents and other village historians were naturally nostalgic about the 'good old days'. They remembered best of all the periods in which harvests were good, bad or indifferent. Indeed, times of scarcity or abundance of food tended to be useful aids to the recollection of their history, as well as, of course, outstanding leaders who had cared for the well-being of the tribe. Their memories connected each event of this kind with a long series of other related events. In this way, the history of the tribe was kept alive.

There is no doubt that the growing of food was one of the greatest achievements of the Shona society of that day. Having the peace, the time and the social structure conducive to the production of food, they developed a remarkably advanced system of agriculture. They discovered which types of soil and conditions were good for their various crops. They understood the various systems of preserving the fertility of the soil, such as crop rotation, letting the fields lie fallow from time to time and the application of manure and humus. As time went on, the VaShawasha people and their kindred tribesmen came to measure a man's worth and standing in society on the basis of his husbandry and industry, as proved by his harvests rather than his boasts, his cunning or physical strength. Thus among the pillars of any Shona tribal grouping were people called *hurudza*. This title, both in the singular and plural, means an agricultural baron or barons, and was given to individuals who had proved themselves to be hard-working, productive farmers.

They were thus accorded a social standing comparable to that of a highly successful industrial tycoon in the capitalist societies of today. A *hurudza*, in this context, was a man not only of sustained and conscientious industry. He was also a man of wisdom, of value to the people of Zimbabwe. He was well connected socially and accordingly played an influential role in all Shona tribal and national affairs.

On the other hand, the opposites of the *hurudza* aristocracy were the *tsimbe*, lazy and improvident people, who were almost looked upon as social outcasts. They did not starve. No one went without food in the midst of plenty among the Shona because their social conscience did not permit the neglect of those in need, however much they were responsible for their own condition. Nor were they entirely ostracized, again for the reason that my people always put every human being above material considerations. But because the *tsimbe* did not work hard enough and might have to be fed by the tribe, they were branded with this name and in most cases they felt ashamed of it. As a result of the stigma attached to this social label and the psychological stress it produced in the unfortunate victims of this tribal intolerance, very few people remained *tsimbe* if they could possibly help it. It proved to be an extremely effective way of deterring people from developing lazy habits and of ensuring a high standard of living for everybody in the country.

One of the lessons I value most from my tribal education is that of work, particularly when it involves growing things. It was well and truly instilled into my mind as the very essence of human dignity. And so I have always despised the white Rhodesian or African foreman who stands about reading a newspaper or with his hands in his pockets as he oversees those who perform work that has been stigmatized by white society's education as 'menial' and therefore below the dignity of an educated man. Until I left Mashonganyika village I could not imagine that any man could lead a life of leisure and get any satisfaction from it. To do so was to degrade yourself and to forfeit the respect and the good-will of black men. And so I had the valuable experience of seeing every able-bodied man and woman in the social hierarchy of the tribe, from Chief Mashonganyika himself down to the ordinary individual, live

43

by the sweat of his or her brow. And they were all immensely proud of it. As they used to say, food-growing was one of the highest forms of human self-expression, whereas waxing fat on the fruits of other people's labour, as many white men did in Southern Rhodesia, was a form of decadence.

I will also add that when I started to travel more extensively in the 1950s, I was utterly astonished to discover that there were certain African tribes in Central and East Africa, such as the Masai, who had not yet reached the stage of being able to grow maize and other crops with anything like the same zeal, discipline and constancy that the VaShawasha and other Shona people had applied in my boyhood, and indeed had been applying for unknown decades before the arrival of the white races. I had taken for granted that the slogging and the drudgery of an agricultural existence, with its rich rewards of crops and the dignity it conferred on man, was one of the most basic joys of life. Until I learnt otherwise, I had thought that this was the one common factor which Africans everywhere had achieved in their civilization. I knew, of course, that in the past the Ndebele had not been keen agriculturalists. But this was due to their preference for the military life and we despised them for it. Anyway, after their defeat in 1893, they came to terms with our way of life and they began to gain a little respect in the eyes of the industrious Shona people.

I still think that the real wealth, self-respect and independence of Africa is in its soil and not in polished office desks paid for by the aid-giving industrial countries of the world. After all, most great civilizations and peoples have been sustained and fertilized by agriculture.

My people practised this philosophy to a high degree. And during this golden age of Shona freedom, the VaShawasha, along with their allies, established extensive economic and diplomatic ties with the outside world. Of these, the commercially enterprising Arabs and Portuguese deserve special mention. Both brought guns, cloths and other products of eastern and European manufacture to central Africa. In exchange, they took away gold, copper, silver and other metals which the Shona mined and refined. In due course there developed an extensive and lucrative trade in these and other commodities, which proves beyond doubt the extent to which the Shona people of Zimbabwe as a whole were advancing in the development of their own mining technology. I saw some evidence of this in Mashonganyika village, where most men of my grandfather's generation did their own extracting, refining and fashioning of iron and copper for domestic use. They remembered and related again and again the prosperity that this kind of trade engendered.

Unfortunately, we do not know for certain to what extent the VaShawasha were associated with the great Shona kingdom of Monomotapa that flourished in central Africa about three to six hundred years ago and is revealed in early Portuguese records on their colonial adventures in east and central Africa. However, the evidence that is available suggests that my tribe, together with most of those in Zimbabwe that never came under Ndebele domination, were very much a part of this great Shona civilization. The founders of the Monomotapa empire are known to have come from the north before A.D. 900. It is reasonable to suggest that the VaShawasha formed part of the empire and were among its citizens, if not its builders. But whether they came before or after it was founded, once they had reached Zimbabwe they took their place in it and were completely absorbed into its culture and civilization. And that explains why pre-1890 free Zimbabwe had strong elements of democracy, a national consciousness and a peaceful and civilized way of life—in sharp contrast to that of the destructive Ndebele, Zulu and Xhosa in South Africa.

There is no doubt that, by the standards of those obscure times, the kingdom of Monomotapa represented one of the greatest achievements of the peoples of Africa. Beginning as a small kingdom in what is today north-east Mashonaland, it grew into an empire or commonwealth which embraced most of what later became Mashonaland and part of Portuguese East Africa. Its unique character lies not only in its existence about the fifteen and sixteenth centuries, when Europeans regarded Africa as the 'dark continent' and Africans as primitive savages, but perhaps more particularly in that the king reigned rather than ruled. He was a symbol of Shona unity, as the Queen is to the British nation, rather than an emperor who had his hands firmly and despotically on the reins of government. He left the government of his tribal subjects to their chiefs and councillors, who derived their power from the common people. They, the chiefs and local government officials, were of course ultimately answerable to the king. This is how the Portuguese found the Monomotapa empire organized. And this was at a time when most or all of Europe was suffering under the oppressive yoke of autocratic kings and emperors.

The empire was fascinating in many other respects. Again according to Portuguese sources, the royal court displayed symptoms of splendour which contradict later European claims that the Shona were a primitive race. Surrounding the king, we are told, were appointed nobles, mediums, historians, intellectuals and various other officials and courtiers, including musicians. In short, here was a civilized society that was conceived and sustained by the Shona people, whose descendants in present-day Southern Rhodesia are being denied the most elementary human rights.

While the kingdom of Monomotapa lasted, it brought peace, freedom, progress and wealth to its citizens and invited admiration and envy from outsiders. Among the earliest visiting traders to the king's court were the Arabs, who were to have a decisive influence in the development of trade in Zimbabwe; later they also contributed, perhaps unwittingly, to the foreign treachery that eventually destroyed both the Monomotapa and the Rozwi dynasties in this part of Africa.

In 1498 the intrepid navigator, Vasco da Gama, discovered what was to be Portuguese East Africa and the sea route to India. Both discoveries were fateful for the African people, for they heralded the beginning of the black and white struggle and the present tragedy of white southern Africa. The territory was settled by the Portuguese in 1505 and they wasted no time in making their influence felt as far into the interior as they could go. Very soon they came into contact with the Monomotapa empire. They were fascinated by its court, its wealth and everything about it.

As all the world knows, the first rule in the Portuguese book of colonial rules, then as now, was to make everyone a Catholic. The Portuguese prevailed on the Monomotapa* himself to become a Christian, while his empire and his subjects entered into a special relationship with Portugal. In other words, these wily people wished to add this intriguing gold-rich African kingdom to their own growing empire. While the Monomotapa took a long time to come to terms with Christianity, he for a time accepted the proffered friendship. The Portuguese, jubilant at this partial success, sent into his kingdom a number of traders, diplomats, teachers and missionaries, such as the famous Jesuit Father Goncalo da Silveira, who arrived in 1560 and eventually baptized the king. They built trading stations, churches, convents, monasteries and other manifestations of their own civilization.

Now, of course, the Arabs, who were there first, did not take too kindly to these developments. Apart from the clash of economic interests, the Cross and the Crescent could not possibly tolerate each other's presence. And it was not long, therefore, before the court of Monomotapa was turned into a centre of Arab-Portuguese intrigue, each trying as hard as they could to influence the emperor into throwing the other out.

Many years ago I read a short biography of Father da Silveira, which described the fascinating, if tragic, circumstances in which he became the victim of Arab scheming and how he was ultimately put to death on the orders of the Monomotapa who had been convinced by the Arabs that his sorcery would soon lead the Portuguese to liquidate him as well as his empire. In the James Bond-like atmosphere engendered by these two parasitic rivals, the Monomotapa became angry and in the end decided to have no more dealings with foreigners.

The change of mood on the part of the emperor, together with the assassination of da Silveira, unleashed a long struggle between the people of Zimbabwe and the Portuguese. The Arabs, who were in the minority, were easily turned out of the country. But the Portuguese were not going to let such a rich prize slip from their hands. The assassination of Father da Silveira offered them a chance to embark on a policy of conquest of the Monomotapa empire. And so in 1569 the Portuguese sent

* Monomotapa means 'emperor' or 'king', or may be derived from *munhu mutapkwa,* 'he who was exiled', or 'he who came from afar'.

47

an expedition under Francisco Barreto to seize the king's mines as well as bring his kingdom directly under Lisbon's rule. Barreto and his forces suffered such losses that they had to withdraw, he himself dying on the way back to the coast. The Portuguese mounted several other expeditions, all charged with the mission of subduing this African state for the crown of Portugal. But for a time the Monomotapa was more than a match for the Europeans and was able to repel their invasion. He ordered all churches, convents and monasteries to be destroyed completely. However, the determined Portuguese would not abandon their objective and in 1629 they succeeded in making the Monomotapa a vassal of their crown. But the Shona did not remain submissive for long, for they rose again between 1629 and 1630 and defeated the Portuguese. Still the latter tried again and from time to time restored their sovereignty until they were finally expelled from what is now Rhodesia.

We shall probably never know the full story of this conflict which was continued into the eighteenth century. The success and determination of Shona resistance should be rated as an epic struggle against a European power which had the relatively vast resources of the mother-country, Portugal, and its colonies, Brazil, Angola and Goa. She was making fortunes from the slave trade and her national pride as a sea-faring and colonial nation, backed by a Papal Bull, was at its peak. Shona resistance which threw the invaders out of Zimbabwe can only underline a very high level of political, social and military organization. But in the long run, the struggle was costly, and caused wounds from which their national life was never really to recover. The various tribal provinces in the Monomotapa empire lost so much in blood, energy and will-power in the cause of the empire that at the end of it there was little left of the loyalty that had kept their commonwealth together. In due course their political cohesion and eventually the central organization, the Monomotapa dynasty itself, disintegrated. What remained was a much looser concept of community of interests between the various Shona tribes, together with their common culture, democratic chieftainships and, of course, their technology. Their demise made way for the Rozwi who were to establish a flourishing empire to the south.

However, these events had occurred such a long time before as to be unremembered in the nineteenth-century Zimbabwe; by that time friendly human and trade relationships had been forged between the Shona in Zimbabwe and the Portuguese in Mozambique. I certainly heard nothing but praise and admiration for the colour-blind Portuguese in contrast to the hard and colour-conscious white Rhodesians. Individuals like grandfather Mizha and a great many other people of his generation often spoke of their good friends—*MaPutukezi*—Portuguese traders who came among them both for business and exchange of ideas. The best known of these was *Kuveya,* as they called him, not being able to pronounce his proper name Gouveia. He was, in fact, a Goanese of mixed parentage holding Portuguese citizenship. He travelled very extensively in the course of promoting his own and Portuguese economic interests. He would appear to have been a man of considerable charm, with a flair for making friends and influencing people. He was spoken of well by all who had met or had known of him, including grandmother Madzidza, whose otherwise inordinately strong prejudices against people of white or almost white colour did not apply to this enterprising man. She admitted to liking him enormously, almost as if he were a person of her own race. He spoke ChiZezuru as well as any foreigner could, was conversant with and observed Shona customs and manners of social etiquette, all qualifications which enabled him to be trusted and treated as a friend. His advice and the news of the outside world he brought from the coast were of special value to the VaShawasha and their neighbours. He sold an enormous number of guns, among other things, to the Shona people, which were to prove a great asset to my people in the rebellion. It can then be seen that he was no ordinary man in the eyes of the VaShawasha.

There were, indeed, a great many other Portuguese personalities who roamed Zimbabwe in quest of riches and adventure and on the whole struck everyone as being amiable, warm, sincere and simple people. But Gouveia outshone them all, having made the most impact on the VaShawasha, and he left a name which was almost legendary even in the 1920s.

I think it is appropriate here to add that this gentleman was still very much present when the buccaneering Pioneer Column reached Mashonaland in 1890 and he became the victim of rough justice from Rhodes' representatives. This was because of rivalry between the Portuguese and Rhodes over Zimbabwe. For some time that portion of Southern Rhodesia called Manicaland had had stronger economic ties with Portuguese Mozambique than with the rest of Mashonaland. The Portuguese had a syndicate which exploited some of its resources. But on arriving at Fort Salisbury, the newly-appointed administrator of Rhodes' company, Archibald Colquhoun, the reckless Dr Jameson, Selous and a few police lost no time in going to Manicaland and duping Paramount Chief Mutasa into signing an agreement, which surrendered his country to the British. When the Portuguese heard of this, they sent Captain Gouveia to Mutasa, with specific instructions to arrest the Chief. On November 15, 1890, Dr Jameson, with a handful of his police, stormed the Chief's headquarters, routed the Portuguese garrison and arrested Gouveia, together with another director of the Portuguese syndicate. They were swiftly sent to Cape Town as prisoners. And that ended the long chapter of association between Gouveia and the Portuguese, and their Shona friends.

However, after the long struggle which ended somewhere between the first half of the eighteenth century and before 1890, the Portuguese were a very positive influence in Zimbabwe. They traded extensively with the Shona, as did the Arabs, who had returned once the country was free of Portuguese colonial control. Needless to say, the guns that the Arabs and the Portuguese sold to the Shona were highly prized acquisitions. They were useful for hunting as well as fighting when the occasion arose. They certainly proved their value when the Ndebele arrived and started to disturb the peace and stability of the country. But at some stage or other, the Shona designed their own guns, appropriately called *zwigidi* (*chigidi*, for one) from the sound they made, which they were to put to very extensive if not too effective use, in the *Chindunduma*, the 1896 rebellion, against Cecil Rhodes' men and the British soldiers who came to help them.

From what I was told, however, *chigidi* was either completely effective or ineffective. In other words, when fired, it was either deadly or made no impression at all. And that depended on all sorts of factors, marksmanship, distance, the quality of its make and the quantity of the powder put in. The powder was made from the droppings of rock-rabbits, of which there were many up and down the country. Apparently, in every case it blew a lot of smoke, which temporarily bleared the vision of the gunman. Jakobo thought that this contraption was overrated. He said that it took a long time to pound in the necessary amount of powder. Then again, he went on, when fired, it was liable to blow to pieces with regrettable results to the unfortunate user. He may well have been joking, but one never knew because he never withdrew any of his wild statements. Other people, however, spoke highly of it. But we can understand that while it answered the needs of a peaceful people, it must have had distinct disadvantages when pitched against the modern weapons that the white settlers from South Africa had at their disposal. All the same, it was a remarkable invention and it was being improved with the passage of time, as indeed were all the other technical achievements of my people. And they were all ample evidence of the steadily developing culture of the Shona and their democratic way of life. All these accomplishments, the guns, mining, smelting and countless others, to say nothing of their system of government and agriculture, are an argument against all later political and racialist propaganda that my people were helplessly primitive and needed to be protected and to be civilized.

Here I must make a point about which I feel strongly. It is that when the people from Europe, first the Portuguese and then the British South Africans, who colonized this part of Africa, put a stop to all these and other manifestations of African evolution towards a higher form of civilization, their role was in many respects comparable to that played by the Vandals, the Goths and Visi-Goths against Roman civilization.

There appears to have been strong traces of intermarriage with the Arabs and no doubt the Portuguese as well. Several people in Mashonganyika and the Chishawasha Mission had distinctly Arabic noses and some traces of European origin splendidly blended with African charm and natural directness. Integration was one of the strongest and most salient features of Shona societies. With marriage within the same tribe being

51

the taboo of all taboos, the VaShawasha were being constantly supplied with new blood, which, together with their eye for beautiful women, produced a breed of energetic and highly intelligent men and women. As was stressed in my tribal education, their guiding rule towards aliens in those days of complete self-determination was to keep an open house and to accept every stranger as one of themselves if he showed no evil intentions. Thus all visitors were expected to remove from their shoulders any weapons they might have and lower them as soon as they approached any Shawasha settlement. Accordingly, they were given friendship, assistance and open hospitality. But woe betide any stranger who sailed in with his weapons on his shoulders! This was taken as an act of supreme defiance. The visitor in question was extremely lucky if he came out of the situation in one piece. I cannot recall a single instance of rudeness or tribal arrogance on the part of the VaShawasha of Mashonganyika village towards outsiders who came among us and were well behaved. All too often strangers were treated better than local people and they could stay as long as they wished.

With this sort of upbringing, I was spared the ravages of tribalistic feelings which are all too common among most Africans and which have caused senseless divisions and anarchy in parts of modern Africa where unity and prosperity should transcend the self-defeating ends of tribalism. Most certainly the Shona people as a whole had a greater regard for all human beings than the European settlers, for the latter have introduced into Southern Rhodesia a type of racialism that has to be experienced from the African receiving end to be understood in its stark dehumanizing reality. The VaShawasha were ever proud to be VaShawasha, but even at the very height of their power, they would never have contemplated designing a system in which they could keep another set of people in permanent subjection. As we shall see, the unopposed entry of Europeans into Zimbabwe was made possible by this universal Shona conception of human brotherhood. And equally the subsequent violent reaction to white rule from the Shona was caused mainly by the failure of the Rhodesian Europeans to respect this timeless philosophy that was the foundation of Shona civilization.

As everyone knows, wherever the Arabs and the Portuguese went in Africa they dealt in slavery and soon enough corrupted the African ruling class of the period into co-operating in this nefarious trade. Here the Cross and the Crescent were at one and deserve to be equally condemned. No sooner had the Portuguese brought Angola and Mozambique under their colonial control than they turned them into sources of the lucrative slave trade, particularly with South America. The Arabs did exactly the same, either by compulsion, if any particular tribe was too weak to defend itself, or by bribery and persuasion. But in Zimbabwe, neither seemed to have made much, if any, headway in this trade. Some 'slave' pits* survive in Inyanga, Manicaland. But I am not aware that they exist anywhere else. Neither do I know of any written records of the slave trade by any of the eighteenth and nineteenth-century hunters, travellers and missionaries who roamed about Zimbabwe. Livingstone came across it on a vast scale in Nyasaland and wrote about it with great horror. But neither he nor anyone else tells us that this pestilential trade blighted the peoples of Zimbabwe. Although most of the tribal elders I knew in Mashonganyika were able to remember, either from personal experience or from oral tradition, most of the great events of the nineteenth and previous centuries which had shaped their society, they made no reference to this form of commercial activity. My first knowledge of slavery began from seeing pictures of very ugly black men and women on labels of tea or coffee tins. On asking who they were, one or other of my relations explained that they were supposed to represent black people taken by force from Africa to America by avaricious white men.

Admittedly, the great distances from the east coast to Zimbabwe would have made the slave trade a pretty hazardous as well as costly undertaking. But the Arabs and Portuguese traders came this far for gold and other mineral products, so some other explanation must be found for the non-existence of this trade in Zimbabwe. And it is not far to seek. I think we must find it in the democratic organization of the kingdom of Monomotapa, and in the failure of the Portuguese to conquer

*It is now generally accepted that the pits at Inyanga were used for small cattle, not for slaves.

this kingdom and make it part of their East African Empire. The Portuguese would-be slave traders, as also the Arab, must have understood that Shona culture and spiritual tradition did not tolerate this form of commercial transaction. To the Shona the idea of slavery would have been repugnant and resisted at any cost. In our religious system the life of a human being was and still is regarded as being the most sacred thing in this world. To take it away was, and is, justified only in war or self-defence. Otherwise at any other time or for any other reason the killer or killers bring upon themselves *ngozi*, a permanent curse, which visits many generations of the murderer, unless and until the killer or his descendants atone adequately and are cleansed and purified by a reputable medicine man. Life was synonymous with freedom, inasmuch as the body, the soul and the mind made up one whole individual. If you took away a man's freedom, then you deprived, or partially deprived him of his life. In other words, they did not regard physical and mental freedom as separate entities. By taking away one of these essential conditions from a human being, you had committed some kind of murder and therefore you brought upon yourself *ngozi*. Being responsible for a state in which a man lost his freedom, his country and his tribe for all time would, by this definition, have constituted a sin of such gravity that it cried out for vengeance both in this and in the next world.

The tribe was not only controlled by the collective wisdom of the paramount chiefs, but was also guided by the mediums who were supposed to be in direct contact with the spirits of the dead ancestors. The word of the mediums was as good as law, particularly of the senior mediums, speaking with the authority of the spirits of the dead on matters of freedom, life and death. They would hardly have compromised on questions touching on the sanctity of human life. If, therefore, slavery was once a fact of life in Zimbabwe, it must have been under compulsion and the rulers of Shona society would certainly have not touched its tainted rewards. As we shall see, the Shona people put up one of the most sustained African freedom struggles at the close of the nineteenth century, and they did so because the conditions under which they were ruled by the South African English settlers looked to them like a form of individual and national slavery.

One last point on this question is that graft and greed do not appear to have been characteristic of my people. This fact was testified by their egalitarian way of life and, of course, by their initial detestation of the European settlers' acquisitive tendencies which ultimately drove them to take up arms in defence of their land and freedom, especially when they were coerced to work for white employers. The trade they had with the Arabs and the Portuguese seems to have been conducted on cautious terms, thus leaving them uncorrupted by the kind of avarice which overcame very many African kings and kingdoms elsewhere.

Until the Ndebele and later the Europeans came into the country, life among the VaShawasha ran along orderly, civilized lines, if occasionally disturbed by factors over which they had no control, such as droughts, cattle diseases, small pox or the depredations of locusts. Thus they had the time to live fully, to learn to think and to study at leisure, to develop a material and spiritual culture that was strongly allied to the soil and its fruits and to win the friendship and admiration of outsiders who had similar pacific inclinations. Their day-to-day life was in the main governed by the seasons, each season having a definite meaning and functional significance. The rainy season was from November to March and was for ploughing, sowing and weeding, April to May for harvesting, June to July for thrashing, combined with beer-drinking and August to about the middle of October for spirit dances, hunting, fishing, travel and communication with their neighbours. And towards the end of October men and women thought and planned anxiously about their next lot of crops and the work involved to make their harvests bigger and better. Anyone who knows the Shona people and their culture in any depth will testify to their extra-ordinarily rich stock of proverbs and fables, their comprehensive names of trees, herbs and animal life, elaborate customs pertaining to marriage, paternity, social and civic responsibilities and their acute sense of right and wrong, which I am convinced is still superior to that of so-called civilized man. All these qualities and achievements emphasize that they were more preoccupied with the study of man and nature than with power and military feats.

However, we only have to trace Cecil Rhodes' trail leading to the legendary land of Ophir and to look at Southern Rhodesia today to appreciate that in the long run the Shona's philosophy of live and let live was monumental folly. I should like to think that white settlement in Rhodesia might have taken a different shape had my forefathers built up stronger political systems, with the necessary military and economic organization to defend themselves against external destructive forces. I should like to think that Southern Rhodesia, free from the evils of racial supremacy, could have been a great force for good in Africa. If her advanced industrial and commercial systems and the energies of her people, black and white, were freed from racialism and instead were harnessed to the concept of democracy and human brotherhood, it might have guaranteed steady, if not rapid economic and political development of central and east Africa and, indirectly, the rest of Africa. More than that, Southern Rhodesia might in that event have helped South Africa to solve her own racial problems. But this mad dream of mine, for mad it must be, judged in the context of contemporary Rhodesia's political and racial thinking, was doomed from the start. How far my forefathers are to be blamed for having failed to sustain a national system that could have prevented the impending disaster of European occupation before it actually happened in 1890, is a question I cannot answer. Equally, as a Christian, I cannot answer the question why God permitted to happen the whole train of events from the arrival of the Ndebele right up to UDI.

5

*The false claim by Rhodes that all the
Shona were under Ndebele rule; the extent
of Ndebele power in Zimbabwe; the
repulsion of the invading Ndebele army
by the VaShawasha; the Rozwi people;
the mediums; the battle of Chitungwiza
and the capture of Chaminuka.*

Almost up to the Unilateral Declaration of Independence in
1965 the official line on the history of Southern Rhodesia fostered
the belief that the Shona people throughout Zimbabwe were
hapless victims of Ndebele savagery, from which they were grate-
fully delivered by white men. Successive Southern Rhodesian
governments have claimed that the white man's coming brought
salvation to the primitive indigenous population of this part
of the world. White rule, they went on, had conferred on us
a freedom and a future which we would otherwise have not
had as subjects of the blood-thirsty Ndebele, who were intent on
exterminating my people. And to give point and edge to this
claim, white Rhodesians of all kinds until recently used to quote
the famous dictum of Mr Cecil Rhodes in which he promised
'equal rights to all civilized men' south of the Zambezi. I have
no doubt that this promise sounds today to Rhodesian Front
ears like one of Karl Marx's or Lenin's revolutionary sayings.
But in the pre-Rhodesian Front era it was used as the stock
answer to all African grievances and a constant reminder to the
Shona in particular that they had been saved from a dreadful
fate and therefore should be eternally grateful.

But the facts I was told by the VaShawasha elders relating
to their attitude towards and relationship with the Ndebele and
the white settlers, differ widely from most accounts that have
been put forward to rationalize minority rule in Southern

Rhodesia from 1890 onwards. The VaShawasha were not filled with gratitude for their supposed 'deliverance'. On the contrary, they never stopped emphasizing that the occupation of their country was the biggest disaster and curse in the entire history of their national life in Zimbabwe. And they were right, not only because their herculean military resistance was met with more efficient and vengeful retaliation than anything they had known before, but more especially because their defeat resulted in a state of permanent subjection. Looking at Rhodesia today, with all its trappings of apartheid and the determination of the white ruling minority to keep the government in their hands for the foreseeable future, who can doubt that my grandparents were right?

But let us examine this whole question more minutely.

To dismiss the Africans' view of their history, the best argument one could offer would be to say that my grandparents were illiterate and therefore ignorant. Illiterate they might have been. But they were certainly not ignorant of their own history. Admittedly, by the time I was old enough to be able to absorb knowledge of this kind, the Ndebele era of invincible power, real or imaginary, was very much a thing of the past. But the occupation of Mashonaland and the defeat of the Ndebele by the Europeans had only taken place about three decades before. These events and the 1896 rebellion were of such importance that they were always being talked about. Indeed, most of the elderly and middle-aged men and women I knew in the 1920s and the early 1930s, had resilient memories and had forgotten little of the events which had catapulted them from freedom into the misfortune of indefinite subjection by the Europeans. To the men and women I knew in Chishawasha, the freedom of this part of Zimbabwe had been as timeless as the Great Zimbabwe Ruins. This explains the initially tolerant attitude of the Shona to the presence of the white pioneers, as well as their lack of active concern about the implication of the first clash between white men and the Ndebele in 1893. In the 1920s and the 1930s Matabeleland might have been in South Africa or some remote region far from the world of the VaShawasha. We can imagine how even more distant the worlds of the Shona and Ndebele were from each other before the Europeans came and contracted time and distance, by spanning the countryside with roads, rail bridges, telephones and wheeled vehicles. It is untrue that Lobengula, king of the Ndebele, had this vast country and its people under his control. However military-minded and blood-thirsty the Ndebele were, the size and geography of this part of Southern Rhodesia would have rendered the task impossible to achieve. As we shall see, the nearest the Ndebele impis* reached was Central Mashonaland and that was only once, according to my Chishawasha sources. They certainly made periodic incursions into Western and Northern Mashonaland, but the scale of their escapades into these regions was far from that which was accredited to them.

I have already described the long struggle of the Monomotapa people against the Portuguese. Although for a time the Portuguese subdued these people, they were in the end thrown out of Zimbabwe. I have said that the resistance weakened this Shona empire to the extent that eventually it lost its cohesion and distintegrated as a political entity. But this did not affect the essential characteristics of these people. While their central system of government had regrettably disappeared, most of its basic values remained, especially the Shona sense of freedom and their ability to defend it. They were still welded together by the complicated chain of mediums, their common culture and, of course, their advanced development in technical skills and trade. They had guns and support from the Portuguese with whom they were now on friendly terms. I have no doubt that had the Ndebele come anywhere near achieving the complete conquest of Zimbabwe that was claimed by Cecil Rhodes when he had to answer some of the awkward questions which were asked in the wake of the 1896 Mashonaland rebellion, the Shona would not have failed to seek help from the Portuguese or the Arabs. In the event, such a necessity never arose. As we shall see, when the Ndebele tried to go too far in their depredatory escapades and threatened Shona independence, they were successfully repelled. In nothing the historians in Chishawasha said was there evidence that either they, or the people of Mangwende, Chiweshe, Mapondera, Nyandoro, Mashayamombe, Makoni,

* Army (Zulu term)

59

Mutasa or any other member of this great Shona fraternity had ever been a subject race of the Ndebele.

Of course, this claim was made by Lobengula and accepted and endorsed in the Rudd Concession by Rhodes who used it to obtain the Royal Charter that signed away the land and the destinies of the Shona people. But neither Lobengula nor Cecil Rhodes was an honest man when it came to attaining their respective political objectives. Power-seekers throughout the ages have seldom been honest men. Lobengula and Cecil Rhodes should not be regarded as unique. But I am shattered by the knowledge that the British Government of the day allowed the two men to make these claims and to sanction the occupation of Mashonaland without even going through the motions of verifying the facts of the situation. Even the most cursory survey of the Mashonaland of that day would have shown beyond any reasonable shadow of doubt that Lobengula's assertions were false. As already pointed out, the Shona in Western and Northern Mashonaland had been subject to Ndebele raids, but that did not make them a conquered people in any legal sense and most of those in Central, North-Eastern and Eastern Mashonaland had never seen or even heard of the Ndebele until the country came under white rule. As Professor T. O. Ranger says, 'The notion that the downfall of the Ndebele monarch, whose sovereignty many of the Shona paramounts never accepted, involved their own submission to British authority, was incomprehensible to the Shona and had it been comprehended would certainly have been repudiated.'*

As far as I am aware, at no time, either before or after the occupation, were the paramount chiefs of Mashonaland officially informed of the Rudd Concession and the Royal Charter and of what they implied. Consequently, my tribal elders, even in the 1920s and throughout their lives, remained completely ignorant of the legal formula whereby Lobengula, Rhodes and the British Government of the day had come to an agreement leading to the occupation of their country. Professor Ranger is right in contending that the Shona paramountcies would have repudiated the sovereignty of Lobengula if this notion had

*T. O. Ranger, *Revolt in Southern Rhodesia 1896–7* (page 69), Heinemann Educational Books.

been put to them. But as far as I am concerned, repudiated it was, if indirectly, according to the oral teaching received from my tribal elders. They told a simple and straightforward human story of what the country was like when they were masters of their own destiny and what it became like after the spirits of their ancestors and *Mwari*—God—had abandoned them to the wickedness of the 'people without knees'. People like grand-mother Madzidza, Jakobo, Chivanda and a great many other village raconteurs, far too many to mention here, looked at history with naked eyes and did not prevaricate or gild facts just because they were against them. They told everything they knew of the sudden invasion of their country by the ghostly-look-ing white men and the resulting change in their circumstances.

Unfortunately, at my age I was in no position to question any of these facts, though now I wish I had been, for then I might have been able to get a more intimate and detailed account of the lives and times of the VaShawasha people and their kind just before the time of the occupation. Regrettably, these times are something of a mystery, which must deepen with the pass-age of time and with the increasing confusions of politics and race in that ill-fated country.

However, from what I was told there is no doubt that the VaShawasha respected the military reputation of the Ndebele; indeed they knew something of their overlordship of the Karanga, Kalanga and other tribes of the Rozwi dynasty who had not been able to resist these invaders from South Africa. But the Karanga and Kalanga lands were by no means the whole of Zimbabwe. It would appear that once the Ndebele had established their capital at kuBulawayo ('the place of killing') and had firmly established their kingdom in what is commonly called Matabeleland, they started making sorties into the interior. They did this more in search of plunder than for the permanent extension of their power, for which they did not have sufficient numbers or administrative ability. At some point, these daring people, flushed with easy victories and loot, did penetrate as far as the Chishawasha country in Central Mashonaland. That they had overreached themselves soon became clear. Not only was Central Mashonaland far from kuBulawayo, which could not know what was going on or send reinforcements if the fortunes of war turned against them, but here they came up against the VaShawasha, a proud people, who had not yet lost their fighting spirit. They immediately took up arms and taught the invader the salutary lesson, that this part of Zimbabwe was beyond his grasp. According to Chivanda, one of the most authoritative of the oral historians in Chishawasha, the VaShawasha had been briefed about the Ndebele and their way of fighting by the people of Mashayamombe, from Western Mashonaland, who had suffered periodic raids. They had also given shelter to numerous groups of people from Southern Mashonaland who had found life too insecure and uncomfortable under the constant threat of Ndebele attacks to stay where they were. And so the VaShawasha knew in advance what could happen and accordingly kept their war machine in a state of readiness. Happily, when the invading impi came, it was routed, though not without the defenders also suffering heavy losses. I was told that the retreating Ndebele carried with them a number of VaShawasha men and women, who were caught on the wrong side in the confusion of a savage and bloody battle, lasting for several hours. Some of the descendants of these captives are called Ncube in the Matabeleland of today.

This victory of the VaShawasha was very important for the rest of this part of the country. Had they been caught unawares and defeated, from that moment on the Ndebele would have had every encouragement to carry out their expansionist policies farther and farther into free Zimbabwe and undermine the peace, democracy and prosperity which prevailed in this area. Central Mashonaland was the citadel of Shona culture and civilization and its destruction would have had dire consequences for all free Zimbabwe and quite possibly parts of Mozambique as well. My feeling is that if the VaShawasha had been defeated, the Ndebele might have been strongly tempted to settle in this region. After all it had a much better climate and was more prosperous than Matabeleland, for the Ndebele had impoverished their country by their lack of industry and constant harassment of the Karanga and Kalanga people who produced much of the food and meat that fed them.

For some considerable time thereafter, the people of Chishawasha lived in the expectation of another raid or series of raids, perhaps more revengeful or aimed at achieving their complete subjection. They did not realize that their resistance had succeeded in making the Ndebele fear them. For the battle proved decisive and in its importance to the indigenous peoples can be compared to other celebrated battles, such as that of Tours which stemmed the Moorish march on Europe, or Waterloo that finally disposed of Napoleonic ambitions. Exactly when and where this Shawasha-Ndebele conflict took place is something we shall never know, like a great many other things about these fascinating times. But considering that these events were told against the background of the personal experience of men and women who were, at a guess, in their seventies or even sixties in the 1920s, it is reasonable to assume that the event took place somewhere between 1860 and 1890. Again it is reasonable to assume that the locality was in the Mabvuku-Epworth area near Salisbury, which was the headquarters of the VaShawasha people for quite a long time.

Chivanda said that the VaShawasha were so certain that the Ndebele would return that they were plunged into a national crisis because of the difference of opinion between the 'doves' on the one hand and the 'hawks' on the other. The 'doves' were a mixture of those who thought they should enter into a non-aggression pact with the Ndebele and those who advocated the least line of resistance of all, namely to leave Chishawasha altogether for lands farther east or north-east out of reach of the Ndebele. In those days of apparently unlimited space, it was a common enough practice for African tribes to solve awkward problems of this or of any other kind, such as lack of grazing and infertility of the soil, by moving farther afield. But the 'hawks', reflecting the pride and the true martial spirit of the VaShawasha, reacted sharply, saying that such a course of action would be contrary to their tradition of valour and independence. Since when, they asked, had they been cowards and flinched from the pointed spear or gun of an enemy? Would not the Ndebele, drawn by the easy prospect of possessing beautiful Shawasha women and the full granaries of the tribe, pursue his quarry wherever they went? How could they possibly trust and enter into a friendly alliance with a people who had shown so much evidence that they were destroyers rather than builders?

Such were some of the questions from the militants when the issue was submitted to a public discussion by the VaShawasha at their traditional forum, the *Dare*. At one stage, said Chivanda, it looked as if a civil war would break out. Or it seemed the tribe might be split entirely and irrevocably, as indeed it had been when they had left the Fort Victoria area some time before; and this would mean that the 'doves' would go, leaving the 'hawks' all on their own to face whatever the next Ndebele impi had in store.

However, in the end the argument prevailed on the side of war and all its consequences if it was forced on them. They did not even consider asking their neighbours to form a common defensive front. In other words, they were sure after all that they could adequately cope with a similar or bigger raid on their own, said Chivanda. And, thankfully, no civil war broke out.

I was told that in past centuries minor civil wars had not been unknown among the VaShawasha, volatile and emotional as they were. When logic and discipline had failed them over national issues, such as the appointment of a new *Mambo*, paramount chief, a position that was shared by certain houses and therefore more often than not subject to sharp differences of opinion, the resulting chaos and internecine killing was frightful. Yet somehow they usually managed to patch things up in the end and to maintain their tribal unity. But once a decision had been reached through exhaustive discussions on the *Dare* based on the voice of the majority, there was then no room for attempts to reopen a debate in order to reverse the verdict of the tribal council or of public opinion. From then on, it was a question of maintaining constant prayers to their ancestors and consultation with them through the mediums.

But although the Ndebele did not come back as physical conquerors, Lobengula, tyrannical and as fond of empire-building as his predecessor Mzilikazi had been, was just as determined to extend his power. For, unlike his own kingdom of Matabeleland, cursed by little food and an unproductive mode of living, which was the result of their never-ending looting and plundering, independent Zimbabwe was by comparison bursting at the seams with food and riches, the fruits of an orderly existence, of progressive agriculture and of trade. These possible acquisitions glittered like diamonds before Lobengula's eyes and to grasp them became an obsession surpassing all others. Thus we can understand why, when confronted with an opportunity to stake his claim on the various pieces of paper that European concession-seekers were to dangle before him, he had no qualms in contending that he was sovereign king of all Zimbabwe.

Here I must say something about the Rozwi people. The Ndebele were originally part of the Zulu nation. They left Natal under their leader Mzilikazi and for a time settled in the Transvaal. Mzilikazi was running away from the wrath of his master Tshaka, king of the Zulus, whom he had offended over a matter of cattle captured from a conquered tribe. But in the Transvaal he and his people were harassed by the Boers and consequently were forced to leave South Africa altogether and finally came to Zimbabwe in the 1830s. They settled in the southern part of the country. The people whom they conquered and whose country they took over were the Rozwi Shonas. I have never been able to discover exactly where the Rozwi originated before they set themselves up in Zimbabwe. But it is probable that they came from roughly the same area as the founders of the Monomotapa commonwealth. Who reached Zimbabwe first is something we shall never know. However, having arrived, they eventually organized themselves into a flourishing empire.

According to Professor T. O. Ranger, 'The origins of the Rozwi state system date back to the fifteenth century and for a time it co-existed with the Mutapa (Monomotapa) confederacy with which it had many and complex inter-relationships.' But its real period of power and prosperity, Ranger goes on, came in the second half of the seventeenth and the eighteenth centuries, 'when it wrested control of external trade from the declining Mutapas and emerged as the only strong state in the Shona-speaking area.' Based 'on much the same principles of organization as the Mutapa kingdom,' says Ranger, 'its achievements in its period of power outshone those of its predecessor. Where the Mutapas had been undermined by the Portuguese, the Rozwi Changamire dynasty drove them out of what is now Southern Rhodesia. The Rozwi brought the tradition of stone building to a high degree of elaboration, building the most impressive structures at Great Zimbabwe and further royal residences at

65

Khami, Dhlo-Dhlo, Naletale and the rest. The achievements symbolized by those buildings were considerable. A developed economic system, a stable political regime, a complex administrative hierarchy—all these were thought by white Rhodesians in the 1890s to be unthinkably beyond the capabilitites of black Rhodesians, so that the stone ruins were ascribed to a long-vanished race of white colonizers.'*

While they did not elaborate on the history of the Rozwi as Professor Ranger does, the VaShawasha of the 1920s always stressed the importance of these people in the development of what they called 'Chiswina'—Shona culture and civilization. They regarded the Rozwi with a special kind of reverence, particularly in spiritual matters, for they were supposed to be a 'chosen people' in the sight of *Mwari.*

It is clear then that when the Ndebele arrived from South Africa Zimbabwe was occupied by two main groups of people, the Rozwi Shona and the Monomotapa Shona. The Rozwi occupied the whole of the southern portion of the country. It was this area which the Ndebele subdued, thus putting an end to its peaceful existence and economic prosperity. Having enjoyed a long period of peace and a civilized way of living, the Rozwi had unhappily lost the art of fighting and so many became the subjects of the Ndebele which they remained right up to the year 1893 when Lobengula's kingdom was destroyed by the settlers.

During this period of conquest, the Ndebele learned with astonishment that the Shona system of government and life generally were centred on a religious conception which accepted God as the maker of all creation. They were astonished because this was something far superior to anything they could claim to have evolved in their own very materialistic system. Indeed, even after defeating the Karanga and the Kalanga, people of the Rozwi dynasty, and that with considerable difficulty, the Ndebele were so impressed and overawed by the Rozwi deity of *Mwari* that it became part of their own religious system. They called him *Mlimo.*

As far as I know, the belief that God is the maker of all creation is as old as the Shona peoples themselves. It is not

* T. O. Ranger, *Revolt in Southern Rhodesia 1896–7* (page 9), Heinemann Educational Books.

something that was brought to them by white missionaries. Hence in all Shona dialects the word God is *Mwari,* meaning 'above whom there is no one else'. They never had false gods nor carved statues as substitutes. *Mwari* was, has always been, and will always be the Supreme Being, according to whose will human beings must live in this world.

However, there were certain differences in the religion of the two groups of the Shona. The people of the Rozwi origin who came under Ndebele rule and those of some portion of Western Mashonaland also used the word *Mwari* to mean the oracle, who was the connecting link between the living, the dead and the Supreme *Mwari.* But in the case of the Zezuru and the other tribes belonging to the Monomotapa dynasty, the ancestors and *Mwari* were communicated with through the intercession of the spirit of *Mhondoro,* a word which ordinarily means lion or lioness in both the singular and the plural. In both cases these oracular spirits resided in chosen human beings for the duration of their life-span. These cults were at the very heart of Shona life and were involved in all their endeavours.

It would appear that, after the humiliating reception his impi had had from the VaShawasha and after other unsuccessful attempts at subduing the Shona outside his kingdom, Lobengula, desperate for the spoils of conquest, decided to make an all-out bid to bring the whole of Zimbabwe under his control. This he did by taking the extraordinary measure of attacking Chitungwiza. This Shona settlement, situated in the Mashaya-mombe country, the present Hartley-Charter district, had the unique distinction of being the chosen residence of the Shona mediums of *Mwari* and *Mhondoro.* For that reason it had become the Mecca of Shona religious pilgrimage and national aspiration. Lobengula reasoned, justifiably, that, by destroying this centre and killing the mediums, he would eliminate the Shona spirit of resistance and independence. I am tempted to believe that, apart from the desire to extend the boundaries of his kingdom as far as possible, the king did not feel secure in Matabeleland. Not only did he live in fear of being pursued by the land-hungry Boers from South Africa, but there was the possibility that the Shona outside his kingdom might come to the help of their fellows and put an end to the Ndebele supremacy.

At this time, the supreme Zezuru *Mhondoro* spirit was Chaminuka who was manifested in the medium, Pasipamire—translated 'the land is alert'—and who was, of course, resident at Chitungwiza. And it was he, the source of all Shona strength, that Lobengula made the first target for his impi.

Here we encounter one of the most fascinating mysteries of nineteenth-century Central Africa. From the many Shona legends that tell of how this man excelled ordinary mortals in his actions and his wisdom, you may take your pick. He was the greatest prophet of his age, who foretold the advent of the white man and all the consequences of his mischievous nature. He was a miracle-performer, who cured the sick, caused rain to come or go and could turn the clear Zimbabwe skies into thick, impenetrable fog. He was omnipresent and omniscient for he could turn into a spirit that was everywhere at once and that knew everything everywhere in the present, the past and the future. And with these powers, he could scatter the enemies of his people, for as long as his people were pure and obedient in the eyes of *Mwari*.

Yet Chaminuka's powers did not seem to have stood the test of Ndebele fury when it struck. The failure was twofold. The Chitungwiza citadel, though defended by an army of picked regiments from most of the main tribes' in both free and occupied Zimbabwe, was destroyed and Chaminuka himself was captured. The battle lasted for some considerable time, perhaps weeks. But eventually, the Ndebele, short of food and reinforcements and ignorant of the terrain, realized that they might suffer defeat and extinction. As a result of reckless use of their abundant manpower, they had suffered enormous losses. Thus they were compelled to beat a hasty retreat. Nevertheless they at the same time made quite certain that, whatever else happened, Chaminuka must be delivered safe and sound to Lobengula, who greatly looked forward to possessing the medium's person and to being able to fortify his nation with the powers of this legendary man. The Ndebele king had heard such extraordinary things about the Shona miracle man. Without the prophet's capture, this costly battle would have been pointless. Certainly, the Ndebele generals who commanded his troops at Chitungwiza knew they could count themselves dead men if they returned to kuBulawayo without Chaminuka, dead or alive. Lobengula was not only an absolute monarch. He used his powers absolutely. What is more, he was capable of being truly angry and becoming so paranoiac that he ordered the slaughter of those who had crossed him before the very eyes of his people. Fortunately, the capture of Chaminuka and his safe delivery pleased the king and he ordered the killing of no one. He raged, spat and cursed his *induna** for failing to subdue the paramounts of Mashonaland. But the sight of the near-god Chaminuka at his feet helped him to keep his sanity.

Lobengula asked Chaminuka to employ all his spiritual gifts of prophecy, healing and miracle-performing in the service of the Ndebele nation. He offered him all the honours he wished—Ndebele citizenship, indunaship, women and cattle. But the great prophet, who, by virtue of his calling and his spiritual powers, spurned earthly riches, particularly ill-gotten ones, had only one answer to all the offers, pleas and threats. For he was the earthly father of the Zezuru people, their mouth-piece to the ancestors and the supreme *Mwari* above. On no account would he be the instrument of their slavery by the Ndebele or anyone else.

Lobengula's brow darkened and he sweated more and more as the proud yet simple-looking Chaminuka hurled at him answers which no living Ndebele in his right mind would dare to utter without fear of his skull being pounded to pulp by knobkerries at the royal command.

'Tell me,' barked the king, 'what is going to happen to me?'

With a simple gesture of his hand and a quiet tone, Chaminuka unfolded the royal future. Men without knees, white men, more powerful than the Ndebele or any black nation anywhere, would come. Lobengula would resist and the king would perish with only the skies and the stars for his roof.

The successor of Mzilikazi, the Drinker of Blood, Eater of Men, son of the Great House of Kumalo, could bear no more. He ordered the innocent *holi*† to be dashed to pieces and fed to the dogs. Assagais and knobkerries rained on him, but

*General.
†Contemptuous term applied to an inferior person by the Ndebele.

69

D

Chaminuka laughed as if they were merely beating the air, not him. Then he buried the unbelieving crowd and the royal kraal under a thick blanket of white fog, so that no one could see even his own hand. Lobengula nearly burst his blood vessels in impotent rage. But Chaminuka went on and on playing his tricks, thereby not only making the king a fool before his people, but also proving to him that the royal power was limited.

Finally, however, the prophet Chaminuka told Lobengula that he did not want to go on living anyway, for the evils unleashed by the Ndebele and those to come upon the land in the wake of the men without knees were too frightful for his mortal stamina. If Lobengula wished to extinguish the life in his human body, said Chaminuka, he should give a spear to a small boy, innocent of the sins of the flesh and let him do the killing. 'But before you do so, let me tell you this. There will be a great starvation in your land and there will always be a shortage of rain, while your people and mine are the subjects of people without knees.'

The king's madness knew no bounds. He raged, coughed and spluttered, stamped the ground with his feet and cursed to the limit of his Sindebele vocabulary. But he did as bidden by Chaminuka. A young boy dispatched the Shona prophet with a well-aimed assagai through the heart.

As I have said, there are many legends about this particular Chaminuka. But to the Shona of yesterday and today and even to the Ndebele, this spectacular man and his powers were real, and he continues to be the spiritual centre of their political movements, providing an inexhaustible emotional theme for their political poetry, platform stunts and poster slogans. He may sound weird or unimportant to the outside world and white Southern Rhodesia. But all the freedom-hungry black people of Zimbabwe believe profoundly that Chaminuka was both real and truly prophetic. The Shona, in particular, will tell you that his predictions after all came to pass. White men came, saw their beautiful country and conquered it. Lobengula's power was squeezed and squashed like a wild fruit and he himself perished in the unfriendly Rhodesian bush. And my people go on to say that rain has always been short in Matabeleland since Chaminuka. What more proof could you want?

But what happened after the destruction of Chitungwiza? According to my tribal teaching, it was this. The Ndebele would appear to have given up entirely any more attempts calculated to subdue the Shona paramounts in independent Zimbabwe. Perhaps it was just as well for them that they did not try again. For having proved that the Ndebele were not after all invincible, and being outraged by the sacking of Chitungwiza and especially by the capture of their prophet, the paramounts of Mashonaland decided from now on to pursue a more active common defence policy. They vowed to defeat the enemy more completely if he tried again.

Their failure to embark on an offensive move against Matabeleland either immediately after Chitungwiza or at some later stage, is often taken as a sign of their political backwardness and cowardice. But they could not, of course, have known that their various kingdoms and lives would be irretrievably signed away to white people on a piece of paper by Lobengula. Again it may be asked why they did not act on the prophecies of Chaminuka and guard themselves against the danger of being invaded by the people without knees. All one can say about this is that perhaps they did not take this prophecy too seriously until white conquest had become an accomplished fact. The fact was that the Shona paramounts and their people were at this stage ignorant of the black and white conflicts that were being played out in South Africa, let alone their possible extension to Zimbabwe. But even if they had known that white men, not only in South Africa, but also in England, France, Germany and Belgium, were casting covetous eyes on their land, it should be obvious that there was nothing they could have done about it in advance. For, as we now know only too well, the clash of interests between Bantu, Boer and Briton south of the Limpopo, and the burning urge for colonial possessions among the European powers of the day, were so strong that it would have been quite beyond any African power anywhere on the continent to prevent them from spilling out into central Africa. The scramble for Africa was on and Africans, including the Lobengulas of that day, were entirely helpless.

However, for some time after Chitungwiza, little significant seems to have happened. Until white occupation in 1890, this period was on the whole marked by peace and mutual if cold tolerance of each other's independence on the part of the Ndebele and the Shona. There is plenty of evidence, though, that as white pressure from South Africa on the Ndebele increased, Lobengula revived his military sorties into Mashonaland. But these were limited in scope, consisting mainly of short, sharp marauding raids on small, scattered villages, mostly in western and northern Mashonaland. I hazard the suggestion that these tactics were not only the symptoms of fear and insecurity. They must also have been an attempt by the astute Lobengula to impress his white concession-seeking guests that he was lord and master of all Zimbabwe. What king in those care-free days, without the United Nations, world courts and other international restraints, would not make the same claims? Lewanika of Barotseland, confronted with a similar temptation at a later stage, was to do exactly the same thing and signed away all the mineral rights of Northern Rhodesia's (Zambia's) Copperbelt when, in actual fact, it was no more part of his kingdom than independent Mashonaland had been Lobengula's.

It must be remembered that as the second half of the nineteenth century drew to its close, with mining having become a fantastically profitable venture in South Africa, European political and economic adventurers were now more firmly convinced than ever of fabulous concentrations of diamond and gold in the Ndebele and Shona country. Consequently, white agents of every degree of shrewdness and dishonesty, acting either on their own or on behalf of rival Boer, German, English and other European interests, were congregating at Lobengula's kraal like vultures before a dead carcass. They plied him with whisky, with guns, money, diamonds and other bribes, in return, of course, for trading licences. With their sense of geography and power, they enlarged the king's vision of his domains. To make him feel benign and generous, they flattered him and made him feel a much bigger man and a greater king than he really was. Predictably, he, in turn, with characteristic sagacity, combined with vanity and delusions about the grandeur of the Ndebele nation, must have reasoned thus: 'If they say I am master of Zambesia (as white men called it then), then I must be.' It did not matter to him where this kingdom began and ended and what lay beyond the Hunyani and Sabi Rivers. What mattered to him was that he was being acknowledged by representatives of white nations as the ruler of a country whose real geography extended far beyond the areas the Ndebele impis had raided for their supply of food and cattle. Naturally enough, he agreed that he was what they said he was. White travellers of those times would occasionally have witnessed some of the routine Ndebele attacks on their Karanga and Kalanga subjects, as well as on some of the Shona in the areas that were near the borders of Matabeleland, such as the Gwelo and Que Que districts of today. Such displays, no doubt, added substance to the belief held by uninformed Europeans that the whole country was ruled by the Ndebele. Anyway, this kind of evidence was good enough for negotiating business concessions, certainly as far as Cecil Rhodes was concerned.

6

*Cecil Rhodes schemes the acquisition of
Mashonaland; the duping of Lobengula
by Rhodes' emissaries; the Rudd
Concession; the story of Makombe.*

The story of how Cecil Rhodes worked out his scheme for the acquisition of Mashonaland and, ultimately, the whole country is a classic example of the duplicity and ruthlessness which nineteenth-century Europeans employed in dispossessing Africans of their power, land rights and human freedom. It is not my intention to elaborate in this book on all the scheming and manoeuvring the founder of Rhodesia used to attain his objectives. The most important point is that Lobengula, unaware of the true intentions of his white guests, made the false claim that he was the ruler of all Zambesia. It was accepted without question not only by Cecil Rhodes, but also by everyone else who was after trading rights. From that moment on the king knew no peace. White men streamed to his kraal, telling all kinds of lies, and would not leave until they had got what they wanted.

In the end, Lobengula signed what came to be called the Rudd Concession, which gave legal respectability to Mr Rhodes' grandiose schemes and everything else that has happened in white-ruled Southern Rhodesia. There is no doubt that the king signed the document with grave reservations and only because he thought that this act would put an end to his worries. He was tired of playing host to his persistent white visitors and of listening to their begging stories. That he was suspicious and did not act hastily there can be no doubt whatever. Rhodes' envoys, Messrs Thomas R. Maguire, Frank R. Thompson and Charles D. Rudd, arrived in kuBulawayo in September 1888 and negotiations dragged on for more than a month. What is more, Lobengula would not give ground until the Rev. Helm, a local missionary, had assured him that by signing the document he was not giving away his lands. The king trusted missionaries completely. Helm, who had been sent for by Lobengula to act as his interpreter, had just been offered an engagement by Mr Rudd on behalf of Rhodes at a salary of £200 a year, but did not inform the Ndebele monarch of this fact. Without an assurance from Helm that the concession agreement did not involve white occupation, Rhodes' envoys would have had to return to Cape Town empty-handed. But thanks to the word of the man of God, Lobengula signed the Rudd concession on 30th October 1888. It was his death warrant. Some accounts say he was under the influence of whisky, which white men had brought to him in cases.

Understandably, no sooner had the representatives of Mr Rhodes accomplished their mission than they raced back to South Africa as fast as their horses could run. Lobengula, soon after, wished to know if he had not signed his rights away. He called two local missionaries for an independent opinion and on being told that indeed the document gave Rhodes' white men the right to dig for gold even under his kraal, Lobengula was shattered. He shook with anger. Lotshe, one of his indunas, who had been present at all the negotiations and had supported the white men, was disposed of there and then, including his wives, his children, cattle, dogs, his kraal and everything else immediately connected with him.

For granting to Rhodes and his business associates 'the complete and exclusive charge over all metals and minerals situated and contained in' his 'Kingdoms Principalities and Dominions ...', Lobengula was promised in return a salary of £100 in gold sovereigns per month, a cruising boat for his royal pleasure on the Zambezi, one thousand Martini-Henry rifles and one hundred thousand rounds of ammunition. But five years later, white men were no longer crawling in the dust of his kraal on their bellies, but hunting him and his people like animals. They were to take his country and in 1893 he was to die in the blood-bath that they had unleashed in order to establish once and for all their right to the country.

However, soon after he had discovered that he had been

75

duped, Lobengula tried frantically to invalidate the agreement. An appeal to the Great White Queen, Victoria, misfired. Cecil Rhodes saw to it that Lobengula was held down to his side of the bargain. It remained now for time to prove that on the piece of paper where he put the imprint of his thumb he had sealed the fate of the Ndebele and the Shona whose descendants today are facing the ugly consequences of UDI. Never in history have so many people and their country been sold for so little.

Had the British Government of that day or any other subsequent period felt inclined to verify both Lobengula's and Rhodes' claims to Mashonaland, they would have found no evidence for the truth of the statements of either of them. Almost any honest missionary, big game hunter or any of the many rival concession-seekers would have been able to prove to the British Government that Mashonaland was a free country. One of the most knowledgeable Englishmen of the day on both Mashonaland and Matabeleland was Mr Frederick Courteney Selous, big-game hunter, author and journalist. He could have produced the necessary evidence to expose the untruths by which Rhodes was going to acquire a country about five times the size of England for the price of a few golden sovereigns, rifles, ammunition and a boat that Lobengula never received. Indeed, Selous nearly took this course of action, but was appeased by Rhodes, who by this time was so immensely powerful as well as wealthy that he found little difficulty in manipulating men and affairs.

Cecil Rhodes and Selous had been on such good terms that they had on occasion discussed the plans for invading Mashonaland and the latter had given Rhodes useful advice on the nature of the country and on how best to occupy it without trespassing on Matabeleland. But subsequently the two men fell out. Meanwhile Selous had acquired a concession from Paramount Chief Mapondera of Negomo in independent Mashonaland, and from his extensive travels in the country he had incontestable proof that the Shona had never been conquered by or come in any way under the Ndebele. But it so happened that at this time Selous was in financial difficulties and, a writer, he had prepared a series of articles which he was going to sell to British newspapers. When he mentioned to Rhodes that the subject of his articles was about this new country and about the true facts of the relationship between the Ndebele and the Shona, Rhodes realized that he had to silence him. Selous was at once taken on as an employee of Rhodes. He was paid the sum of £2,000 for withdrawing publication of his articles, plus the offer of £3,000 per year for guiding the Pioneer Column to the country of the Shona.

Thus, the lie that the Shona were hapless subjects of the Ndebele was perpetuated.

However well or badly treated a conquered people may have been by their masters, they never go into a conspiracy of silence about their past. An experience of this kind in the life of any tribe or nation becomes part of their consciousness and lives on in their history, in their folklore and in their poetry as well as in their music. But the European-inspired stories of the subjection of my people by the Ndebele never even formed the background to any of the thousands of the legends and fireside folk tales that were told by my elders and were such an essential ingredient of our evening entertainment.

I can recall no more than one individual in Mashonganyika village who admitted to having had some personal experience of Ndebele rule. His name was Makombe. He lived with his tribe until he reached manhood somewhere near Que Que. A great portion of this part of the country, being so close to Matabeleland, was within range of the Ndebele impis and as a result suffered heavily from constant attacks. According to him, Lobengula's soldiers visited his unfortunate people and their neighbours on every kind of pretext. One time they would come for no other apparent cause than to kill the *Maholi** and destroy their houses and other belongings. The next time they attacked a chosen tribe for some named misdemeanour, and the next for the acquisition of women, cattle and, of course, food. It was obvious, he used to say, that the Ndebele had little knowledge or inclination to grow food for themselves. They thrived mainly on tribute and loot from their vassals.

Makombe's recollections would have been treasure to the public relations employees of the Pioneer Column who were in search of material with which to antagonize the British public opinion of that period against the blood-thirsty Ndebele and

*Plural form of '*holi*'.

77

bless the white man's mission to liberate the unfortunate Shona. The Ndebele, he said, came in and out of his people's land as they pleased. Usually they arrived at dawn or in misty conditions when their intended victims were least prepared. Otherwise, if they thought they were numerous enough, they arrived at any time of day. As if they were hunting animals, they rushed forward and attacked men, women and children, including domestic animals, using assagais, guns, knives and other lethal weapons. When they had had enough of this orgy, they embarked on a systematic destruction of huts by battering them and burning them down, until the whole place turned into a spectacle of flames and clouds of smoke and a heart-rending cacophony of the voices of dying men, women and children. The main features of their strategy were to achieve a maximum degree of surprise and confusion, to kill as many of their victims as possible, particularly old men and women, and to instil such fear that the subject tribe would not entertain any notion of opposition to Ndebele power. If they were not satisfied with the results of any attack or found the kraal deserted, they combed the surrounding countryside, searching and prodding every bush, thicket, cave and rocky fastness for signs of human life. This they did by hurling spears and threats, and, if a human voice cried out in pain or fear, more spears rained into the shelter whence the noise came, to the great joy of the warriors who whistled and cheered.

It was a savage, jungle-animal relationship because 't was completely devoid of any of the finer feelings, such as pity and kindness, which are normally associated with human beings, Makombe used to say. The Ndebele were the hunters and his tribe the hunted and there was no question of talking over problems, wrongs or demands. The Ndebele made no attempt to reach some understanding whereby they could get what they were after from the subject tribe without that savage killing and looting.

These raids came, sensibily enough, mostly during or after harvest when the invaders were sure of being rewarded for their efforts with food and fat cattle. And, of course, they always left enough men and women who would be able to gather up again the threads of their tribal existence, grow more food and rear more cattle and goats for the future replenishment of their larders. The survivors would always be warned that if they tried to flee, they would be tracked down and exterminated. The king's domains had no beginning and no end, the Ndebele would say.

For a time Makombe did indeed believe in the endlessness of Lobengula's empire. But one day he plucked up enough courage to go and find out for himself. He kept travelling to the north, wandering all the way through Mashayamombe's country, until finally he reached Central Mashonaland. There, realizing that he had travelled far enough from his Ndebele-plagued country, he asked for and was given asylum by the VaShawasha.

Makombe's was no mean achievement in those days of thick bush, wild animals, strange and sometimes hostile men, and swollen, bridgeless rivers.

I came to know Makombe when he was a very old man, very stooped, very grey and heavily-leaden with filthy rags and the accumulation of scales of sweat and dust on his never-washed body, which sent out the most offensive smell I have ever encountered from a living human being. Yet he was young enough in mind and body to be able to reconstruct the scenes of some of the battles that his people had fought with the Ndebele. Sometimes he lived up to his reputation of not being quite right in his old head. But sane or not, he seemed to remember it all. At the snap of anyone's fingers, he gave realistic dramatizations of the fury and violence of Ndebele attacks. Being a natural artist, endowed with wit and an amazingly retentive memory, he re-enacted his experiences in such a picturesque language that we, his young audience, listened with rapture. The only thing that was wrong with Makombe's instant battles was that if you were unwise enough to stand within the grasp of his massive hands, you were liable to be snatched into a vice-like grip and quite possibly flung against the nearest tree, rock or wall. He was unaware of his animal strength. Anyway, he did this in order to make you experience what he had had to put up with when he was a young man. For this reason and, because of his polecat-like smell, we kept well away from his lunges and parries.

When he died, Makombe was greatly missed, particularly by the young, to whom he was such a great source of entertainment and information on the unique experience he had had of living under Ndebele oppression. No doubt it had been a terrible life for him. But in telling us about it, he raised the memories of these times into something of a romantic historical saga and with such style that it all sounded more like fiction than fact. No one else had this background, and I am convinced that the VaShawasha people had never been under the Ndebele and therefore did not need European protection. If they had, I cannot believe that one of the most uninhibited people on the African continent would have undertaken this conspiracy of silence, much less succeeded in maintaining it.

7

A broader look at southern Africa;
the discovery of diamonds and its
consequences for the African; African
freedom is doomed; the arrival of
Cecil Rhodes and the Scramble for Africa;
Selous in Zimbabwe and the subsequent
arrival of the Pioneer Column in friendly
Mashonaland.

Like the Battle of Britain to the British people, or that of Stalingrad to the citizens of the Soviet Union, Chitungwiza is unforgettable in the memories of the Shona. It represents the finest hour of Shona unity. So greatly is this event cherished by all sections of Shona society that Chitungwiza has come to stand for the most respected political philosophy, indeed, the only acceptable political faith to hold for any self-respecting African in Rhodesia today. Thus when we say that a man 'talks Chitungwiza', most politically conscious Rhodesian Africans will understand at once that the individual in question would never sell out, but is uncompromisingly for majority rule.

But in my boyhood the name was revered even more than it is today. In Mashonganyika, for instance, it was a household word, constantly recurring in the reminiscences of the village historians; Chitungwiza, like Chaminuka, was a permanent memorial to their past glory. It evoked memories of their once flourishing civilization, of their freedom and, of course, of the names of the great Shona leaders who fought in this battle and won the victory which made it possible for their people to live in peace and prosperity for a time.

However, the fruits of this military triumph at Chitungwiza were not to be enjoyed for long. The VaShawasha and their compatriots were to realize that their limited brush with the

Ndebele was an omen of infinitely worse things to come. In the distant south, the clouds of human folly were darkening fast. Once South Africa had revealed its diamond and gold treasure trove to the eye of the white man, that was the beginning of the end of the black man's era of self-determination. As it happened, at the time of Chitungwiza, either just before or after it, in South Africa the stage was set for the forces of economic enterprise, racial passions and lust for wealth and power to explode into a fierce struggle and one which had no comparison anywhere else on the African continent.

The process began in the late 1860s. The first sensational news of the mineral prospects of South Africa swept across the world in 1866 when the first diamond was picked up at De Kalk, a farmstead situated in the Hopetown district of the Cape Province. Later more 'finds' were made and by the beginning of the 1870s, the existence of diamonds in exploitable quantities was no longer a matter of speculation, but one of solid fact. It was the most tantalizing piece of news from Africa since the dauntless Portuguese navigators, Diaz and da Gama, had rounded the Cape of Good Hope and discovered the sea route to India more than three centuries before. In the chance discovery of this gem, which the dictionary defines as 'a crystallized form of pure carbon', Africa, particularly its southern half, had suddenly become more important than at any other time in its history. The whole future of southern Africa, if not the entire black continent, was to change politically, economically, and indeed even geographically.

But more immediately, these sensational discoveries, which were rapidly to be followed by the finding of gold, started a phenomenal movement whereby the white world, including Australia and America, oblivious to the Africans' interests, began to offload its human flotsam and jetsam onto the African soil. For the Africans, it was as if the white man was letting loose a wild beast, whose ferocious appetite and savage capacity to devour and destroy surpassed anything the African people could contrive in defence of their freedom. White men from all corners of the world, of all degrees of greed, perverted values and ruthlessness, poured into the subcontinent and trailed to Kimberley, where this, one of the most valuable of all gems, was to be found. They all desired to be rich men and they started a diamond industry which boomed.

Among the early arrivals in South Africa at this time, in 1870, to be exact, was one, Cecil John Rhodes, who nursed a bigger dream than that of simply acquiring wealth for its own sake. His overriding ambition was to paint the rest of the map of Africa with clear, lovely British red colours. By the very look of things at the time, fortune could not have been kinder to any other man. Kimberley, with its glittering diamonds and the economic philosophy of its merchant adventurers, provided all the necessary ingredients for Mr Rhodes to translate his dreams into reality.

In retrospect, it is easy to see how favourable the prevailing circumstances were to those Europeans who, like Rhodes, set out to acquire wealth, power and land in Africa. At this period of history, the African, compared with the lowest white man from the slummiest sections of any English, European or American city, seemed to be the most backward and primitive member of the human race. He was puerile and untidy in his thinking. Africa and the Africans did not have the ordered existence of European civilization as expressed in literature, architecture and such things as roads and other systems of communication. Africa seemed no more than a primitive land, affording shelter, sunshine and food only at their very elementary levels to a people who were still in their sleep of centuries, almost totally incapacitated by the debilitating diseases of tribalism and animal forms of violence against their own kind. All in all, Africans appeared to be spending most of their energies in destroying one another rather than in developing their vast natural resources.

This is how Africa and the Africans looked to most Europeans of that day. It was both convenient and desirable for them to think of the Africans in these terms, as white Rhodesians are doing today. Otherwise they would not have been able to rationalize what they set out to do, which was not only to dispossess black men of their land and deprive them of their independence, but also to initiate a racial system, whereby Africans in most of southern Africa were destined to suffer human degradation for the foreseeable future.

It was in this atmosphere that representatives of various European governments gathered at the Berlin Congress of 1884. But to make their colonial brigandage in Africa sound respectable and appear conceived from noble motives, they paid lip-service to the rights of black people whose possessions they were about to plunder. However, their insincerity in this respect is scarcely in doubt—not only in the light of what colonialism turned out to be in practice (especially in places such as German West and East Africa, and the Belgian Congo where Africans were tortured and maimed for such reasons as failure to pay their taxes or to bring in the required weekly amount of rubber from forest trees) but also in the massive document of sixty thousand words brought out by the Congress, of which only two hundred had direct reference to the black man. They were, as Felix Gross rightly says, 'two hundred words of hypocrisy, bigotry and lies', which exhorted every participant in this monumental act of international robbery to 'watch over the preservation of the native races, and the amelioration of the moral and material conditions of their existence ... to educate the Natives, and to lead them to understand and appreciate the advantages of civilization.'* Splendid words—which have as much meaning as a rosary wound round the knife of a murderer.

One of the many facile arguments that white South Africans offer in defence of their policy of apartheid is that the Bantu are, like themselves, immigrants to South Africa. Not only is this argument irrelevant as a basis for separate development and second-class citizenship; it has the added mischief of distorting the true history of the African people. Whether or not the Bantu reached South Africa before the arrival of the white man in 1652—and it is now generally accepted that they did—it is nevertheless true that, having come to it, they stayed there long enough to establish themselves as what were, in some cases, admirable democratic societies. I refer, of course, to such people as the Zulus whose military prowess, particularly under Tshaka, was one of the greatest achievements that the country has seen and took, as every South African knows, an extraordinary amount of sweat and blood for the white man to subdue. I refer also to the equally renowned Xhosas, as well as the Pondos, the

*Felix Gross, *Rhodes of Africa* (page 90).

84

Sothos and various other black people of South Africa who were by no means primitive in the sense in which that term was used by white immigrants to give respectability to their acts of injustice.

What is significant is that before 1870 there was a measure of respect for the rights of the African people. Britain, in particular, showed real concern for the territorial integrity of black men and in the eighteenth and nineteenth centuries tried to prevent the Boers from encroaching on the freedom of the Africans in South Africa. Even the Boers, wherever possible, sought to live in peace with Africans, admittedly strictly on a separate territorial basis. So much was this a feature of European thinking that most of the African tribal and national institutions in southern Africa were intact and reasonably secure until the second half of the nineteenth century.

But the discovery of diamonds and, later, gold changed the outlook of both the white settlers and their mother countries, particularly Great Britain. Aside from astute exceptions like Moshoeshoe of Barotseland, Sobhuza of Swaziland and Khama of Bechuanaland, whose lands held no prospects of mineral wealth, most of the African kingdoms and paramountcies were to be toppled one by one like houses of cards. African land, with its attractions of space, diamonds, gold, sunshine, had become too precious to be left untouched simply because of the presence of its pathetically innocent indigenous people. As Kimberley revealed more of its valuable secrets and mining shares boomed in London, Paris and other European cities, the interests of the African people became less and less important in the board-rooms of white big business corporations and the parliaments of colonial powers.

There was nothing that the Africans, so completely forsaken by fate, nor even their white missionary friends, nor the British liberals who had fought so hard and for so long for the abolition of slavery, could do to stem the tide of the nineteenth-century technological progress. Admittedly, this phenomenon promised all sorts of potential material benefits to the b'ack man—which were indeed hailed and explained to suspicious Africans and white liberals by the more tactful supporters of colonialism. But we who live in these times know better than to believe that white enterprise in southern Africa has only brought the 'advantages of civilization' that were so glibly promised by the Berlin Congress of 1884.

Instead of bringing syphilis, tuberculosis, and the evils of political and economic subjection, the arrival of the white man could and should have been the most positive historical event in the development of Africa. If the white immigrants and their descendants had had the foresight to see their true role in Africa in relation to the sum total of human progress and happiness, they might have become the greatest benefactors as well as sharers in the economic and human revolution that is taking place in Africa today. Had the white Africans and the black Africans accepted their common interests, South Africa, including Rhodesia, might have become a natural and most acceptable elder sister of the new African nations, the one best qualified to guide them in their complex programmes of development. The amount that South Africa could have contributed to the material and spiritual values of Africa would have been immeasurable. Her scientists, teachers, missionaries, let alone her capital and industrial goods would have been welcome everywhere in her sister African countries and brought corresponding benefits that could have increased her economic prosperity several hundredfold. Who knows, she might have been able to spearhead the creation of a united states of Africa, which, I am convinced, is possible and would pay untold dividends to the peoples of that otherwise sadly divided continent.

But, regrettably, the situation took an entirely different turn. The Boers, inspired both by the Bible as well as by the fear of the numbers and the ferocity of the Zulus and other Bantu tribes, had always conceived the philosophy of permanent separation between black and white. When in due course the English came, they also adopted this policy, no doubt with slight liberal modifications and subtle sophistications that suited their own phlegmatic temperament. Although right up to the Act of Union in 1910 Britain tried hard to uphold her traditions of liberalism, the fact remains that the majority of individual Englishmen who settled in South Africa soon fell into line with the Afrikaners on the racial question. It was from their ranks that Cecil Rhodes picked the men who were to create a new country for him in

Zimbabwe. Though most of them had English names and wished to see British power and standards of government prevail all over southern Africa, their thinking on the race question was basically the same as that of the Boers, whom they both feared and despised.

With the discovery of mineral wealth, the racial struggle in South Africa was intensified and colonial imperialism quickened its pace in search of more territories and more minerals. As these developments gathered momentum, black freedom became more restricted, giving way to insecurity and degradation among the African people, particularly those within reach of white economic enterprise and the fierce political rivalries that followed the struggle between the British and the Boers for supremacy in South Africa.

In Zimbabwe no people were more aware of these dangers than the Ndebele. They were right in the path of the great winds of change from South Africa, particularly as the queue of white concession-seekers at Lobengula's court became longer and more menacing. Having come to Zimbabwe as fugitives from the violence of the Boers, they had every reason to feel apprehensive.

Knowing what they did of white cunning, mendacity and military superiority, one would suppose that the most logical course of action would have been for the Ndebele to alter their imperialistic concept and come to terms with their Shona compatriots to defend their common interests. But instead of making an alliance with the Shona, they decided to assert their authority even more than before over their Karanga and Kalanga subjects and to display even more unfriendly intentions to the Shona living on the borders of Matabeleland. In short, they thought that their reputation was a sufficient guarantee against white mischief.

For the VaShawasha and the Shona world to which they belonged, these distant rumblings were not yet audible. Even if they had reached Shona ears, one wonders whether they would have been heeded. Since the Portuguese had been driven out of Zimbabwe such a long time before, the Shona had become an essentially peace-loving and trusting people. The whole drama of economic, racial and political struggle bedevilling South Africa was completely outside their national experience. The only people who could have educated and alerted them in these matters were the Ndebele. But there was no communication between them. As a result, the Shona had no compelling reasons to feel anxious or to suppose that their land and freedom were in peril at the hands of white men, in spite of Chaminuka's warning.

Yet had they not been so simple-minded and so ready to think that most people, except the Ndebele, were as uncomplicated and decent as themselves, they might have been able to draw certain conclusions from the signs of the times and alert themselves to the possibility of outside interference. But this is to enter the realms of conjecture. However, as time went on it became more and more apparent to them that the oceans were no longer effective barriers between black and white. They noticed that as years and months and even as weeks went by, white faces were appearing in increasing numbers. To the number of the comparatively simple Portuguese who had been their friends for decades were now added a growing number of fairer men who were not only very much less friendly, but also whose business in these plateau savannah lands of the Shona was as vague as anyone's business could possibly be. My grandparents remembered that this new species of white men looked shifty and generally eccentric, unlike the Portuguese who mixed easily and did not cause suspicion. But perhaps this was an opinion formed afterwards as a result of the occupation of Mashonaland, for which some of these early travellers were preparing.

Probably the best known of these visitors among the VaShawasha and other Zezuru-speaking Shona, as indeed among the Ndebele, was Frederick Courteney Selous, whom I have mentioned earlier and who, as events subsequently proved, was not only a big-game hunter, but was also a pathfinder and spy in the interests of Cecil Rhodes.

However, in his own very English way, Selous was a charming man and won the confidence of the VaShawasha people, who treated him with their traditional hospitality and a measure of trust. It was only after the Pioneer Column, which he had guided into Mashonaland, had taken over the country, that they realized that their trust had been misplaced. But in the years preceding the occupation he was probably the most familiar English man in both Mashonaland and Matabeleland. Had his real intentions been known to my people he would have had quite a different reception. He made several trips into the country and many of the old people in Mashonganyika claimed to have actually met him. They called him Seruwe. I was told that he paid his due respects to the then Paramount Chief Mashonganyika. This gesture of peace having been made, he was allowed to roam at large in the beautiful and friendly country of his hosts. They admired him for his remarkable courage and marksmanship as a hunter while they regarded his restlessness and his extensive travels as signs of the general madness of white men.

'He did not trade like the Portuguese. . . . Only after the occupation did we realize that there was a kind of shiftiness about him. . . . But then we had really nothing against him. . . . We just put his curious ways down to his race,' my grandfather Mizha remembered.

Grandmother's strong dislike of white people in general seemed to have had its origin in the treacherous role played by Selous and the other white men who paved the way for the white occupation of Zimbabwe. 'We fed them, but they bit us afterwards,' was her eternal song.

Throughout Africa, even among the Ndebele, the Zulus and the Xhosas, individual Europeans were, generally speaking, taken at their face value, and they in turn exploited the ignorance and the hospitality of the African people. For small presents, such as a case or a bottle of whisky, or a few yards of cloth, some Africans parted with their lands and political rights. Indeed it can be said with justification that Africans greatly contributed to their own loss of political independence. But it was not only a question of ignorance versus education. Much more important, it was also one of innocence and trust against the cunning, greed and corruption of the so-called civilized man. There was no doubt as to which of these forces was going to prevail in the struggle for the control of the resources of Africa and Zimbabwe.

However, to get back to Mr Selous, while purportedly big-game hunting, he was studying the geography of the land and the characteristics of the various tribes inhabiting this country which by now was earmarked for white occupation and exploitation. The VaShawasha must have proved an interesting case study for this versatile man who was an amateur anthropologist, psychologist, politician and empire-builder all rolled into one. Although he eventually fell into line with Rhodes, he too was, after his own fashion, in the running for African land and minerals that could be acquired so easily by coaxing African rulers to sign pieces of paper which they did not understand and indeed were not intended to understand. Among the educated VaShawasha of the 1920s and 1930s there was a school of thought which held the view that it was Selous who advised Rhodes to hand over the VaShawasha and their country to the Jesuits. There seems to be no written record of what Selous thought of the VaShawasha people. But some of our historians said that in his survey he stated that most of his contacts, including those of Matabeleland, reported that the VaShawasha were like the Ndebele in character. And so, believing in the efficacy of religion as a means of taming a bellicose primitive people, he advised Rhodes to let the Jesuits take care of these potentially dangerous tribesmen and women. This story may be unfounded. But if true, he could not have had much difficulty in persuading Mr Rhodes to make this arrangement. Cecil Rhodes was a great admirer of the members of the Society of Jesus, their efficient organization, stern discipline and missionary zeal and I do not doubt that their eventual assignment among the VaShawasha was cordially approved, if not entirely decided by him.

There is some evidence, however, that Selous was not a racist. Not only was he popular for a time among the Shona and the Ndebele, but he also married an African woman and had a son by her. I take pride in having been a personal friend of Selous junior who died only a few years ago and who was an intelligent man and, throughout the years I knew him, spoke out ceaselessly against racial injustice and colour discrimination in Southern Rhodesia. He lived in the 'Hunter's Lodge', a house built by his father at the bottom of the Harare Kopje in Salisbury and bequeathed to him by the famous man.

For the time being, however, the VaShawasha continued to

regard the intermittent presence of men like Selous and various others as a passing curiosity. They did notice in time, though, that the whites from the south and those from Mozambique heartily loathed one another, and were only too ready to ingratiate themselves with the Africans at each other's expense. The Portuguese pointed out to their Shawasha allies that the English were mischief-makers, while in turn the English were not slow to say unpleasant things about the Portuguese. But as the VaShawasha could not make sense of this white rivalry, they attached little importance to what these foreigners said about one another. They had been free for as long as they could remember, and despite the increasing number of European travellers in their country, they had no reason to think that the future would be any different. To have had any misgivings about their independence would have implied a lack of faith in the power and goodwill of their ancestors. After all, the role of the spirits of the dead was, at all times, to safeguard the security and the well-being of the living as well as to guarantee the integrity of their national homeland. This was one of the central doctrines of Shona religion and was deeply embedded in their national consciousness. Despite Chaminuka's prophecy, this faith remained unshakeable and unchallenged. The VaShawasha and their kindred tribesmen had never been let down by the ancestral spirits or by *Mwari*. Why should these heavenly powers suddenly forsake a people who had always trodden the path of truth and righteousness?

And so, committed to this kind of semi-superstitious reasoning, Shona society as a whole refused to entertain any thoughts of danger. Whereas the Ndebele, with their history of adversity and their firsthand knowledge of white colonial rivalry and aggressive intentions, were smitten with remorse and an almost paranoiac state of panic as soon as Lobengula realized the mistake he had made in signing the Rudd Concession, the Shona had no such apprehensions. Even when the Pioneer Column, armed to the teeth, lumbered with its lugubrious ox-wagons into the very heart of VaShawasha country, no one was sufficiently alarmed to think of haranguing the people to arms. The year was 1890. Life was normal. Since Chaminuka, no oracle had made ominous prophecies. There had been no hint from anyone, sage or clairvoyant, that anything spectacular would occur. The rains and the harvest had been good and the people of Mashonaland as a whole shared a state of euphoria and optimism in their future.

The Pioneer Column chose to pitch its camp at the base of a lonely hill called Harare or the Kopje, as the white Rhodesians were to call it. Selous had instructed them to make their final encampment at the hill he named Mount Hampden, about twelve miles farther north. But, as he was absent, they mistook Harare for Mount Hampden and settled there permanently. The place was named Fort Salisbury, in honour of Lord Salisbury, the British Prime Minister who had sanctioned Cecil Rhodes' occupation of Mashonaland.

In the event, however, Harare, where now stands the beautiful city of Salisbury, had historical significance. Firstly, it was situated at the common boundary between the tribal territories of the people of Chishawasha, of Seke, of Mashayamombe and of Chiweshe, and because of its inter-territorial position, it was used mainly for hunting and fishing. Secondly, in the distant past it had been the settlement of a renowned Rozwi chief, by the name of Zharare, after whom the name was corrupted to Harare. I understood that his power was destroyed by one of the Monomotapa kings and Zharare himself had perished in the final battle.

But none of these reasons would have influenced the leaders of the Pioneer Column who were not concerned with the local history. I imagine too that to these ragged freebooters any place where they could disband after such a long, tiresome and anxious journey was as good as another. They were, understandably, impatient to be let free in order to grab the land they had been promised and to prospect for the minerals in which Mashonaland was supposed to abound and for which they had made this hazardous undertaking.

In passing through Matabeleland, the Pioneers had taken extraordinary measures against possible attacks from the Ndebele who by now were fully aware of the white man's treachery. Such precautions included, for instance, huge naval search-lights, which Selous had specifically recommended as a means of frightening away the superstitious Ndebele. And his idea had worked. For although they were fully armed for battle and watched the Pioneer Column travel through their country, the Ndebele were too mystified to risk a fight.

But once the Pioneers had reached Mashonaland, they were among a friendly people, as Selous had rightly told them. They arrived at Harare without having encountered a single act of hostility from any of the Shona tribes throughout independent Zimbabwe. As I was told in Mashonganyika village, initially the ghostly-looking new arrivals were little more than a spectacle of extraordinary entertainment. What could be funnier than the sudden, unheralded appearance of several hundreds of men without knees, *vasina mabvi,* as they were called, and known from then on because their legs were covered by long trousers and their women by long dresses! My father, who was a very young man at the time, said that these people, with their long, animal-like hair and beards, wild eyes, uniforms, hats and shoes, as well as horses, ox-wagons and other accoutrements, were like a circus. For several weeks, all the Shona society around Harare would be irresistibly drawn to gape and often split their sides in wonder and amusement. Most extraordinary and ridiculous were the Pioneers' habits of living, such as military formations, drilling to the barks of their commanders, bugle-sounding and the hoisting and unhoisting of their flag. These strange antics, never seen before, were greeted by the Shona as signs of incomprehensible eccentricity and conclusive evidence that the people 'without knees' were mentally deranged. They were like beings from outer space, my father used to say.

A more friendly welcome to any occupying power it would be difficult to find in the annals of history!

But, as events have since proved, this friendly reception was taken for gratitude as well as stupidity on the part of the Shona by the cocksure European settlers. As we shall see, the new arrivals were not impressed by the so-called 'gratitude' and 'stupidity' of my people. This, to my mind, is the worst aspect of the Rhodesian tragedy. If the Europeans had had any foresight or real appreciation of human values, they might have turned this friendly reception to good account and used it as a foundation stone upon which to build the new society that was the object of their endeavour. The attitude of the Shona to the

Pioneer Column which they allowed to come into their country did not stem from their supposed feelings of 'thankfulness' or 'cowardice'. It went much deeper than that and if the Pioneers had tried to analyse the character of the people whose land they were taking, they might have saved themselves much of the racial tension that Rhodesia has known since 1896. The civilization that my people had built up had elements which could have made it possible to build a country where black and white people might be spared the passions of fear, hatred and repression. The foremost virtue in the character of the Shona was a love of peace, which, coupled with the tradition of hospitality to strangers, was unwittingly and innocently extended to the Pioneers who had come into our country.

Before the white occupation, Chishawasha stretched from the eastern bank of the Mukuvisi, which white Rhodesians corrupted to Makambudzi river and which flows through today's Salisbury, to the western bank of the Mapfeni river in the north more than thirty miles away, and from south-west near Marandellas to the vicinity of Mazoe in the north more than fifty miles away as the crow flies. In those days, however, boundaries, except in respect of hunting rights, were not considered important. All the tribes living in this part of Zimbabwe were essentially the same in language, customs, and religion and lived amicably together. Not only did they intermarry. They were constantly in communication with one another over questions of trade, national affairs and above all religious practices, which were probably the strongest of the many links that existed between them.

The people 'without knees' wasted no time in disturbing the peace, dignity and freedom of the Africans who lived in this area. The Pioneers soon proved that they recognized no local authority, law or rights except their own. They did not consider it necessary to explain their presence or their intentions, let alone consult anyone about anything. Such niceties were a waste of time to them, and they proceeded to appropriate for themselves whatever attracted their greedy eyes, from a black population that had not committed a single hostile act against them when they had marched into the country. Using a code of behaviour like that of the Mafia or the Spanish *conquistadores* in South

94

America, the Pioneers wrested whole tracts of the best land belonging to the VaShawasha people and other Shona tribes nearby. The era of the triumph of the strong and ruthless had well and truly arrived in the peaceful country that had nurtured a civilization which gave justice and protection to the weak as well as the strong. No people could have been more ill-prepared for a misfortune of this magnitude. Although the Shona were now wide open to flagrant plunder it was some time before they lost their patience completely, and by then any political advantage they might have had was irretrievably lost to them. The white man, having cunning, education and the modern weapons of destruction all on his side, was master of Mashonaland. He knew it and he used all these advantages without the least qualm of conscience as to the past, present or future of the black Africans.

The land was the white man's first concern. For the land was not only where the minerals were to be found. It was also to serve as a status symbol, giving testimony to individual power and possibly wealth as well. I am sure that every member of the Pioneer Column had dreams that matched those of their master, Cecil Rhodes, who had shown what money and power could achieve. And he had not achieved these earthly possessions by sentimentality either. His code of behaviour became the criterion for their own conduct in this new country. And so land was what they went for, as far as was allowed by the terms of their contracts.

The African victims of this expropriation were pressed and squeezed into pockets of land which the white man had not found convenient to confiscate. This did not happen overnight, of course. But it was done blatantly, and the indigenous population soon noticed that white men were helping themselves to land all over the country. As grandmother used to say, the Europeans took what land they fancied. My tribesmen, living so near the centre of white power—Fort Salisbury—were among the first Africans in the country to feel the impact of this land-grabbing process. Within a very short space of time, they saw their once extensive piece of country shrink to a tiny remnant of its original size. In fact, in the end they had no land at all. Because of its natural beauty, the fertility of the soil, its possible mineral deposits and because of the suspected bellicosity of the VaShawasha, the best part of Chishawasha was given to Father Hartmann. He was a Jesuit priest who had acted as Chaplain to the Roman Catholic members of the Pioneer Column. How these men reconciled their religious views with their piratical mission is something that always puzzled me when I was a devout Catholic. However, they obviously did, just as many of their descendants in present-day Rhodesia do not seem to have suffered crises of conscience as a result of the contradiction between their Catholic beliefs and their support for the Rhodesian Front racial philosophy.

Father Hartmann, as far as I know, received this piece of land as a reward for his services to the Pioneer Column and took title to it in the name of the Society of Jesus to which he belonged. In this way, the once proud, independent VaShawasha were handed over to the spiritual, and in a sense to the physical, possession of the Jesuits. Father Hartmann established a mission station which he called St Ignatius of Loyola Mission, after the gallant founder of the Society. But the more popular name became, appropriately enough, the Chishawasha Mission. And henceforth it was to teach Christianity and the other mysteries of Western civilization to a people who, to European eyes, looked very much in need of salvation from the physical and spiritual barbarism of their way of life. If they ever thought about this whole drama at all, I suppose Father Hartmann and the other good Fathers of the Society must have felt that the wrong of their participation in sharing the land of the conquered Africans was more than counterbalanced by the blessing of Christianity that they were bringing to the Africans. However, whether they thought about it or not it made little difference to the VaShawasha who, from the moment their territory was expropriated, became a landless people and were to live on what was previously their property entirely at the pleasure of their white missionary landlords. Many of their Shona countrymen were in the same position. Fate had decided, utterly mercilessly, against the people of Mashonaland.

8

*The mood of a friendly people changes in
the face of exploitation by the white
strangers; the Shona are perplexed:
the settlers take their land, coerce them to
work and use the sjambok; driven to
desperation, the Shona at last decide to act
against the strangers.*

Very soon the friendliness and the sense of wonder and, no
doubt, of admiration with which the African people had greeted
the Pioneer Column gave way to harsher feelings. The white
strangers, it became obvious, were far from being harmless
eccentrics. They were in fact wielders of power and insatiable
land grabbers. The VaShawasha watched their activities with
growing apprehension. And like all sections of African society
throughout the country, they became dismayed and frightened as
well as angry at the blatant robbery which gathered momentum as
the Europeans spread and asserted their authority farther and
farther into their territory.

How long was the white man going to stay in the country?
How much more land was he to take? What else was he
intent on expropriating after his land-hunger had been satisfied?
Even more intractable was the question: what could be done
to stop the white man behaving in such an arbitrary manner?
The Shona were in a state of indecision and mental anguish. They
were to remain so until six years after the occupation.

Once more Shona tradition was acting against its architects.
Once more they were imprisoned by their love of peace, their
non-violent ethos and by their innate faith in the intrinsic good-
ness of men. Consequently, they hung on to the mistaken
belief that the foreigners' presence was not going to last. Being
the ignorant optimists they were, their thoughts alternated

between the hope that the Europeans would quit the country when they had found what they were looking for, and the hope that they would sooner or later see the error of their ways and thus become reasonable human beings with a sense of right and wrong in their relationships with the African people. The Shona were misguidedly applying their own standards of motivation, thinking and morality to the settlers.

The Ndebele on the other hand did not give the Europeans this benefit of the doubt and soon realized that war was inevitable. Although the settlers had not so far arrived in Matabeleland, the Ndebele were already convinced that the occupation of Mashonaland would lead to the loss of their own part of the country, and accordingly kept themselves ready for battle.

Much of the time that the Shona spent in considering this problem was passed in open speculation and philosophizing. But their fantasies were not without a tinge of realism. Their patient thought was designed to avoid the mistakes made by the Ndebele, such as the occasion when their king precipitously signed the Rudd Concession and then, in 1893, found himself at war, without considering the cost to his people. And yet what in other circumstances would have been an admirable quality in the Shona, that of patience and consideration born of a tradition of peace and democracy, proved a serious weakness. Unfortunately, then as today, this national characteristic played right into the hands of the European settlers, who threw all caution and any sense of guilt they might initially have had to the winds and helped themselves to as much of the Africans' land as possible. Rhodes had given Frank Johnson, the leader of the expedition, a cheque for £94,100, or was it £87,500—the sources vary. Anyway it certainly did not cost more than the higher figure to acquire this whole country, with all its enormous natural resources.

That the Shona were mistaken in their optimism and their hope for a possible change of heart on the part of the Europeans became more and more apparent as time went on. They were in for a systematic policy of shock-treatment in the course of which their education in white attitudes to black races and their economic systems was to be acquired painfully and agonizingly. They learnt that the white man's nature was governed by different norms from their own and that there could therefore be no prospect of change or alleviation of their lot in the immediate future. They learnt that the European was almost entirely motivated by greed and aggression and that he had nothing but contempt for the African. All these traits were a sharp blow to Shona pride. Where the Africans expected justice, they received injustice, where they looked for compassion, they received callous and inhuman treatment. And so, the people in Mashonaland moved progressively to the realization that their interests and those of the white settlers would remain irreconcilable for a long time, if not for all time, unless they did something about it. That something took some time to evolve, and still longer to be endorsed by all leading sections of the Shona society of that period. Unfortunately, the longer these people took to register some kind of national protest, the more confidence the European settlers gained in running the country.

The process of strangulation of the native people spread with ruthless efficiency. The European community, either individually or as a group through their administration, found any excuse for this, that and the next course of action without taking into account the feelings and the rights of the Africans, whose growing sense of despair and bitterness remained undetected right up to the day that the 1896 rebellion exploded upon this once peaceful country.

It was curious, my grandparents used to point out, that the Europeans who had visited them before the occupation had been human, polite and considerate and had taken nothing that they had no right to take. But now that they had arrived in large numbers, they behaved like gangsters, they became insufferably arrogant and demanded instant obedience. They disregarded all the good manners and common decencies that the VaShawasha and their Shona countrymen had mistakenly thought were the common heritage of all human beings. 'Many of them treated us as if it was a crime for us to exist,' I was told.

But worse things were still to happen. My people soon learned that to the white man's voracious appetite for land was added the need for black labour. It was a big shock, a bigger shock than the others they had experienced so far. The concept of hired labour was completely unknown to my people, and this innovation cut right across the most sensitive area of what the Shona understood by personal freedom. It was bad enough that the Europeans were taking their land. But by demanding their labour as well they were stripping the Shona of the last vestige of the little freedom that they still possessed. This brought about a much more direct personal confrontation between black men and white men than before, for apart from wishing to retain some personal independence, the Shona could not in any case see any reason for selling their labour to anyone, least of all to white men whom they now detested heartily. Their traditional economic system was rooted in agriculture, which protected the individual from any of the humiliating stigmas associated with the master-and-servant relationship of the Rhodesian way of life. They had little need for money, and were unlikely to want to work for it under a white master. They had enough food of their own, they had enough meat, adequate shelter and warmth and, of course, they felt they had the freedom not to want most things of white origin. They thought they had a right not to do what they regarded as irksome and purposeless. And they were convinced that most things European were irksome and purposeless, particularly work that went on from sunrise to sunset, from Monday to Saturday, season to season and from year to year. Such a mode of existence was singularly barren and reduced human beings to the level of cattle or donkeys, as my elders used to say. So they did not respond to the white man's call for their services.

On the other hand, the economic system which the Europeans were establishing in the country could not begin to function smoothly and profitably unless it had a sufficient local labour force. They were starting absolutely from scratch. It was all 'bush' country, covered with trees and grass and teeming with wild animals, apart, of course, from its black inhabitants, who had been content to leave it as it was. The settlers, coming from a culture that measured civilization in visible human achievements, had every intention of giving 'their' country a new look. They must build roads and bridges and houses. They must construct railways and develop their farms and mines. For all these and numerous other undertakings, they required plenty of labour, and the cheaper it was, the better for their profit. What was more natural and logical than for the Europeans to look to the victims of their spoliation to provide the muscles for their enterprises. They, in fact, felt that they were doing the Africans a great favour.

Imagine their shock and fury when they discovered that the Shona would not stir from their villages nor respond to their call for paid labour! This shock and this fury had many aspects. The Europeans were angered not only by the supposed sloth and primitive state of evolution of the Shona, but perhaps more so because the black people of Mashonaland showed a defiant indifference to the religion of money and fortune-making which had brought the settlers this far. The Shona, it seemed, were making an indictment of the European system as well as holding the white man's authority in contempt. To allow them to withold their labour in this way would mean acceptance of all kinds of unpleasant implications, political and economic. It was a sharp point of ideological conflict and it unleashed every sort of racial passion on both sides of the Rhodesian colour structure.

However, the Europeans, having the power to enforce their will, decided on coercion. After all, the blacks were part of the country's assets, which they had acquired by their bold venture into central Africa.

The people of Mashonganyika village had extremely unpleasant memories of their experience with the white men who invited themselves into their homeland. Forced labour was among the biggest of a number of grievances that turned their amused reaction to the occupation of Mashonaland into one of bitterness. Not only did it militate directly against their concept of personal freedom, it also carried the added humiliation of taking orders and doing tasks which were not to the Africans' liking. The average white pioneer outside the administration was very much a law unto himself, and as far as my people were concerned, he did not seem to accept guidance from any law, if he was in need of labour. Once he had found the men to work for him, he used them as if they were his personal property. He did not know about the delicate African customs, which demanded that a man be treated according to his age, social rank and other considerations. As for the psy-

101

chology of the African and the tribal approach to the whole question of why and under what circumstances a man should work, they were the least of his worries, even if he was equipped intellectually for this enlightened attitude, which he usually wasn't. He ignored the plain fact that Western standards and disciplines relating to paid employment were abrupt innovations to Shona society as a whole. He did not appreciate that, even with the best will in the world, it would take time and patience to break these people in before they could respond satisfactorily to incentives of employment, money and the values it represented.

On the other hand, the Africans too made no allowances for the white man's failings. Why should they, considering the wrongs they had suffered? They simply saw the European as a lawless thug, both individually and collectively. Not being fools, they clearly understood that all the white man valued in them was their brawn and sweat. Pioneers in search of black labour, said my tribal sources, roamed about the villages and demanded that the men should come out and work for them. But as most refused, a great proportion of these prospective employers resorted to force and beat up those reluctant individuals whom they judged to be fit enough to toil for their profit in return for very little pay, if any in some cases. Short of shooting or maiming the African people, as the Belgians did in the Congo towards the end of the nineteenth century, the early white settlers in Southern Rhodesia used every form of intimidation that they could think of to get African manpower for work on their farms, in their mines and in various other undertakings. But far from being the passive and stupid people they were supposed to be, the Shona showed that they had a stubborn streak in their character and, wherever possible, resisted this intimidation. Often they did so by answering force with force, as I was told, and many a settler soon learned to be tactful in his search for local African labour.

There was a Government. Yes. But it was obviously not on the side of the Africans inasmuch as it never did anything to curb the activities of these farmers and miners. Neither was the Administration itself above reproach. Like the rest of the white community, it needed as much African labour as it could get, particularly for public works like making roads and building bridges and for what Africans described as *kutakura mangwanda*, carrying heavy loads such as machinery. Understandably, when a white farmer or miner could not get labour, he looked to the Government to procure it for him. As the local Africans were not prepared to work for anyone but themselves, the Administration had to use force, overt or covert, against them. The Government put African chiefs and headmen under the legal obligation to supply native workmen whenever required to do so. If the chiefs failed partially or altogether to produce the specified number of men, they were punished. This gave rise to a situation where the unfortunate chiefs and headmen, left with no other choice but to serve the interests of the strong, became instruments of force against their own people. It was a more serious development than any action the Europeans had yet taken against the African people. Although no doubt unaware of its implications, the white Administration was driving a wedge between the traditional Shona rulers and their people. The inevitable effect of this imposition was that the ordinary people not only became contemptuous of their chiefs, but disobeyed them as well. That shook Shona society to its very foundation. White Rhodesia was to pay dearly for such ill-advised measures. If the Europeans had examined the structure of Shona society realistically, they would have discovered that the paramounts as well as the ordinary chiefs were invested with both temporal and spiritual power. But at the same time, and this was the nub of their position, they could not use that power independently of or against their own people. I should like to think that, having made this assessment, the white government of the day would have understood the dangerous implications of making the chiefs labour agents for the profit of white men. Any honest African would have told them that this course of action was like sticking a pin into the most sensitive part of the human body.

The Africans reacted with growing anguish. They bitterly complained, but only to each other, which made no difference at all to their problems. If only they could have met these strangers and discussed and thought together as equal men constrained by fate to live together should, then there would have been light instead of darkness. This is what my grandfather

103

used to say. 'We were like dogs and were expected to obey, not to answer back,' he said.

And so, whether the European settlers realized it or not, they added one grievance to another in the ever-growing chain of labour demands, land demands and others too numerous to mention here. As my people said, almost every settler thought that it was his right to be respected by every African. While many of them did nothing to deserve this privilege, as I know only too well from my own experience, they were highly offended if, for instance, Africans did not take off their hats to them from a great distance. Because very often what constituted good manners to the African, such as sitting down before addressing a person as a mark of respect, was regarded as rudeness by the European, personal black and white relationships were bedev-illed by constant, unnecessary friction, which grew worse as more and more Europeans came into the country.

The Shona people were soon made aware that European rule entailed restriction on their freedom of movement, of residence, of expression and even of the choice of employment. And so, whatever virtues the settlers might have prided them-selves in possessing and whatever benefits they might have believed that they were conferring on their black fellow country-men, were not apparent to the Shona. What dominated the thinking of my people was that their position was becoming increasingly insecure, not only because of actual loss of freedom, but also because of white boorishness and a whole host of other petty, but painful pinpricks.

But, like today, the Rhodesian Europeans were out to govern and they had to be seen to be doing just that. After all, they had to make life more secure and more pleasant for themselves in an otherwise 'hostile' country. It seems that to the white Rhodesian of that period as of today, the right to govern carried with it the right to abuse the black man. One has only to read the correspondence columns of Rhodesian papers of any period since the occupation to appreciate that this privilege has always been greatly relished by white Rhodesia. Reading of these times, one is left in no doubt that the black man was not to the liking of most Pioneers. Even when he did what he was told, he had very little to commend him to his white masters. He was regarded generally as a thief, actual or potential. He was a liar and a lay-about. He was a parasite and, of course, he was most definitely a danger to the lives of white men, women and children, if not a potential rapist as well.

With evil, macabre aberrations such as these in their fear-ridden minds, the European settlers were not to be restrained either by compassion or expediency, nor would they soften their harsh attitudes towards their fellow black citizens. Their preju-dices reached dizzy heights particularly after the war of 1893 which put an end to the Ndebele power and completed the occupation of the whole country. Although the Shona had so far done nothing hostile, except refuse to work for white men, especially on the farms and in the mines, they were lumped together with the Ndebele as a source of trouble. Now they were subjected to even cruder forms of treatment.

Two important measures were introduced at this period. One was that the native population should pay a hut tax. This had a twofold intention, to make the Africans contribute to the cost of being governed and indirectly to force them to work for wages, if only for the purpose of finding the money to pay their taxes. The other measure was the establishment of a black police force. This was intended not only to provide more security for white Rhodesia which imagined itself to be surrounded by all kinds of perils, but also to identify some sections of the Shona and the Ndebele people with the administration of the country. Like everything else in Southern Rhodesia connec-ted with African affairs, then as now, both steps were taken arbitrarily and without any careful study of how the people would react to these decisions. A compassionate and more far-seeing ruling minority would have realized that a people who had had their own government for countless generations would need to be convinced of the necessity of paying taxes and of being policed. But for them, native opinion did not count. The prerogative of power, to rule and decide what was right and proper for the African population, rested with the white man. It was a policy that white Rhodesians were to stick to with the stubbornness and tenacity of Lisbon or the Vatican, regardless of its obvious hazards. And so, for the first time in their lives, my people were forced to carry the burden of taxation

105

by a foreign government in which they were not represented. For the first time in their entire remembered history, they were placed under the humiliating authority of a policeman, against whose abuse of power they had no protection whatsover.

I shudder each time I recall what the elders of Mashonganyika told me followed. But what happened then could not have been fundamentally different from what is happening in Rhodesia today and anywhere else where the concept of master-race prevails. From the accumulated evidence that I have, and this includes not only my ancestors', but also my own experience in Southern Rhodesia and South Africa, I no longer hold much respect for man, black or white, and his vaunted superiority over the rest of the animal kingdom. In the final analysis we are all brutes. My belief is simply that most men and women are 'good' and 'law-abiding' and help each other only if they are encouraged or compelled to do so by good laws and a corresponding climate of opinion. But otherwise I think it is the evil side of man which most easily comes to the surface and takes over; I believe that in a situation where racialism or the domination of one set of people over another is a cherished principle, it is the sadist and other such basically violent people who assume power for its own sake, for the opportunity and sheer pleasure it gives them to inflict fear, pain and suffering on their fellow human beings. For this reason I contest strongly the consensus of world opinion during and after the Second World War that cruelty was peculiar only to the German people or that section of the Germans which actively supported Hitler. I do not expect that I would behave any differently if I were trapped into a position where I was expected to uphold the domination of one group of people over another. I hope that I shall never be so unfortunate. If, however, my observations are ill-founded, how is it that some American soldiers have been accused of massacres in Vietnam? How is it that British immigrants, who in the United Kingdom were ardent advocates of democracy, justice and fairplay, became rabid racialists in Southern Rhodesia or South Africa?

Understandably, the Rhodesian authorities did not lack black recruits for their police force. The lure of the uniform, the handcuffs, the sjambok and the personal power which went with this position made the police force the only form of employment that black men did not shy away from. It gave its members a superior status and a share of the spoils of power which they would not otherwise have had. It went to their heads almost like the whisky that white men drank. Its effect was even more devastating.

To those who know the facts, no proof is needed that the sjambok played a substantial role in taming southern Africa. But it also fermented a great deal of hatred and trouble for the white man. This short whip, thick on the holding side and tapering at the other end, was made usually of hippopotamus hide. Like the gun, it was very much a symbol of white authority and was widely used against Africans as well as against horses, mules, donkeys, cattle and dogs. It did not break any bones or kill, if administered with reasonable force. But it caused pain of a special kind, sharp, penetrating, excruciating and lingering. My people called it *chamboko* and came to regard it as the weapon which more than anything else epitomized the nastiness of the institutionalized violence of the new society. Law and order had to be maintained at all cost, reasoned the Administration, but it did not seem to dawn on them that this supple whip, placed in the hands of uneducated black men and white men reared on the South African philosophy that Africans were both subhuman and dangerous, might be used in such a way as to defeat the very ends which it was intended to serve. Every man in uniform was issued with the sjambok and let loose to do his duty as he thought fit.

Black policemen, both local and those brought from South Africa, were, as it happened, in the forefront of the sjambok reign of terror that was unleashed against their own people. Ignorant, underpaid and treated by their bosses little better than any other Africans, they carried out their task with a particular devotion, and proved to the stupefied and terrified Shona, as also to the Ndebele, the truth of the saying that a slave in authority is more cruel than his master.

'They were continually among us. To them we were not people like themselves,' recounted the VaShawasha tribesmen who had the misfortune to be alive during this period. They came into the African villages for all sorts of reasons and were a law unto themselves, just as was the European. They used the sjambok freely. They were arrogant and insulted everybody without cause. Each man in uniform insisted on being addressed as *mwana we ngosi,* son of the Native Commissioner or the Government, a self-aggrandizing title which was accepted as meaning that whatever they did or said had the full backing of the white power that they represented. Dealing with a people who did not know the first thing about their legal rights, if they had any at all, let alone the limits of police power, these police-men did as they liked.

Having no protection against this bullying, the Shona and the Ndebele submitted as best they could. The people of Chishawasha said that they tried to please the 'sons of the Government' as much as possible. They gave them, on demand, food, especially chicken and ground rice and plenty of beer. They killed goats or cattle for the policemen. If they failed to satisfy any of these wishes, they were sjamboked or arrested on some trumped-up charge or both. As a result their stocks of grain and their numbers of goats diminished. Neither the black nor the white police took the trouble to observe their social customs. Least of all did they heed the tradition that those invested with tribal authority should be revered. Fathers, headmen, councillors and other highly respected men and women in Shona society were abused and humiliated in front of their families and followers. Even Paramount Chief Mashonganyika, the very fountain-head of the VaShawasha, as the Aga Khan would be to the Ismaili or the Pope to all good Catholics, was an object of contempt and maltreatment. No longer did he nor any other African chief wear the mantle of that especially exalted power which trans-cended life and death. He was regarded as just another black man, except that he was expected to be the instrument of the Government and to supply ready labour from his tribe at the behest of the arrogant policemen. Under the new order, all black people were the same, and inferior to anyone in uniform.

As my informants told me, the police were more terrifying than the white men who employed them. For over a long period their possession of power to inflict pain and suffering on their fellow men blunted any feelings of wrong-doing they might initially have had. They became more and more addicted to their practices. They pitched their demands higher and higher. Not the least among the fruits of office was sex. But as the Shona of that day and age were strict as regards prostitution, promiscuity and love-making outside the state of marriage, the only means open to these men to achieve this particular objective was the sjambok. When they were intent on a good time, they usually came early in the day and drove the village menfolk out before settling down to a long day of feasting and raping.

The central authority seemed to remain ignorant of the sins that were being perpetrated in its name. This was perhaps because it had confidence in the professional standards of the force, or because it did not care so long as the Africans were kept in their places. It therefore took no action to curb the excessive zeal with which law and order were being enforced. From my own experience of Rhodesian white officialdom, I think it was a mixture of both ignorance and indifference. In the view of most white Rhodesians and particularly of the Government, Africans are the special responsibility of the Native Affairs Department and of the police, whose primary duty is to ensure that they keep within the bounds of their segregated world. Under this general directive and with the aid of the complicated laws of discrimination that have been passed over the years, the Native Affairs Department officials as well as the police carry out their duty on the general principle that the end justifies the means. African human rights are of secondary consideration, if at all. Thus they have in the past been able to get away with many forms of injustice against the African people without the Government or white society in general being aware of what was being done in their name. This happened even during the liberal administrations of Mr Garfield Todd and Sir Edgar Whitehead. It cannot be difficult, therefore, to imagine what the policeman could and did do in those rough times when every white man felt that force was the only means of survival in the country he had just robbed.

Some of this will not seem credible except to a Rhodesian African who is well-informed on the history of his people or to a student of what documents are available relating to the causes of the Mashonaland and the Matabeleland rebellions of 1896.

I doubt whether there exists a complete and truthful account of how the African police so deliberately and freely misused their authority over fellow Africans, especially the womenfolk. One relevant piece of evidence, however, is that after the rebellion the sjambok ceased to be issued to the police and it was made a legal offence to use it on anybody without written authority.

When one considers that these abuses continued unchecked from 1890 to 1896, one might be tempted to question the moral courage and honour of the Southern Rhodesian Africans. But we must bear in mind how other conquered people in history, before and since, have behaved in conditions of subjection. How soon, for instance, did the Europeans overwhelmed by Hitler's Third Reich in the last war react to the slavery, the plundering, the arrogance of their conquerors and all the other forms of humiliation inflicted by the invading armies? Indeed, how effective and successful would their resistance have been without the combined physical and material resources of Great Britain, the Commonwealth, the Soviet Union and the United States of America to help them? We must remember that it took nearly six years for these otherwise highly organized and sophisticated nations to overthrow the Nazi empire.

The advocates of white rule in Southern Rhodesia will, of course, be horrified at any attempt to equate the system in white Rhodesia with that of Hitler's Germany. I certainly would never suggest that there has been in Rhodesia anything like Auschwitz, Dachau, and the other camps of mass murder. But in their first Pastoral Letter, the Roman Catholic bishops of my country described the Rhodesian race policy as being little different from Hitler's. And the fact that their condemnation did not stir the rest of the world into action against white Rhodesia does not make any difference to the essential truth of their judgement. Certainly, to the Africans of Southern Rhodesia, like myself, who are condemned from the cradle to the grave to live by the racial system of white rule in that country, it seems that the difference between Hitler and white Rhodesia is one of degree and not of kind. However, I believe that if the situations were reversed and Africans, either in Rhodesia or Zambia, treated their white fellow citizens as black people are treated in Rhodesia, the problem would be seen by the outside world exactly for what it is and has been since the day the Pioneer Column raised the Union Jack at Fort Salisbury on September 12, 1890.

According to our elders, discussion between the leaders of the Shona tribes about how to deal with the white man started shortly after his arrival. But the Shona were divided between those who preached caution and those who seemed to have understood at once the perils of white presence in their land and would have gone to war almost immediately the Pioneers' wagons rolled into the country. The VaShawasha were very much in the forefront of the war-mongers. For apart from anything else, the VaShawasha were close to Salisbury and felt the injustices of white society more acutely than most others. The presence of white missionaries at Chishawasha Mission, of course, had the effect of muting Shawasha discontent. But to Paramount Chief Mashonganyika and his hot-headed councillors we must add Paramounts Kunzwi-Nyandoro, Mashayamombe, Makoni and Muchemwa the son of Mangwende. These people were very militant up to 1893. Then the defeat of the Ndebele, the news of which would have been spread with relish among the Shona by the Native Commissioners, had the effect of dampening their enthusiam. The pacifists pointed out, with good reason, the folly of going to war against a people whose strength was clearly superior. For a time, their arguments held sway. Had there been effective channels of communication between the Shona and the Administration the impending catastrophe might have been averted. But no such channels existed.

The local Native Commissioner whom the VaShawasha called *Vuta* (Mr Campbell) was described by them as a particularly unpleasant person. *Vuta* means 'full of airs'. People like my grandfather said that he was a tyrant and they held him responsible for most of the sins perpetrated by his fellow men and particularly by his black hirelings in uniform in the Goromonzi and Salisbury districts. Time and again Mashonganyika and his councillors tried to discuss matters with him in the hope of settling their differences peacefully, but with little success. Either they were prevented from seeing him by his native staff who said that he was too busy to attend to them, or, if they did see him, he took what I know to be the typical attitude of Native Commissioners in Southern Rhodesia. All he was inter-

111

ested in was preaching to them about white power and white benevolence and the duty of the VaShawasha people to do as they were told. My people got nowhere at all, however hard they tried. The man was harsh and refused to entertain the idea that the police were misusing their power. It is understandable that he became a marked man and the VaShawasha tried to kill him first when the time came.

There is no reason to suppose that other Native Commissioners were judged differently by their own Africans. Both the good and the bad ones represented an evil system; they were all guilty men.

9

Mashonaland rebellion not incited by the
Ndebele; the death of Lobengula in 1893
leaves the Ndebele demoralized; the
Shona mediums revive their spirit and
inspire them into an alliance with the
Shona; both people rebel after firm
reassurances from the mediums; the bitter
struggle in Mashonaland.

A great many books have been written about the occupation
of Zimbabwe and its immediate aftermath. Of those I have
read, I suggest that Professor T. O. Ranger's *Revolt in Southern*
Rhodesia 1896–7 is certainly the most impartial and analytical,
bringing out, as it does, new facts and facets of the rising which
have either been suppressed by cautious officialdom or remained
unknown through lack of scholarly research. Most previous
writers have tended to rely too much on official sources and have
been influenced by partisan considerations; they have interpreted
the events of these stirring times mostly in terms of white achievements, with some admiration for the courage and plight of the
Ndebele. I contend that those who have ignored the point of
view of the Shona, have failed to put the situation in its proper
perspective. One obvious distortion that many writers have
perpetuated is the view that the Shona were incited to rebel
by their erstwhile masters, the Ndebele. This was the view of
the settlers at the time when they were suddenly faced with an
unexpected country-wide revolt by a people whom they had
thought to be among the most primitive, cowardly and defence-
less in the world. The Shona had been the victims of land-
banditry, police thuggery, forced labour and the hut tax, to
mention only a few of their grievances. The notion that they
would have borne all these injustices indefinitely with stoic

patience had they not been stirred up by the Ndebele is, to my mind, ridiculous. It is equally absurd to suggest that the Shona rose purely because they were afraid of Ndebele reprisals after the white man was driven out of the country, if they didn't. The only people who might have felt in need of this kind of insurance were those directly under Ndebele rule, namely the Karanga and Kalanga. But, as it happened, many of these people stayed completely out of the rebellion.

The facts indicate that the people of Mashonaland took up arms in a genuine desire to recover the freedom which they had always enjoyed until 1890. This was the sole reason for undertaking a task which they knew, even before they began fighting, would entail colossal sacrifices in men, sweat and blood. I had no hint of any kind from my tribal elders that they reached their fateful decision to rise against white rule at the behest of the Ndebele. The imperative to fight came from the Shona themselves. I will explain what I mean.

The swift defeat of the Ndebele in 1893 was, without doubt, demoralizing for the proud and powerful people who had dominated a sizeable proportion of Zimbabwe for several decades. The defeat had robbed the Ndebele of the main source of their national strength, Lobengula, who had died in the struggle. This had created the problem of finding a successor of the same stature and calibre as the late king, and they could not hope to settle such an important issue without interference from the victorious European administration. In the past, the Ndebele had met catastrophes of this kind by moving away altogether to new areas. But this was no longer possible. Lewanika of Barotseland made it known that he would send them packing, back to Southern Rhodesia, if they tried to cross the Zambezi to find a new settlement in his domains. He knew their troublesome character only too well and understandably did not wish to have them as neighbours. Neither the Shona nor more particularly the white man in control would permit them to march through Mashonaland to the north or east. Even if that had been possible, the Portuguese would have reacted very strongly if lands under their jurisdiction had been trespassed upon by such a notoriously war-like people. So the

Ndebele had to remain in the same country and accept their misfortune until better times.

The one hope left to them was in the spiritual inspiration of the Shona mediums, whose influence, as explained above, acted as binding factors between the two sides of the Rhodesian African world. By now, with Chaminuka's prophecies fulfilled, the Ndebele were ardent adherents of the *Mwari* or *Mlimo* cult. Without this influence, I doubt that they would have undertaken another war against the Europeans, particularly so soon after their costly rising in 1893. And so, while great courage and love of freedom were the main ingredients of the struggle that the Shona and the Ndebele put up together, the mediums provided the yeast which fermented the whole movement and enabled the participants to co-ordinate their policies and tactics. Without the oracular forecasts and spiritual assurances of the *Mwari* and *Mhondoro* spirits, I doubt very much whether the two tribes would have been as united as they were.

There is no doubt that the overthrow of the Ndebele monarchy and independence in 1893 had been a turning-point in the affairs of all the black people of Zimbabwe. This defeat brought home to the two nations that they had mutual interests in defending their country against the white invaders. It made them recognize for the first time that their fate was one. I think that, while their unity lasted, it was a moment of greatness for the Ndebele and the Shona. For, despite the fact that the Ndebele king had signed the rights of the Shona away on a piece of paper, the two people were able to sink their differences and join to fight the common enemy.

I contend, however, that the attitude of the Ndebele *per se* was not the decisive factor in the Shona's resolution to free themselves from the chains of white rule. They would still have gone to war even if the Ndebele had held back. The behaviour of the Europeans and the whole system of administration were too repressive for them to tolerate any longer. This is the impression I got from my tribal teaching. Apart from this, the Shona were in several respects much stronger than the Ndebele. Their morale was higher. They had not yet tasted the white man's military medicine. Their institutions were intact and they had an unshakeable faith not only in the justice of their cause, but perhaps more important still in the spiritual strength of their oracles and ancestors. It was natural that they should be more confident than the Ndebele, who had nothing better to show than the memories of their broken power. In other words, Shona confidence, as expressed through the mediums, was the mainstay of Ndebele hopes of liberation.

Exactly how the Shona mediums were inter-related and how they operated before and during the rebellion is something no living person today can honestly profess to know. I will not pretend to be an expert on the subject, which is clouded by contradictions and any number of exaggerations from the few who think that they know something about it. But what happened, broadly speaking, is as follows:

The arrival of the white man in 1890 was, for the Shona, a phenomenon, whose meaning they immediately looked to their mediums to unfold. This is how, traditionally, they had always approached national problems. And, in spite of Chaminuka's dire predictions about the coming of the Europeans and its consequences, their actual arrival still opened up considerable speculation as to what was going to happen next. Such situations of national importance always demanded the closest consultation among the Shona paramount chiefs as well as between them and their kith and kin under Ndebele rule. This was a role that only the mediums could undertake with any degree of success. As it happened, there were now other problems of national concern. There were droughts, cattle rinderpest and locusts, the causes of which could only be spelled out by the mediums. The mediums spoke out unequivocally. The message went throughout the country that the white man was not only an oppressor. He caused droughts, cattle sickness and locusts, all of which would lead to starvation and the extermination of all black people. Everyone believed this. The evidence against the guilty white man became more solid and irrefutable when the Administration, in order to arrest the spread of the rinderpest, ordered as many cattle as possible to be destroyed. This made the urge to fight it out irresistible.

However, there were a number of mediums, particularly the *Mwari* in Matabeleland, and they did not all subscribe to the prevalent feeling among the Ndebele and their vassals that another war was necessary. The Kalanga *Mwari*, for instance, refused to participate in the impending rebellion. As a result the people in that area stayed out of it. It would be interesting to know what would have happened if all or most of the *Mwari* oracles had taken the same stand. My feeling is that the decision to fight once more would have been postponed for further reflection by the people of Matabeleland. But in the circumstances, the majority of the *Mwari* mediums understood the mood of the moment, backed it, and, what is more, promised certain victory and the ejection of the intolerable white man from Zimbabwe. Nothing could have suited the Ndebele leaders better. These leaders were particularly encouraged in 1895 with the news that several white men, including the reckless Dr Jameson, had left the country to start a revolution in the Transvaal. Yet we will never know to what extent the oracles were brain-washed or intimidated into toeing the Ndebele line, just as modern Church leaders are pressured by their governments.

In Mashonaland there were also several mediums in a complicated relationship, consisting of lower, middle and upper *Mhondoro* and *Mashave* spirits, which I cannot describe here. The most senior of this Shona ecclesiastical hierarchy were Nehanda and Kaguvi (*Gumboreshumba*, 'the lion's leg', to call him by his proper name). In naming the various personalities who left their mark on these times, the Mashonganyika village historians made no reference to Chaminuka. And all these years I have retained the impression that after the death of Pasipamire, the Chaminuka who was captured at Chitungwiza and put to death by the Ndebele, his particular oracle ceased to exist; some people on the other hand are of the opinion that it continued to function during these later developments. But even if it did, the evidence I heard from my people showed that the Chaminuka oracle was completely overshadowed by Nehanda and Kaguvi so far as Central, Eastern and Western Mashonaland were concerned. It is quite possible that one or two people may have posed as the vehicles of the spirit of Chaminuka. But they did not carry the universal popularity which Nehanda and Kaguvi commanded, and they most certainly did not live long enough to give a convincing account of themselves. Nehanda

117

and Kaguvi, on the other hand, did so and in an unmistakeable manner.

Nehanda has always been a woman, and affectionately called *ambuya*, grandmother, by all her Zezuru adherents in Central Mashonaland among whom this particular one operated during the rebellion.

Kaguvi, being the main leader of the Shona rising, was active practically throughout the length and breadth of Mashonaland and was also the main link between the Shona and the Ndebele planners of the rebellion. He was very well equipped for this immensely responsible role. Being something of a cosmopolitan citizen in the Shona society of that day, he wielded unique influence. Born of the Chief Chivero family in the Hartley-Charter district of today, which is in Western Mashonaland, he was also a son-in-law of the VaShawasha Paramount Chief Mashonganyika in Central Mashonaland. He had lived among the people of Chikwaka, not very far from Chishawasha, for several years before the rising. And not only did he possess a very strong personality and gifts of prophecy, which he proved, for instance, by being able to forecast where hunters could find game, he also had the distinction of being acknowledged as the natural brother of the late Pasipamire, the legendary Chaminuka. He was therefore the most obvious choice when the men who shaped Shona national policy in these momentous times looked around for the man best suited to meet the challenges of the coming war. They must have been fully aware that the fortunes of this conflict would be decided above all by their ability to maintain national solidarity and the highest morale both among themselves and their Ndebele allies. Kaguvi could play this role.

There had always been a great many *Mhondoro* and *Mashave* spirits among my people and they became particularly important in times of national stress. But, like the modern fortune-teller or psychiatrist, they enjoyed, or suffered, a wide measure of intrinsic scepticism in the public mind. They had to work very hard to prove that they were not charlatans. In this endeavour, Nehanda and Kaguvi seem to have proved themselves much the most genuine and successful *Mhondoro* of the time and became the foremost mediums among the Shona.

It was a remarkable achievement, considering the number of claimants to this profession which carried immense prestige, especially in a society as deeply religious as the Shona.

As a man of such great substance and intelligence, Kaguvi would have been very much involved with the politics of this period. He would, no doubt, have been conspicuously active and vocal against white rule right from the moment the white man pitched his tents and hoisted his flag with flamboyant impunity on the hunting grounds of the VaShawasha people. Accordingly, when consulted, he dutifully communed with the ancestral spirits, who in their turn gave assurances of victory over the infernal *vasina mabvi* if the VaShawasha and their fellow countrymen should decide to make a combined effort to drive them out of their country. Believing himself, as he must have done, to be the true reincarnation and heir of his illustrious brother Pasipamire and the Chaminuka oracle, Kaguvi did not equivocate in any way. On the contrary, he came out with most emphatic and reassuring answers. He was a fiery nationalist and a patriot, who fully shared with his people the desire to be free in their own homeland.

With his revolutionary spirit, his popular appeal and the strong connections he had throughout Mashonaland, he emerged as the national leader of the Shona people when he was summoned from Chishawasha by Paramount Chief Mashayamombe of Western Mashonaland in 1896. Mashayamombe, 'he who needs cattle', was not only geographically nearer Matabeleland, but was also one of the foremost divine rulers of the Shona people. It was very natural, therefore, that Mashayamombe should be visited by the main medium of Matabeleland, Mkwati, a priest of the *Mwari* cult, for whose benefit Kaguvi appeared at Mashayamombe's court and with whom the Shona-Ndebele war policy was worked out. There can be little doubt that various messages had passed between Mashonaland and Matabeleland before Kaguvi and Mkwati met. But their meeting officially in the presence of Paramount Chief Mashayamombe put the final seal to the Shona–Ndebele pact.

On the other hand, my Chishawasha sources suggested that, initially at any rate, Nehanda was not an enthusiastic supporter of the impending rebellion and at that stage added her voice of authority to those of the pessimists who shrank from it all. Her oracle gave a most chilling account of things to come as a result of this war. Her body shook with paroxysms of horror. She cried like a child, unable to stomach the sight of blood, death, starvation and the subjection of her people that were to follow. She writhed in physical and mental anguish as she saw it all in her spiritual transformation, men with their brains and blood spattered in all directions, their limbs torn off their bodies and the countryside littered with rotting human and animal corpses for the vultures and the beasts of the forests to feed on. She saw the white man, filled with hate and fear, kill her people as if they were game or vermin and she asked the spirits of the ancestors again and again why they had brought this evil curse on her people. 'If it were possible to prevent this darkness and evil, I would. But I can't,' the spirit of Nehanda is alleged to have said.

This is an intriguing and unprovable piece of information about the dark past of the Shona people. We do know for certain, however, that Nehanda ultimately became the spiritual military leader of the rising in Central Mashonaland. This means that she must have changed her mind at some stage. She could, of course, have stuck to her original stand. As a medium and spiritual law-giver, she had no need to shift her original position, but she must also have felt that a struggle against white rule was preferable to silent national stoicism. If I am right, her attitude would have been somewhat similar to that of the majority of black Rhodesians today. Though basically peace-loving and non-political, most Africans I know in Southern Rhodesia have, sooner or later, been driven to the philosophy of violence as the only means left to them to eliminate the existing exclusive white minority rule. Nehanda was a person of very strong principles and character. Her defiance of white rule to her very last breath is evidence of the fact. When she was sentenced to death at the end of the rebellion, she was again and again coaxed and cajoled by the Rev Father Richartz, of Chishawasha Mission, in Salisbury gaol, to repent, be baptized and die fortified with all the last rites of the Church. But she refused absolutely and died without the least act of compromise with the Church and

120

State. On the other hand, Kaguvi gave in at the last moment and died a Christian.

The rebellion in Matabeleland began early in March 1896 and was over by the end of the same year, largely because Cecil Rhodes himself intervened with his famous Matopos *indaba*.* On this historic occasion, Rhodes, completely unarmed, convinced the Ndebele leaders that their fight was hopeless. But he also bribed them out of their struggle with promises of reforms in the hated oppressive police and the provision of adequate land. These promises are as dead as Rhodes himself in present-day Rhodesia.

But in the quick surrender of the Ndebele we see once more the unfortunate divergence between Ndebele and Shona interests. There is not the slightest evidence that, when the opportunity arose to wring concessions from the leader of the white settlers, the Ndebele felt any moral obligation towards their Shona allies. In saving their own skins by accepting hollow promises the people of Lobengula merely proved how naïve, ignorant and parochial they were. However, one understands their terrible misfortune and maybe the Shona would not have behaved any differently.

The Shona people started their revolt, variously called by them *Chindunduma†* or *Chimurenga*, in June 1896. It was to last into 1898 with the hanging of Nehanda, Kaguvi and other Shona leaders in March of that year.

If the Ndebele rebellion was something of a surprise, that of the Shona was even more so. With the great myth that had been built up about their cowardice and gratitude for being saved from the Ndebele savagery by the Europeans, no white settler nor even Native Commissioner in his right mind would have believed before June 1896 that these people would rise against their 'saviours' and fight with far more tenacity, cunning and sense of national purpose than the Ndebele themselves. Yet this preconceived notion, having been exposed for the fallacy it was, gave way to an angry reaction from the settlers, one that would seem to have had something in common with Hitler's reaction to the Poles when they dared to challenge the Aryan race in the

*Tribal conference
†Shona terms meaning strife, or rebellion

121

last war. How dared the Shona rise against the white man, most settlers asked themselves. They would have to be treated with a special brand of rough justice. And rough justice my people received.

But there were uglier political implications in the Shona rebellion. Up to now Rhodes had convinced the otherwise sceptical British Government and sections of the British public that his adventures into Mashonaland would be to the benefit of the primitive Shona who had previously groaned under the yoke of the savage Ndebele oppression. But here were these selfsame recipients of the benefits of white civilization and its liberalism proclaiming to the world, by their fanatical rebellion, that Cecil Rhodes and his henchmen were liars. Here were the 'primitive' and 'grateful' Shona demonstrating that the 'facts' presented to the British Government by the settlers contradicted the truth. Not only were they exposing the misrule of the Pioneers, but, most infuriating of all, the Shona were disputing the legality of the basis upon which their country had been occupied.

This particular rebellion had to be quelled and stamped out quickly, so that the Shona rebels should never be in a position to dispute, either in Rhodesia or in Britain, the terms of the Rudd Concession or any other legal or moral instrument by which Mashonaland was occupied. Like Smith today, Cecil Rhodes plugged every loophole through which the Shona paramount chiefs at war with his community and his Administration might express their national feelings about white rule. I understand that Cecil Rhodes, like most settlers, did not like the Shona as a people. He now had even better reason to dislike them than before.

Of all Cecil Rhodes' faults, surely the most unattractive were his double standards in the handling of the two risings. In Matabeleland, when the moment came, he realized that a negotiated peace settlement would be a better solution than fighting to the finish, and he extended the quality of mercy to the majority of the rebel Ndebele leaders. He not only restored them to positions of some authority among their own people. He made them the paid servants of his Administration.

In Mashonaland, however, he did precisely the opposite. He

allowed the war to be fought to its bitter end. When my people were finally vanquished, Rhodes had all the Shona personalities that were found guilty of leading the rebellion convicted and hanged, including my own great grandfather, Paramount Chief Mashonganyika, not forgetting, of course, the woman medium, Nehanda, whose guilt could not have been any more heinous than that of any of the Ndebele *indunas* whom the founder of Rhodesia had pardoned. Rhodes argued that the Shona were a divided people and did not have one central authority and that therefore they should be treated as traitors. I see no logic in this kind of thinking, only callous political expediency.

On the other hand, we cannot blame him for everything, for there was a British Government with the power to stop him and his hirelings indulging in these excesses. It was represented in Southern Rhodesia and must have been fully briefed on all aspects of the rebellion. To the extent that it was ultimately the supreme authority, I say that the final blame for these and all the other injustices connected with the occupation of Zimbabwe lies fairly and squarely with the British Government of the day. How strange that this very act of powerless indifference should be repeated seventy years later by a much better informed British Government and a Socialist one at that. I sincerely believe that had the Imperial Government firmly stepped in and insisted on remaining in control of the country until full African participation in the government of Southern Rhodesia was realized, the present UDI tragedy would have been rendered impossible. I should like to think that, had this happened, present black and white Rhodesians would be living in a country that we could all be proud of, offering every citizen humanity, equality, freedom and prosperity. We should then all have remembered Rhodes as a great man.

In the circumstances, however, the then Government at Westminster allowed Rhodes to handle things in his own way. He proceeded to treat the rising in Mashonaland with a much firmer hand than its counterpart in Matabeleland. Against this background we can understand why there were to be no epic battles or Shona heroes in Rhodesia's authorized history books. White Rhodesia, of course, remembers its own valour in such incidents as the Mazoe patrol and men like Blakiston.* But black men whose courage was the occasion for white courage are never heard of and are recorded only in age-worn, fading archival documents, which, to most white Rhodesians, serve only as fearsome reminders of the black dynamite that they are fated to live with as their servants for the foreseeable future.

The one thing that did not go quite according to Rhodes' wishes in Mashonaland was the length of the rebellion, which says a great deal for the courage and determination of its people. It dragged on much longer than the struggle in Matabeleland and came to an end only because Imperial troops were brought in through Beira and imposed exceptionally harsh conditions. The British troops pursued a scorched-earth policy, which included burning down African houses, food stocks and dynamiting the rock caves and fortresses where Shona men, women and children were suspected of hiding. Nehanda had been quite right after all, recalled the surviving old men and women of Mashonganyika. When the local white community had got over the shock of the unexpected challenge and their spirits had been raised by the arrival of British troops under Lt-Col. Alderson, they set out to settle scores with the Shona in the only way they knew, giving no quarter, and expecting none. Having superior weapons and organization, the white troops found it easy enough to fight in every type of terrain; they killed a far greater number of Africans than it was possible for the Africans, with their erratic *zwigidi,* and old, rusty Portuguese guns and spears, to kill them. When supplies of dynamite became available, even the shelter of the rocks and caves could no longer serve as effective protection. The dynamite, *daramete,* as the Shona came to call this fiendish white invention, split and blew the rocks into thousands of pieces which became quite as lethal as the white man's bullets themselves. In this way, thousands of Shona men, women and children were killed, wounded and maimed. But as there were no medical facilities for the rebel African population, a great many were left to die slowly. As the historians of Mashonganyika recalled,

*Blakiston led a small patrol to save the settlers in the Mazoe area. This mission, undertaken in the teeth of African attacks, made him a hero, and he is remembered with gratitude by white Rhodesia.

the countryside echoed with the booms of the guns, big and small, the screams of the fleeing and the dying and for many days, nights, weeks and months, rotting bodies lay strewn everywhere for the vultures and jackals of the Rhodesian bush to feed on.

It was, however, by no means a one-sided affair. In the initial stages, the Africans had the advantages of secrecy and many white people, especially in outlying districts, were surprised and put to death. Those who had been noted for their arrogance and harshness towards black people were the first objects of attack. Understandably, African policemen, messengers and others who were associated with the use of the sjambok and complete subservience to the white man at the expense of their own people were the early targets of Shona fury. Called *imbga dza vasungate,* 'white men's dogs', they were killed with an even fiercer hatred than that felt against the foreigner.

Right from the beginning, Paramount Chief Mashonganyika, urged on by his impatient and highly militant councillors who resented subjection probably more than anyone else in the country, took a prominent role. Indeed, without his support, the struggle in Central Mashonaland would probably have died even before Kaguvi thought it fit to leave for Mashayamombe. The VaShawasha people were traditionally in the senior grade of the Zezuru tribal organization, and because of their military tradition they were logically expected to identify themselves with the movement for national liberation. It was natural then that once Chief Mashonganyika had given his blessing to the fateful undertaking, there could be no change of mind on the part of Mashayamombe, Nyandoro, Mangwende, Seke or any of the main paramounts in Central, Western and Eastern Mashonaland. But by the same token, the VaShawasha and their close neighbours such as Chiweshe, Mangwende, Seke, Chikwaka and Mashayamombe had to bear a much bigger share of the fighting. Not only were their areas nearer Salisbury, but they had also been picked first for prospecting and farming operations, which gave them a much more lively sense of injustice than that of the other Shona not so blatantly despoiled.

And so, whether they liked it or not, the people of Chishawasha had to throw themselves heart and soul into the

Chindunduma. Once it was agreed to start fighting, Mashonganyika picked one of his sons, Gukwe, my grandfather, to lead
the VaShawasha contingent. This was to team up with
Chikwaka's people, whose general briefing was to drive all white
people out of their districts and then converge on Salisbury for
the final assault on the white settlers. Gukwe decided to attack
the seat of Native Commissioner *'Vuta'* at Goromonzi first, it
having been agreed by all concerned that he was the most
reprehensible white official in their area. But before he marched
his men for this particular objective which was not far from
Mashonganyika's capital, Gukwe sent a section of his warriors
to Chishawasha Mission. Their object was to drive out the white
missionaries from the Mission, which the VaShawasha, not un-
reasonably, suspected of being a spy centre in the service of the
Administration.

I was told that this was a most agonizing decision and had
not been reached in haste because it involved delicate considerations of conscience, a moral question that brought in the Shona
conception of right and wrong. Of all the white men in the
country, the missionary community at Chishawasha was seen as
representing the highest of what little good there was in the
values of white civilization in Southern Rhodesia. Although now
they owned part of what was the country of the VaShawasha,
they stood quite apart from the majority of their mercenary
race. They were just, unselfish and compassionate to the
VaShawasha people. What is more, they had established a school
for the teaching of reading, writing and training in technical
skills and generally came much nearer than any other white
people to treating Africans as human beings and children of
the same God who had created all humanity. They were, of
course, not all the same. Father Biehler, for instance, with his
harsh discipline and general high-handedness, was suspected
of being anti-black. But he was more than counterbalanced by
the majority of the others, especially Father Richartz, the
Superior of the Mission, who despite the incomprehensibility
of the religion he represented, was the kindest white man in the
eyes of the VaShawasha. What were they to do with this
community, which was above injustice, greed, cruelty and all the
other malpractices of white power?

126

This knotty question had confronted the VaShawasha elders for a very long time indeed. It was not easy to resolve, especially when they looked at the reverse side of the coin, namely, the possibility that once the fight had started, the white missionaries might choose to side with their fellow white men, whatever their private feelings might be and whatever their religion had to say on the subject. However, one of the influential VaShawasha chiefs, Chidyausiku, 'night-eater' or 'prowler', had no such qualms and tried very hard to talk everyone out of merciful sentiments. He held that these were dangerous to the freedom of the tribe. In fact, he was so hell-bent against the unfortunate Fathers that one day he left for the Mission on his own. He had a sword hidden in his coat and on reaching there asked for a special audience with Father Richartz. The priest, whose sixth sense suspected his would-be assassin, refused to grant him the interview and so was saved. This happened before Gukwe gave official orders to attack the Mission and only after it had been established that it was being or was going to be used as an intelligence centre.

While Gukwe and his men were on their way to Goromonzi, they met '*Vuta's*' brother, who was a trader in the district. The white man was attacked and killed by the VaShawasha warriors. Whether '*Vuta*' himself was aware by now that something was going to happen, it is not possible to say. But at this particular point he had left his place of office on horseback, somehow heard about the death of his brother and decided to go and ask Paramount Chief Mashonganyika about this killing. Mashonganyika denied that his men had been responsible for the crime. And '*Vuta*' never got down from his horse. When he had failed to elicit the information he was seeking from the chief, he galloped away, this time making for Salisbury. When he reached somewhere near Ruwa Siding, about fourteen miles from Salisbury, he ran into Gukwe's troops, who attacked him. '*Vuta*' was saved by leaning over one side of the horse, and escaping at full gallop. The VaShawasha warriors, not being confident of catching him, made for the camp, where they joined Chikwaka's men and together attacked the settlement. They killed many of the African staff and destroyed what property they could lay their hands on. This done, they made sorties on

127

pockets of white settlement and isolated farms in that area and in the Chikwaka-Mangwende districts where they joined other Shona combatants in a general mopping up operation. They had hoped that they could quickly kill or clean out all the Europeans in this region and then make a general march on Salisbury. But by this time the Europeans had formed themselves into defensive positions. Also relief white troops had been sent from Salisbury which were able to pin down the Africans in the district for a protracted struggle. As far as I know, the Africans never reached anywhere near Salisbury during the rebellion.

In the meantime, the group that made for Chishawasha Mission found that the Jesuit Fathers had been warned beforehand of the impending assault by some of the Christian Africans, who were members of the tribe. The white missionaries had taken refuge in one of the Mission buildings. This building, which had previously served as a warehouse, was well built; it was here that the white Fathers put up a stout resistance against what must have been tremendous odds. As it happened, the site of the Mission commanded a very good view to the north, west, east and to some extent south sides, so that whichever direction the attackers came from, the missionaries could fire at them with good effect. Among them were some first-class marksmen, particularly Brothers Biermann and Puff, who, I was told, were able to hold their own against the quivering spears and the slow, unreliable *zwigidi* of the VaShawasha. They defended themselves so well that they did not suffer a single loss of life or injury until they were rescued by Government forces from Salisbury. The VaShawasha attacking force actually stormed the building and tried several times to break in. When I went to school years later, I saw evidence of this siege in the battle-axe scars left on the main door where the warriors had attempted to smash it open. However, it must have been a very amateurish job, considering that it was a wooden door. This seemed to bear out the truth of Jakobo's description of this encounter. Jakobo never altered his view about the bungling and lost opportunities which contributed to the defeat of his people. Of the Mission episode, he said that once the VaShawasha had reached its precincts, at great loss to themselves in dead and wounded, the bulk of their men were more interested in what they could loot than in achieving their objective. Without a strict commander, such as Gukwe would have been, the besiegers, finding that it was not going to be easy to dislodge the white community from their stronghold, relaxed their efforts. Instead of maintaining their vigilance and discipline, they turned their attention to the bread, jam, sugar, meat, biscuits and the great quantities of wine in the Mission's cellars on which most of these men became so roaring drunk that their commander could not control them. Little wonder that the missionaries were eventually rescued.

On the other hand, it is very possible that the tribe did not intend to kill their former teachers and friends, but merely wished to scare and remove them from their presence. As Chivanda used to say, the VaShawasha did not really want the blood of the missionaries on their hands. But because they were identified with an evil system, which had robbed the tribe of everything that it had possessed, except the houses in which they lived and the plots of land that they cultivated, the least that the VaShawasha could do was drive them out of their area.

As a schoolboy, convinced by the teaching of the Catholic Church, but at the same time not yet fully aware of the many ramifications of white rule in Southern Rhodesia, I always carried a strong feeling of guilt for what seemed to me a most sinful course of action by my forefathers who had tried to kill the finest white people to be found in the country. But men like Brothers Krechel and Puff who had survived these bad times, discussed this story with myself and other Shawasha boys and did not think that there was any cause to worry about it. Showing a remarkable lack of bitterness, they were content to dismiss it as one of the hazards of missionary enterprise. Indeed, I am certain that they had nothing but admiration for the VaShawasha people. Brother Puff used to say that my tribesmen could have killed all the missionaries if they had really wished to do so. There is a lot in this, or else how does one explain the fact that, although the VaShawasha had a completely free hand once the Fathers had escaped to Salisbury, they never attempted to desecrate or destroy any of their buildings! They completely emptied the Mission larder, but did nothing more.

Subsequently, the same people, their Chishawasha Mission

assignment completed, headed for Salisbury. But they do not appear to have gone far in this direction. The vicinity of the town was well guarded by white soldiers. In any case, this small body of men was ordered not to move in a hurry, they had instructions merely to harass the enemy until the general body of the Shona freedom fighters from other parts of Central Mashonaland were ready to converge on Salisbury for the final battle. According to my information, this force fought many skirmishes as it tried to advance on the town and some were overwhelmed and surrendered while others retreated and joined their fellow men in the neighbouring districts, where by now they were on the defensive.

Not far from the Mission in the direction of Salisbury by the side of the Arcturus road there can still be seen the lonely grave of a man called Stevens. I imagine that Stevens was killed by this section of the Shawasha fighting forces as he and his fellow soldiers were trying to rescue isolated Europeans, including the priests and lay brothers of Chishawasha Mission. Because of the terrible penalties some of the Shona leaders paid in the end, and the fear that the white man would always seek vengeance on the guilty, the VaShawasha of the 1920s and 1930s were very circumspect, particularly in cases of individual involvement in the killing of Europeans. And so I never was told who killed whom.

10

*International opinion deceived in the
question of right and wrong in the struggle
in Rhodesia; Rhodes has powerful friends
in England; the powerless white liberals,
Henry du Pré Labouchère and
Olive Schreiner; the British Government
sends military help to the settlers;
the defeat of the Shona and their
misfortunes under the 'no-mercy' policy
of Cecil Rhodes.*

The climate of international opinion towards all Africans eighty years ago was infinitely less enlightened than it is in our times. To the majority of Englishmen in their own country the wronged people of Mashonaland, as also of Matabeleland, were just faceless savages without rights. White men who had a taste for adventure joined in the hunting and killing of a people, who protested and rebelled against the theft of their country. There was nothing like the United Nations, the League of Nations or the World Court to make even a token expression of mankind's conscience on behalf of the Shona. There was no television or radio journalist to slip through a quick interview with a black chief and let the world or a portion of the world know what my people felt about their calamity. As far as the British Press was concerned, Rhodes had several supporters, particularly W. T. Stead of the *Pall Mall Gazette,* Sir Sidney Low of the *St James Gazette* and Flora Shaw of *The Times.* These journalists were among the writers who moulded the British political opinion of that time. They never transferred their loyalty from Rhodes to the Shona. Flora Shaw, who became the wife of Lord Lugard of Nigerian fame, so believed in Rhodes' African mission that she was personally implicated in the abortive

Jameson Raid into the Transvaal Republic, which the founder of Rhodesia had engineered behind the scenes. At Westminster the attitude of Members as a whole was not pro-African. As for the Government, it was wholly behind the settlers and proved it by despatching professional soldiers to help them in suppressing the rebellion. Having no adverse world opinion to contend with and being aware that the bulk of the British public would expect it to protect the European settlers against African rebel savages, the British Government of the day considered that it had a duty to carry out. It is possible that those in power secretly regretted the mistakes and the injustices committed by Rhodes' white community in Southern Rhodesia. But publicly they defended the settlers and made it possible for them to put down two rebellions, of which the Shona was a particularly determined one.

There was, however, some genuine concern in England among the liberal people against the piratical actions of Rhodes. Foremost among these critics was Mr Henry due Pre Labouchère, Member of Parliament and proprietor/editor of a weekly paper called *Truth*. Labouchère represented the exact opposite of Flora Shaw's attitude to Cecil Rhodes and kept up a consistent campaign against all his imperialistic schemes in Africa. But, as we have experienced in the sorry story of UDI, not one word said by men like Labouchère was of any practical value to the friendless African tribesmen. In South Africa there lived at this period of time one of the most courageous torch-bearers of liberalism of this or any other age. She was Olive Schreiner, a distinguished authoress and political commentator. Though an admirer of Cecil Rhodes initially, she later became his bitterest adversary and that mainly because of his theft of Mashonaland and particularly the massacre of the Shona, for which she held Cecil Rhodes entirely responsible. Her revulsion was appropriately expressed in her novel, *Trooper Peter Halket of Mashonaland*, in which she portrayed Rhodes' mercenaries as a gang of murdering, raping, thieving marauders. Rhodes was a monster and she felt it her Christian duty to expose him and did so in this book which was published in 1897, causing tremendous sensation in England because it did not gloss over the gory acts of the settlers against the Ndebele and the Shona.

But, of course, Olive Schreiner's campaign and exposures made no difference to the plight of my people in the end.

It is easy to appreciate now that the Shona could not at the start of the rising have had any inkling of the forces which were ranged against them. However, as weeks and months passed, it became clearer and clearer that they had overestimated their own strength. By any reckoning, my people realized, they could not match the white man's resources and so they began to reconcile themselves to eventual defeat. This fact became all the more poignant when it was obvious to them that they were very much on their own now. Their Ndebele allies had opted for peace with mercy and salaries. The enemy, having pacified Matabeleland, was now able to put more men, energies and other resources into the war against the stubborn Shona. Naturally enough, they lost the initiative that they had had in the beginning and began to be on the defensive in all sectors of their struggle.

And what of the mediums, who had promised certain victory and the miraculous transformation of white men's bullets into water? What of the ancestors upon whose power and goodwill they had relied? They had believed in all sincerity that they would see them through their misfortunes. Rotting bodies upon rotting bodies, burning, charred huts and crops piled up all over the countryside were proof that all the prophecies of Kaguvi and of all the other seers had been false. Perhaps for the first time in their history, the Shona people were shaken out of their blind faith in the *Mhondoro* spirits and the protection of the ancestors. It was a shattering realization and, as we shall see, the disillusioned Shona for a time lost confidence both in themselves as a people and in their traditions. It also made most of them, especially the young, ready material for Christianity and gullible converts to Western materialism. I am convinced that if the Administration had at some stage or other offered to talk peace, to right wrongs and so end this appalling race war, the paramounts of Mashonaland would have responded in the same way as their Ndebele counterparts had done. But this gesture was never made, as far as I know.

The military forces were given a free hand in the execution of their duty, but their methods of warfare were hardly neces-

F

sary. It appears the white soldiers were more interested in killing Africans than in capturing them alive. That was the impression gained by some of my people who lived to tell the tale of this conflict. The manner in which men like Paramount Chiefs Makoni and Mashayamombe met their deaths certainly confirms that the European soldiers were totally devoid of compassion and magnanimity towards their black foes. I shall say more about Makoni and Mashayamombe later. Yet the people of Mashonaland struggled on doggedly until they realized that if they went on any further they might be exterminated altogether, particularly through starvation. The thorough destruction of their food stocks by the white troops was ultimately the determining factor, said the VaShawasha people. They were reduced to existing solely on wild fruit, roots and field rats. Many of them died from starvation. Some of the early settlers who experienced the Shona rebellion admitted that the Shona were a great deal more determined and tenacious than the Ndebele. They must have angered the Europeans even more by their methods of fighting. Unlike the Ndebele whose military tactics took the form of massive charges and therefore provided excellent shooting targets, the Shona operated as guerrillas, striking only when it was to their advantage and disappearing into natural cover before the enemy had time to recover his balance. This was particularly galling to the enemy who wished for a speedy end to this expensive war and who did not care how many blacks were killed. I suppose that this was one of the reasons why the white soldiers resorted to such gruesome methods as the use of dynamite. If Mashonaland had had thick forests, like parts of Kenya and Malaya, for instance, the odds against the African people might not have been so overwhelming.

However, sooner or later they had to give up the struggle. As they were cut off from one another and contact became virtually impossible, each tribe or group of people began to surrender individually. By the end of 1897, the rebellion was practically over.

Thinking of the tangled problems of my country, as I have done every day of my adult life, I return again and again to this ugly drama of 1896. I am sure it was inevitable, given the state of affairs at the time, but I have come to believe that it was this war, more than anything else, which degraded Rhodesia, both black and white.

It degraded the African, because it destroyed his political balance, his hope, his dignity. It profoundly undermined his self-confidence. From the time of the 1896 rebellion, my people have tried to find a common platform from which to assert their rights. There have been many African organizations, of all kinds, political and social, led by fine men. Of course organizations everywhere suffer division and debate, but disunity and acrimony have eroded our attempts to further African progress. This is in spite of the example set by our forebears in 1896. This is in spite of the example of unity given us by white South Africans and white Rhodesians—the unity of white reaction everywhere. I believe that our comparative lack of political maturity (which is fortunately showing signs of improving) is due to the humiliations of the 1896 defeat, and the savage reprisals we suffered afterwards. We have lived too long as a conquered people in a conquered country, and have not found it easy to recover our national self-respect.

As for white Rhodesians, I believe the 1896 struggle degraded them even more than it did us. They are in possession of a wonderful, rich country. But it is an African country, just as England is a country of the English people. They tyrannize a peace-loving, friendly, adaptable people, who long for freedom, education and equal opportunities to use their constructive energies, to create the material and spiritual wealth that would improve the quality of life for everyone, including their white compatriots. By using the best values of Western civilization, of Christianity, white Rhodesians could make a special and lasting contribution to all Africa. But instead they threaten and defy Africa, and African dignity. They impose on their fellows, the black people, miseries and humiliations that the civilized of the world repudiate because they are repugnant and obnoxious to everything that Christianity and the family of man stand for. And their behaviour is dangerous to themselves, for history teaches that conquerors will in their turn be conquered. They do not seem to be able to learn from the facts of their situation. They are inflexible and stupid. I think the reason for this is that they have never been in anything else but the position of

135

conquerors, who do not understand, let alone feel what it is to be black and to be permanently underprivileged. They entered the country as if it already belonged to them. They crushed the Ndebele in 1893, and then the Ndebele and the Shona together in the rebellion of 1896. Might has always been right. They have never tried to use the ways of respect and humanity. And now perhaps they have forgotten how to do so, having created a society and a system of social, economic and political values based on the philosophy of might and race. They do not know themselves how backward, how brutal, how heavy-handed they appear to their African captives and to the outside world, white as well as black. They have corrupted themselves by the abuse of their best qualities and are more savage than the very people they have always insulted by calling savage. The great Goethe and Booker T. Washington, the author of *Up From Slavery*, said : If you are going to keep a man down in a ditch you have to stay with him. Thus as long as the Rhodesian Africans, my people, remain in the ditch of apartheid and the physical, moral and psychological as well as spiritual degradation that go with this system so must their oppressors remain there with them.

Perhaps it was in the aftermath of the rebellion that the white man showed himself at his most short-sighted and vindictive. It is certain that it was then he set patterns of subjugation which he has not softened since. The Administration gave itself wide powers of arrest and extortion of evidence from anyone suspected of having been a rebel. Once again the police and the security forces were let loose on the Africans. They went to all the outlying areas of Mashonaland. According to my tribal informants, they were ruthlessly cold-blooded and efficient. And so, to the hundreds, perhaps thousands of Africans who had been killed and maimed in battle were added hundreds of others whose chances of escaping the hangman's noose were as slender as had been those of the men dynamited in the caves escaping death or crippling. We do not know how many people were hanged for their crimes nor do we know what evidence was cited against them. The numbers remain secret, as the battle-field casualties are secret—if anyone ever bothered to count them. I was given the impression by my elders that they were very

136

considerable. But dead men tell no tales and we shall never know.

The VaShawasha people, who knew the methods used by the Administration to obtain evidence to convict the accused, thought that some rebels escaped hanging, while other innocent men were sent to the gallows. Naturally, they had no access to the processes of the law. Their friends and relations just disappeared and were never accounted for. According to some people, Africans have been disappearing—remaining unaccounted for— in Rhodesia since UDI. So it is easy enough to imagine that in the much rougher conditions of Rhodesia in the 1890s, the need to remove troublesome black human beings would not have caused the slightest embarrassment. However, the VaShawasha thought that miscarriages of justice were mainly due to lack of reliable evidence. Many of the Africans subpoenaed either would not give evidence, or submitted facts which were of little or no value to the authorities. And the few committed government informers were such notorious liars that they testified against innocent people. As the Smith regime is doing today, the law officers of that time encouraged informers and spies of all kinds.

Against outstanding personalitites such as Nehanda, Kaguvi and Paramount Chief Mashonganyika, however, the testimony was overwhelming. They were to be executed with little political or moral compunction. Native Commissioner *'Vuta'* could not possibly have forgotten and forgiven the killing of his brother, the trader. In any case, as the administering officer of the Chishawasha district, *'Vuta'* had made it his duty to study painstakingly every clue as to who were the most influential rebel leaders. All the evidence he had collected pointed to the proud, cunning Chief, who came directly under his jurisdiction. The Native Commissioner remembered that Mashonganyika had proved himself particularly unamenable to the white man's authority. The leader of the VaShawasha people had refused to be submissive and had been generally deceptive. Indeed, *'Vuta'* recalled that, but for the grace of God, he himself might have been killed by the Chief's men. Accordingly, the Native Commissioner submitted a case against Mashonganyika. Once the Chief was arraigned before the white court of justice (just

137

as the Rev. Ndabaningi Sithole, ZANU's president, was arraigned before Mr Smith's court of justice for the alleged crime of planning political murders), the process of trial, with its procedure of cross-examination, was a mere formality. At the end of it, Mashonganyika, who had been one of the chief pillars of Shona society, was hanged like a common criminal—for trying to recover the freedom of his people and his country.

His colleagues, Mashayamombe and Makoni, had preceded him. The manner of their deaths bears out the truth of the statement I made before, that decency and magnanimity were wholly lacking in the methods of warfare used against the Shona. In both cases, they had emerged from their granite strongholds, wishing to negotiate with the white soldiers. But the soldiers had been given sweeping powers and chose not to accord these African leaders the right to be arrested and to be given even a semblance of a just trial. They were both shot on the spot by individual soldiers whose orders did not include that of capturing rebel leaders alive. The man who shot Paramount Chief Mashayamombe even expected to receive a reward, for this great and brave Shona leader had put up such fierce resistance in his area of Western Mashonaland and had cost the attacking white forces so many casualties that a price had been put on his head. When he finally came out of his rock fastness, he was quickly disposed of, to the jubilation of the beseigers and to the glory of the officer who made the kill.

As for my grandfather Gukwe, fate had a different twist, if the following account is to be believed and I do not see why it should not be, seeing that this is very much a family matter. The evidence against him was not sufficiently conclusive. Yet the authorities strongly suspected that he was guilty. And so they remanded him in custody, with specific instructions to the police to use every method they knew for extracting confessions from an obstinate prisoner. The police proceeded to make him confess his guilt. They crushed the palm of his right hand with several hammer blows. But this did not make him talk. Medical facilities in those days were crude and the pain must have been terrible for Gukwe. At a later stage, the hand was amputated from the wrist. Still he did not talk. Then gangrene set in and it was thought advisable to cut it off from the elbow. Gangrene

138

set in again. Yet again the brave man did not make the desired confession. They finally removed what was left of his arm from the shoulder joint. But by this time diarrhoea and other complications had overtaken his once robust physical frame. He died subsequently, without having said a word in admission of his alleged crimes.

However, this meting out of 'justice' was only a part of the general policy of ensuring law and order and consolidating white rule. The confiscation of arms from the Shona was the most important operation for making the country really safe for the white population. This was to take a very long time indeed, involving, as it did, the entire Shona population whom no one was prepared to trust nor could regard as being harmlessly stupid any longer. Once again, the law officers were given maximum freedom to use their discretion in this task. They grilled their victims indiscriminately. They contrived various forms of torture which were intended to make the native people reveal any hidden guns, spears and other weapons that could be used again should they attempt another rebellion. The VaShawasha and their allies were not to forget this experience for the rest of their lives. They said that it was almost like another war. Perhaps it was worse since they were now unarmed and could not fight back. Apart from sjambok lashings and the crushing of men's testicles, other cruel methods were employed against them. People who proved particularly stubborn were tied hand and foot and held in such a way that their backs were partially roasted on flames of fire. They were treated in this way again and again until they gave useful information. And sure enough, in the majority of cases, these tactics worked and resulted in the revelation of large quantities of arms, which had been hidden in rivers, caves, old mine pits and various other places. Whether or not the Shona had intended to rebel again, we shall never know.

For the people of Mashonaland, this was now perhaps the most painful and humiliating phase of their subjection, for it was being impressed upon them that they could no longer consider themselves a free people. The right to carry weapons and to use them wherever occasion demanded was no less important to the Shona than their freedom to worship in their traditional ways and to revere their chiefs. You were not a man, let alone a free man, unless you carried a spear or two, better still a gun, the possession of which assured you that, when necessary, you could defend yourself, your family or your tribe and you could kill game to feed your wife and children. This right was now taken away. It was, to them, the final act of submission. But there was nothing they could do about it. And so, those that could not help it gave in their weapons, including the Portuguese guns and their own *zwigidi* which had been their inseparable friends in war and providers of meat in the days of old Zimbabwe. However, very many proud and obstinate men revealed nothing and surrendered nothing. Yet in a way it all came to the same thing, for they were never able to retrieve their arms wherever they might be without risking severe penalties, possibly death. And so, many such weapons were to rot to dust in the silent Rhodesian bush.

11

*The aftermath of defeat; Chishawasha
Africans are fed and sustained by the
Jesuit Fathers; Chishawasha School
proves that the Shona can be regenerated
through education; Lord Albert Grey's
impressions; the settlers entrench their
position.*

From the ashes of this complete defeat and this national humiliation, the Shona people inherited a fear which was to last so long
that even in the late 1950s prominent white Rhodesian politicians could boast that since the rebellion the Europeans had
never fired a bullet at the African in anger. The Ndebele had
been given certain assurances by Rhodes and for a time could
comfort themselves in the knowledge that they had some kind
of security and had found favour in the eyes of the white man.
But they were black and in the long run they too would receive
the same treatment and come to realize that the promises of the
founder of Southern Rhodesia were as empty as the memories of
their illustrious kings, Mzilikazi and Lobengula. For the blood
money which Lobengula had been promised by Cecil Rhodes
for surrendering Mashonaland to white occupation the Ndebele
was now paid in the form of permanent subjugation. It must
be one of the worst cases of injustice in world history. On the
land question alone, the Ndebele were worse off than the Shona,
for when they were defeated in 1893, white men exercised less
restraint in taking their land than they had done in Mashonaland. If Rhodes had not intervened in 1896 and put a stop to
this plunder, the Ndebele nation might well have become a
landless people in the end. But whatever temporary security and
safeguards they obtained, there were no fundamental differences
between their lot and that of the Shona. Rhodesia was a white

141

man's country now and he started to lay, stone by stone and brick by brick, the foundations of a system which offered permanent subjection, colour discrimination and lack of opportunity to all Africans.

Would the Africans of Southern Rhodesia have been given a better future if they had not gone to war against the white settlers? My feeling is that they would not. But there is no doubt that the 1896 rebellion quickened the pace of white reaction and debased whatever decent human values they might have had. Instead of having to wrestle with their consciences before embarking on their racist native policies, as they might have had to do, particularly when dealing with the British Government, now they had an excuse to be inhuman to the Africans. As my people would say, by killing Africans in an unjust cause, the Europeans had brought *ngozi* upon themselves and would not therefore be able to think and act rationally. As an African, I find it difficult to dismiss this simple, if superstitious kind of logic. The white community in Southern Rhodesia is a complete puzzle to me, a concentration of irrationality. I cannot repeat this fact too often.

But to go on with the story of the VaShawasha. Like everyone else, they found themselves at the end of the conflict completely without food. This long struggle had made it impossible for them to cultivate any new crops. What food they had had at the start of the rising was exhausted. In this total war the white forces had destroyed everything that could possibly help their black enemy. I was told that, until life returned to some order, the tribe as a whole was reduced to a form of existence little better than that of animals, without shelter, without hope or dignity. Many families were broken up either temporarily or permanently. Most people lived on wild fruit and berries, which were far from nourishing, but nevertheless prevented the strong from dying, while the not so strong wasted away and went to their graves. They were now completely dependent on and at the mercy of their victorious white enemy and could not assert themselves in any way whatsoever.

Fortunately for the VaShawasha people, this state of destitution and despair did not last long. The Jesuit Fathers, who by now had returned to pick up the threads of their Mission enterprise at Chishawasha, assumed a role which made even the most anti-white and anti-missionary feel ashamed of the unhappy fate they had originally designed for this religious community. Father Richartz, benevolent and influential man that he was, appealed with success to the VaShawasha to look upon his Society and the Mission as agents of mercy and sustenance for soul and body. Having influence in the corridors of power in Salisbury, he obtained food from the Administration and distributed it liberally among those starving VaShawasha who responded to his call. More than that, he knocked at the door of every white person of any standing and compassion, pleading for charity and forgiveness for the defeated. He was treated with ridicule and, in certain cases, he met such anger and callousness as must have severely tested his own faith in the Western Christian civilization that had been transplanted to Central Africa, of which he was representative and interpreter to the VaShawasha. At least he was supplied with food for them, which was almost the only thing that mattered at this dark hour. Over and above all this, he and his fellow missionaries gradually relieved my people of the despair of defeat and the consequent emptiness of life. By giving them the assurances of religious teaching and by organizing such activities as Church and school meetings, they strove to relieve bitterness and boredom, particularly among the young whose minds and bodies were adaptable. In short, out of the tragedy of war, the Jesuits reaped the advantage of a more amenable, if captive, audience in the VaShawasha people. They had almost unlimited scope to do good and atone for the wrongs that had been committed by their fellow white men. They gave clothes, seeds and hoes. They solved family and neighbourly problems. They offered advice on all kinds of human difficulties and, most important of all, they could now teach with greater conviction and effect that all men were the children of God and that the lowly would gain richer rewards in the Kingdom of Heaven.

Some of the authorities were highly impressed by this missionary undertaking, carried out so efficiently and unselfishly, and responded to Father Richartz's earnest pleas not to exercise too much official control on the VaShawasha under his care. As a result, the police and other security men gradually became less conspicuous in the Chishawasha area. This removed anxiety and restored the confidence of the black community.

Before the rebellion, the Church had worked in a mainly barren environment. During that phase, the VaShawasha had been indifferent. They were deeply cynical and in many cases hostile to the missionaries. The Church had made little, if any, impression on a people so rooted in a religious system of their own.

But now the situation was entirely different. The white man's superiority in the field of battle had turned the minds of the VaShawasha people from a state of indifference into that of highly receptive sponges, ready to absorb almost any piece of knowledge, fact or fiction, dropped from the lips of a European. Only the most obdurate remained unmoved by the recent bloody rebellion. The majority, especially the young and middle-aged, were, at least for the time being, thoroughly shaken out of their belief in the religion of their ancestors. They had every reason to be. After all, they had prayed fervently to their ancestors for victory. They had made the necessary sacrificial offerings. They had killed cattle and brewed beer for the pleasure of the dead. They had, in fact, done everything to ensure that the power of their departed, who could speak to the Supreme *Mwari,* would be on their side. But all their efforts and their hopes had been repaid with utter defeat and humiliation. The tribe as a whole began to search for something better and stronger than the *Mhondoro* and the ancestors who had turned a deaf ear to them in their greatest hour of need. So manifest was this spirit of change and co-operation that Father Richartz and his fellow priests rejoiced deeply, convinced that out of the recent evil had come all the opportunities which they had prayed for in vain since they had come to the new country. The new Chief Mashonganyika, appointed by the Government on the strength of his non-involvement in the revolt, urged his people to co-operate with the missionaries. It was an extraordinary breakthrough in trying to reach men's minds. And, of course, once the Chief had given this directive, most parents encouraged their sons and daughters not only to be baptized, but also to attend school at the Mission. The children responded beyond the wildest expectation of the Jesuit Fathers. The class-rooms and the

144

Church filled up with young people of both sexes, who were willing to make a break with their tribal past in order to attain the bright new world which Christianity held out to them.

Among these young people who answered the call to the Church and the school was Alphonse Vambe, my father, son of Gukwe, the commander of the VaShawasha fighting forces in the recent rebellion, and grandson of the rebel Chief Mashonganyika. Also among the first girls was Agnes Dambudzo, my mother, who died not long after my birth at the end of the First World War and whom I never knew.

Father Biehler, the spartan priest from Alsace Lorraine, was then the principal of the newly-established Chishawasha Boys' School. Under the unusually favourable conditions that had arisen, he soon made this institution a kind of show-piece for the whole country. With a mixture of Germanic efficiency and Gallic versatility, he deliberately set out to prove to the doubtful, cynical Europeans and the diffident Africans that the black man, given the opportunity, was as good as anyone else in his intelligence and his reaction to civilizing influences. Leaving sentimentality and paternalism to his superior, Father Richartz, Biehler laid down his own strict standards of learning and was so harsh in maintaining them that many of his pupils believed that he disliked Africans as a people. His school disciplinary rules, as described to me by some of his former pupils, sounded as if they were copied from the French Foreign Legion military syllabus and were imposed in some cases with inhuman harshness. Yet, years later, some of his students were to remember that their material success and ability to break down some of the racial barriers in Southern Rhodesia were due to his stern training.

Being a musician, Father Biehler introduced brass instruments into the school and in a short time organized a band that came to be looked upon by many in the white community as such a miracle of achievement by the black people that it was invited to play at official functions in Salisbury. When Mr Joseph Chamberlain, the Colonial Secretary, visited Mafeking at the turn of this century, the Chishawasha band was given the honour of entertaining him.

Interestingly enough, this band, like most musical bands everywhere, drew large crowds from all over Chishawasha to

145

the Mission at public performances, particularly on Sundays and special feast days when it rendered a wide repertoire of musical compositions, especially marches. Pieces such as 'Under the Double Eagle', 'Rule Britannia', 'Kleber' and many other English, German, French and American works were common to the ears of most Chishawasha inhabitants right up to my time. It is not unreasonable to suppose that many individuals became Christians initially simply because of the attraction of this band. Even my own grandmother Madzidza was deeply impressed by it and used to talk of the time when she joined crowds of other people who flocked to the Mission for this entertainment. But it did not turn her into a Christian.

The Jesuit Brothers taught skilled trades such as carpentry, stonemasonry, bricklaying, shoe-making, black-smithing and horticulture, while the Dominican nuns taught their girls domestic science and child care. In this way, the Mission and the academic and technical standards it pursued acquired a unique reputation throughout the country. It became the pride and joy of many VaShawasha people and the envy of neighbouring Africans who had no facilities for education at all.

From all this evidence, there is no doubt that, despite their identification with the conquest and subjugation of the Shona, Father Richartz and his religious community were sincerely trying to make amends for the terrible wrongs that had been committed against my people. They were attempting to give the VaShawasha a new hope, dignity and sophistication which would help them to cope with the challenges of the white man's civilization. In doing so, they also hoped to confound the Europeans' deep-seated belief that Africans were permanently inferior. Ignoring all the white prejudices and without much, if any, Government financial support, they embarked on a programme of academic and technical training which turned out some first-class industrial craftsmen, whom white Rhodesia did not particularly want, teachers the Government would not take, and organists and other musicians who could play Wagner, Mozart and Beethoven, but would not find a cultured society that could adequately appreciate their talents and enable them to earn a decent living once they had left the academic oasis of Chishawasha Mission. Indeed, the Fathers unwittingly gave their boys and girls the impression that they would be as good as white people once they had been trained to use their heads, hands and hearts. The VaShawasha, unaware that they were the gullible victims of a vicious system, expected that they would be treated as well as white people were.

Since they were cared for in this way in these difficult times, the African people in Chishawasha fared infinitely better than the majority of their fellow countrymen who lacked this kind of missionary benevolence. As a consequence, they were able to adjust more easily to the conditions imposed by white rule. They were an intelligent, adaptable people and they fully justified the Chishawasha missionary experiment, bringing a flicker of hope to the hearts of the few liberal white settlers that there were.

Soon after he arrived in Mashonaland, Lord Albert Grey, the third Administrator, made a visit to Chishawasha in 1897 and was deeply impressed not only by the efforts of the Jesuits, but also by the capacity of the Shona to learn. From this experience he drew the conclusion that the Shona could be regenerated by education and recommended to his Administration and other missionary bodies to carry out this undertaking more seriously than they had done before. He was particularly in favour of industrial training, which would produce skilled African craftsmen and so make them useful citizens. Professor T. O. Ranger says, 'Grey's plan ... was a revolutionary one in its context; nothing less than a government attempt to emulate the Chishawasha approach and to take the lead in the transformation of Shona society through education.'*

Unfortunately, there were very few white liberals in the country and so the enthusiasm of Lord Grey had no result. But after he had gone, the Jesuit Fathers at Chishawasha Mission continued their enterprise and made it an even bigger success than what it had been when he visited them in 1897.

In most other parts of the country the conditions of defeat and adjustment were very different. Here Africans were mainly in the care of Native Commissioners. These men had been bad enough before the rebellion. After it, they were certainly in no

*T. O. Ranger, *Revolt in Southern Rhodesia 1896–7* (page 314), Heinemann Educational Books.

mood to emulate the example set by the Jesuits at Chishawasha. As officials of the Administration, theirs was a more worldly approach. Admittedly, the Government was now more cautious and more aware that Africans had grievances. But far from being more benign and democratic in its dealings with the African people, it used the rebellion as the excuse for a policy of greater vigilance and firmness. This responsibility fell directly onto the Native Commissioners. It was these officials who had to implement, for instance, the new land policy, whereby Africans were moved into the Native Reserves which were set aside for each tribal grouping. This measure was deeply resented by the African people, and of course, it made the Native Commissioners all the more unpopular. Thus the way was paved for the system of racial segregation, which was to be consolidated over the years by various laws and practices, but particularly by the infamous Land Apportionment Act that has become the basis of the present apartheid policy of the Rhodesian Front 'republican' regime.

In those early stages of white rule, however, legal segregation took the form of the creation of Native Reserves, which strikes us today as being very mild, though it did not appear so to the Africans at the time. Officially, this was explained to the African people as a way of protecting them from the land-hungry white settlers, who had the money and could soon buy up all the land, leaving them without any form of security. This was the thin end of the wedge and it led to the now inviolate philosophy and practice of race separation.

Another turning-point in the lot of the African people was the position of all Shona chiefs, who had previously ruled by consent as well as by virtue of their spiritual symbolism. Their status was now severely diminished. They were reduced to mere puppets, whose duty was, in effect, only to the Government and not to their own people. The Ndebele chiefs were also treated in the same way. From now on, these unfortunate repositories of traditional African power and independence became no more than what we used to term 'political footballs' of white Rhodesia. In the majority of cases, they became as comical as the man who is immortalized in the ballad of 'The Vicar of Bray'. Even under the most liberal administrations (using the word

148

liberal in the context of the Southern Rhodesian concept of liberalism), and these have been few, most African chiefs have been no more than personal servants of the Native Commissioners, to whose individual whims and foibles they have had to pander, as an office boy panders to the temperament of his employer. In some cases men were made chiefs merely because they had supported the Government in the rebellion. A well-known case is that of Samuriwo. In Chishawasha a man called Joseph Minyonanyane from the Mtoko area was made a Christian chief because he had actively sided with the settlers by agreeing to be sent ahead of the white column to persuade his chief, Gurupira of Mtoko, to provide supporters in March 1897. However, in the 1920s he was a completely changed man. Disillusioned by white rule, Joseph Mtoko, as all VaShawasha called him, now had nothing good to say about Europeans, including the priests. Although he continued to attend church services and held on to his title of Chief Mtoko, he openly expressed his virulent opinions against white rule.

But for the VaShawasha people, life became normal sooner than it did anywhere else. They organized their tribal existence as best they could. The discipline and the dedication to work, to husbandry and to spiritual contemplation fostered by the Jesuits were very much in accord with their own way of life. And so the Chishawasha community became properous and progressive, particularly in the production of food. This made it so self-sufficient that in time it was able to supply Salisbury with maize, cement, beef, timber and a certain amount of wheat, barley and grapes. If the Government and the white population had wished to assess the capacity of the African to profit by white teaching, as Lord Grey did, Chishawasha would have provided abundant evidence to disprove their misconceptions.

But they were not prepared to make this assessment. Their attitude was identical to that of the present generation of white Rhodesians who see nothing but evil in African independence even where its success is proved by massive statistical evidence in every field of human endeavour. The mood of the white settlers of early Rhodesia was shown in the Government's refusal to finance African education. It was also manifested in the general tone of the white politicians who, even at this early stage, started agitating for white self-government to replace the rule of the British South Africa Company. One only needs to read Hansard to see the outbursts of anti-black sentiment that were common to the spokesmen of the settlers in their legislature and to appreciate the extent of white racialism among the rest of the European population. Fear and guilt are written large. While the young people of Chishawasha were sincerely trying to come to terms with the new way of life by accepting its virtues and blessings and by seeing a better future for themselves under the teaching of the Jesuit Fathers than they could expect under the tutelage of their tribal elders, white men were hatching different ideas. All around, the walls of racial prejudice were being erected as fast as the white population gained in numbers and self-confidence.

One of the silliest, but most characteristic, products of white Rhodesian racial prejudices came into being almost from the very beginning. It was the municipal bye-law that made it an offence for any African to walk on the pavements of the towns. And so in large towns such as Bulawayo and Salisbury, with numerous animal-drawn wagons and other forms of traffic, any African pedestrian took his life in his hands. The road to apartheid was being systematically paved with sharp stones over which the Africans and their liberal missionary sympathizers must pick their way with increasing caution. Men like Father Richartz protested against the intemperate tones of white politicians and against the general trends of white opinions on Africans. But their words, then as now, fell like water off a duck's back, and they were described as cranks. That description has also since been applied to such Members of the British Parliament, both Labour and Conservative, as have dared to sympathize with the Rhodesian African, no matter how mildly or indirectly.

When the First World War came, it found the African population still largely indifferent and ignorant of world politics and also timid and confused about their own position in Southern Rhodesia. But among the settlers the biggest topic, apart from the black peril, exercising their minds was the question of their relationship with the Government of the Chartered Company. Although they owed practically everything they possessed to the British South Africa Company, most of them ganged up together to get rid of its political power. An Imperial Order in Council of 1896 had provided for the creation of a Legislative Council, which contained a number of 'unofficial' members who were Europeans. From that time they had kept up a persistent campaign for increased representation and during the years preceding the Great War, the 'unofficials' had attained a majority in the Council. But this was not good enough for them. What they were after was complete control of the executive. This was the core of their agitation, which reached fever pitch as the Great War was coming to an end.

Partly to counter this settlers' movement and partly to achieve administrative efficiency and cut down expenses, the Board of Directors of the British South Africa Company proposed in 1915 that Southern and Northern Rhodesia should be amalgamated. The Company had been allowed to take control of Northern Rhodesia during the 1890s and felt that now was the time to make it one country with Southern Rhodesia and, if necessary, to settle the whole issue of government for the two territories once and for all. When the proposal came up for public debate in 1917, the representatives of the settlers in Southern Rhodesia fiercely opposed it. Their leader, Sir Charles Coghlan, a lawyer, of Irish descent but born in South Africa, put forward arguments which illustrate vividly the fear and prejudices that have long tormented white Rhodesia even at that stage when African political consciousness was practically non-existent. He said that amalgamation would delay the attainment of responsible government for the settlers and that the white population in Southern Rhodesia would be swamped by the blacks. Although the Company's proposal was carried through the Council, the settlers' views, as expressed by Coghlan, won in the end. The British Government, having heard the passionate sentiments of the white politicians, vetoed the plan.

Strange as it may seem, the Rhodesian settlers were supported by left-wing and liberal elements in Britain, whose antagonism to the political and economic monopoly of the British South Africa Company made them think Coghlan's line was the lesser of two evils. Lacking a proper appreciation of the white Rhodesian mentality, British liberals and Labour Party men thought that the white settlers had a good case against their

151

powerful landlord, the Chartered Company and its multifarious financial interests. In other words, the beginnings of white self-government in Southern Rhodesia found its strength mainly in British Socialist circles. However, this marriage came to an end not long after Southern Rhodesia had become a self-governing colony.

In the mid-twenties copper had become important and the Southern Rhodesians then woke up to the valuable assets of the Northern Rhodesia's Copperbelt. Their Prime Minister, Howard Moffat, proposed, in all seriousness, the amalgamation of the two countries. But by that time the British Colonial Office was firmly in control of Northern Rhodesia. Not only was Britain also interested in the wealth of the territory, but most British liberal and left-wing politicians realized now that African interests were paramount and should not be sacrificed to the prejudices of white Southern Rhodesia. A British Commission that was appointed to make a study of this question reported in 1929 and did not support Moffat's case. Although another attempt was made to amalgamate the two countries in 1937, Southern Rhodesia and Northern Rhodesia went their separate ways until they were joined together in 1953 in the now defunct Federation of Rhodesia and Nyasaland. Had the two countries been amalgamated in the 1920s, it is logical to suppose that African political advancement in Northern Rhodesia would have been reversed. There would be no Zambia today and none of the exciting development that has been achieved in that country under President Kenneth Kaunda, whom I admire greatly, would have been possible.

However, neither the Chartered Company nor the white settlers in the period between the rebellion and the end of the First World War would have thought it necessary to consult African opinion in Southern Rhodesia on the question of self-government or amalgamation. But the Africans did not remain silent for long. No doubt as a result of the winds of change that the war had stirred around the world and the glaring injustices affecting them, some Africans began to question their conquered status. The result of a general feeling of frustration was that a small body of people decided, at the end of the war, to form a political organization. They called it the Southern Rhodesian

Native Association. Some of its founders and early members were Shona, such as Messrs Abraham Chirimuuta, Office Chanakira and Aaron Jacha. It soon attracted many supporters, including African chiefs, particularly in Mashonaland, who hailed its formation as a great event, which promised them the first chance of being able to speak with one voice to the Government of the country. By comparison with subsequent African political movements it was tame. But for those days it was a bold move. The first organized African political association in Mashonaland since the rebellion, it heralded the advent of nationalist movements, led and inspired by educated people who wanted justice for all Africans in the country rather than for a particular tribe. Since the day that this Association presented its manifesto to the white Rhodesian authorities, the African people of Southern Rhodesia, under various banners, have continued to knock at the door of white rule and white privilege. Unhappily, the harder they have knocked the more viciously they have been treated.

There is no evidence to suggest that any great effort was made to interest Africans in Southern Rhodesia in fighting the Germans as was made in the Second World War. With the memories of the rising in 1896 being so fresh in the minds of the Europeans, the last thing they wished to do was to put guns in the hands of black people and train them for warfare. Such a move would hardly have made any impact in Chishawasha, run, as it was, by German Fathers, loyal to the Kaiser. In any case, knowledgeable VaShawasha felt that there was nothing to choose between the white antagonists. Thus, they were untouched by the war fever that swept through white Rhodesia, whose own position was gravely threatened by the German settlers in what was then German East Africa, later Tanganyika and now Tanzania. If anything, most politically-minded VaShawasha, as also other Africans, hoped for a German victory, if only so that white rule in Rhodesia, as it was organized, would come to an end. That this did not happen was a source of great disappointment, for, as we shall see, the end of the war witnessed a greater influx of white people into Southern Rhodesia and a corresponding worsening of the Africans' position.

As the war drew to a close, another blow fell upon the

Africans. The VaShawasha and other Shona called it 'Furu-wenza', the influenza. It struck with great ferocity and was devastating in the number of deaths and the social upheaval it caused. In loss of life among the VaShawasha, it was more catastrophic than the 1896 revolt. For, as they said, the 'Furu-wenza' was a 'ghostly foe' and, unlike the tangible white man, it was immune to spears and guns. It defied all the combined powers of the witchdoctors and the ancestral spirits. In short, they had no defence against it whatever. According to those who survived it, it killed men, women and children, by day and by night, week after week and so fast that the traditional duty of mourning for the dead was no longer physically possible; indeed it lost all sense, for burying the dead was more important than shedding sentimental tears. The 'hidden reaper', as they called it, mowed down people like grass everywhere. In this devastation the VaShawasha, who, in spite of the great number of their own people killed in the *Chindunduma*, had cherished the secret hope of returning, some day, to their former days of national freedom, were further reduced in size as a tribe. Scores of their tribesmen and women, including some of their finest leaders who had survived the 1896 struggle and the aftermath of arrests, hangings and imprisonment, perished at the hand of a visitation which seemed to be a final act of conspiracy against them by unknown powers. Hardly a household escaped its share of this undeserved retribution. In some cases whole families disappeared in one week or one day. In other cases families lost two, three and more members. Some of those who were working in Salisbury and other European settlements died in the bush as they tried to flee in panic to their homes. In consequence, the number of widows, widowers and orphans multiplied, leaving the tribe with far more dependants than its human and material resources could provide for. Food became short because sickness and death prevented men and women from tilling the soil and raising new crops. Dead bodies rotted in people's homes and in the forests because there were not enough able-bodied men to dig the graves and bury them. Once more, the tribe was plunged in sorrow and lost hope for the future. Indeed, while this calamity lasted, which was from October to November 1918, it seemed to them that they had been as completely abandoned again by the Creator Himself as in the *Chindunduma*. As they said, never in their remembered history had death been so defiant and sure of its mastery over men; never had it laughed in their faces and shown its hand so ruthlessly, making their own prayers and those of the Church, the incantations and herbs of the medicine men, and all faith in the protective benevolence of the ancestral spirits so utterly futile. Many felt that the end of the world had come. Some, having lost all hope, wished that their own deaths should come at once rather than that they should be given a few more days or weeks of life to suffer the horrible anguish of seeing the endless deaths of their fellow men, and their women and children. Such was the extent of the influenza and the impact it made on the VaShawasha.

Naturally, in the midst of this human destruction, they cast their minds back to the suffering and bloodshed of their struggle for freedom and survival, some twenty years before, and they connected it with this tragedy, thus coming to the conclusion that fate was pursuing a blind vengeance against all black men. They let their minds wander through those fields of metaphysical reasoning that were their intellectual heritage. But both events were unfathomable and were to be explained only in the context of divine punishment for some unknown wrong. For, in the spiritual world of the Shona, evil did not come without the agency of some directing hand. But then what had they done to deserve this series of Nemesis? The one had cost them the loss of their country, their power, dignity and certainty for the future. The other was taking away even their right to live and to hope. Some muted prophets said it was because the Shona people had offended their ancestors by failing to defend the life and property of Chaminuka. Others said it was because white men had desecrated the sanctity of Zimbabwe and in their blind rage the ancestors were meting out indiscriminate retribution. The more worldly-wise, however, let it be known that the white man, with his evil turn of mind, had caused the influenza in the hope of wiping out black men so that there would be no repetition of the events of 1893 and 1896.

Obviously, this kind of reasoning was faulty, for they noticed that some white people were also dying from the same unknown cause. To be exact 514 Europeans in Southern Rhodesia died from this 'flu which was in fact world-wide, but is reported to have become particularly virulent when it reached southern Africa.

Fortunately, once more the Jesuit Fathers came to the rescue of the VaShawasha under their care and gave them all the help they could afford. They gave medicine, food and rational, if suspect, explanation as to what this strange sickness was and why it was so prevalent.

My own family were recipients of this help. When my mother died from this 'flu after I was born, Father Richartz made a firm order that my two older brothers, my sister and myself, the youngest, should at once be brought under the care and up-bringing of the nuns at the Convent of the Sacred Heart at the Mission. My father readily agreed. But my mother's parents did not. Mizha and Madzidza, being such punctilious observers of African tradition, received this news with alarm and were extremely forthright in saying that this sort of problem had nothing to do with white men. But Father Richartz, I was told, would not take no for an answer and somehow eventually succeeded in overcoming my grandparents' objections. I was a very sickly child and it seems that the priest pointed out that if I was kept at home and died, Mizha and Madzidza would be in trouble. That secured our release from the determination of my well-meaning grandparents to keep us.

The four of us therefore were bundled to the Convent in due course. But in the end, the arrangement did not work out quite as Father Richartz had expected, for after a little time, both my brothers and sister ran back to the safety and more familiar environment of our family. The priest relented and said that I could also be taken home, but on the strict condition that my mother's sister, Catherine, would undertake to look after me and agree to walk to the Mission every day to fetch the milk specially prepared by the nuns for my benefit. Clearly, the implication was that I might not live if I was left entirely to the nursery ways and the diet of my family.

Whether or not Father Richartz was right in his supposition as regards my possible fate, if left entirely in the hands of my family, I have never lost my sense of gratitude to him and the Jesuit Society in Mashonaland for this concern.

The reason why John, Joseph and Mary ran away from the Convent sounds quite nonsensical today. But not so then. They said that the place was visited at night by spooks, witches and wizards. As it was, the cemetery, where so many African victims of the 'flu must have been buried, was only a few yards away. Most Africans I know have a strong aversion to and fear of death and cemeteries. Certainly this particular cemetery excited many African minds at this time, believing, as they did, that under cover of darkness it became alive with wandering spirits and witches. While my two brothers and sister had never seen any of these spectres and wizards themselves, all the other grown-up boys and girls at the Convent talked about them every morning and night, so that they became real in their imaginations. As time went on and everyone continued to talk on the subject as if they were speaking from personal experience, John, Joseph and Mary were so terrified that they chose to provoke the wrath of the priest by running away rather than to stay on and face the risk of being seized by these nightly prowlers. Anyway, it was a very good excuse for them to return to the intimacy of home life.

When years later I went to the Convent to be educated, these fearful spooks and witches were still being talked about. They were the first topic of conversation every morning before lessons started. They sounded then like fairy tales. In any case I was a day scholar and they did not affect my enthusiasm or love for the teaching that the nuns offered, which was excellent in every respect.

*After the First World War; the beginnings
of a policy of segregation; the settlers are
divided in support of self-government or
incorporation into South Africa;
the 1923 Constitution gives complete
power to the settlers; the conflict between
the Church and African traditions.*

The great war was over. But while it had caused much suffering
and uncertainty to white Southern Rhodesians, it also ushered
in a new age in which they were to gain many advantages. The
episode had put Southern Rhodesia on the world map through
its men who had fought in Europe, in East Africa and South-
West Africa. The most immediate effect of this was the increased
flow of white immigrants who came to swell the ranks of those
already in the country. This was a most welcome turn of events
for the tiny white minority. The new immigrants brought in
greatly needed skills, capital and other valuable assets. The
menace of German imperialism in Africa had been effectively
eliminated, particularly in nearby Tanganyika. Once again for
white Southern Rhodesia the future was rosy.

But for the African people, white immigration and the growing
confidence that it engendered among the earlier settlers tipped
the scales even more against their already shaky position. As they
had observed before, once the white man felt secure in the
company of his own kind, he almost inevitably became arrogant
and intransigent, and his capacity to make the black man feel
insecure became correspondingly greater. These were the ugly
realities that the decade of the 1920s ushered in for my people.

As early as 1915 the VaShawasha people had heard vague
rumours that white people were entertaining the idea of dividing
the country more precisely into black and white areas. These

rumours came in the wake of the appointment of the Native Reserves Commission in 1914 to make final recommendations on the allocation of land for African communal occupation. It published its report in 1917. According to some of the VaShawasha people these rumours of new measures to entrench the policy of segregation had been put to them very circumspectly. The barnyard metaphor that sheep and goats did not mix had been used and it had been urged that there was everything to be gained from separating Africans and Europeans. For one thing, said the Government opinion-makers, mostly Native Commissioners, the white man was a compulsive mischief-maker, who, if he were allowed to mingle freely with black tribes in their kraals and reserves, would, without doubt, violate black women and ultimately wipe out the black colour. Indeed, this process was already in evidence in the crop of coffee-coloured children that had been and were being born everywhere where white men and black women had come into close contact. For another thing, white men had plenty of money and could soon buy up all the land and leave Africans landless.

Expressed in this way, the segregation policy which the Europeans were trying to work out to perfection sounded highly plausible. And so, although white people were generally considered to be congenital double-dealers in their approach to African affairs, some VaShawasha felt that the Government might be thinking along the right lines. They no more relished the prospect of their colour being rubbed out than they looked forward to the wealthy white men buying up all African land.

The recommendations of the Native Reserves Commission which largely ignored African opinion considerably worsened their position. The Commission recommended the reduction of African-owned land and assigned the best agricultural areas to Europeans, leaving the worst to my people. In this case, the Shona were the chief victims. These recommendations which were officially described as 'the final' settlement of the land question were accepted by both the British and the Rhodesian governments.

But it was in fact a lie to say that this was the 'final' settlement. When responsible government came into effect, it appointed the infamous Morris Carter Commission to go into

159

the same subject, which went about the country 'consulting' African and European opinion on the matter. This was obviously another bluffing attempt at convincing the African people and the British Government that justice was being done to everyone. But I am old enough to know that the white settlers, through their government, knew exactly what they wanted and needed no African opinion to enlighten them on the system they were evolving. All the same, they went through the motions of sounding out African public opinion on a process whose basic intentions were directed at reducing black people to the state of permanent political, economic and racial inferiors. According to Mr Charles Mzingeli, who in 1929 became the organizing secretary of the Industrial and Commercial Workers' Union in Salisbury, a much more radical body than the Southern Rhodesian Native Association, the Morris Carter Commission did not commend itself to educated Africans. They understood at once that the policy of land segregation was a foregone conclusion and many of them boycotted the Commission. When it interviewed many Africans, particularly the untutored people in the rural areas, the Commission's enquiries were slanted so as to draw out the opinions it needed to back up its conclusions. By asking rhetorical questions, by accentuating the virtues of segregation and by other sophisticated arguments too devious for African chiefs and headmen to see through, it was able to extract the verdict it required. When it submitted its report in 1925, it stated that black and white Rhodesians were in favour of possessory segregation. Thus it set the stage for the enactment of the obnoxious Land Apportionment Act of 1930 upon which white Southern Rhodesia was to build its citadel of supremacy.

But after the war, the immediate issue was to replace the unrepresentative and unpopular administration of the British South Africa Company with a government controlled by the settlers themselves. The majority of the settlers were as united on this as they are today on independence under their minority rule. But they were divided on the form that this government-to-be should take. One faction was for incorporation into South Africa. There, men like General Smuts and other prominent politicians and businessmen were more than ready to receive Southern Rhodesia as the fifth province of their country. Cecil

Rhodes had dreamed and worked untiringly for the unity of southern Africa under the British flag. In 1910 this dream was partially fulfilled when the Cape Colony, the Natal Colony and the Boer Republics of the Transvaal and the Orange Free State became one country under the name of the Union of South Africa. That Southern Rhodesia should become a part of this immensely wealthy British dominion would have been entirely consistent with Mr Rhodes' cherished dreams. South Africa had many good things to offer white Southern Rhodesia, particularly economic and psychological security. Many prominent white Rhodesians and, of course, the British South Africa Company thought that this was the most sensible course to take. They formed a political group and called themselves Unionists.

But the rest of the white settlers, particularly artisans and junior civil servants, wished to have no political ties with South Africa, preferring instead internal self-government. Their group was called the Responsible Government Party, which was an extension of the Responsible Government Association that had been formed in 1917. Their foremost spokesman and leader was Sir Charles Coghlan, the successful Bulawayo lawyer, whose over-riding ambition was to see white Southern Rhodesia forge its own future and its own character. Just as he had fought the proposed amalgamation of the two Rhodesias, he fiercely opposed the suggestion that his country should be joined to South Africa.

In due course, these factions presented their case to the British Government. When they met the Colonial Secretary, Winston Churchill, their views were sympathetically received. There was no African on this delegation. But it made no difference, for, especially at this time, even the British Government agreed that Southern Rhodesia was a white man's country. However, Mr Churchill not only shared the dream of a bigger and stronger British dominion in southern Africa. He was also a great friend and admirer of General Smuts, whose arguments in favour of the incorporation of Southern Rhodesia into the Union of South Africa made more political and economic sense than those of Sir Charles Coghlan. Without being too partisan, Churchill urged the Rhodesian delegation to consider incorporation more seriously. But the two possibilities, internal self-government and absorption into South Africa, could best be decided by the voters of Southern Rhodesia, he suggested.

When they returned from London, the Unionists and the Responsible Government Party representatives entered into a country-wide political campaign, whose purpose was to muster public support for their respective causes and decide these issues by a referendum. The campaign was a hectic and often a rough one, for apparently the Rhodesian European community had very strong feelings either for or against South Africa. The referendum which took place in 1922 revealed that the majority of the white voters were fiercely against joining the Union of South Africa. It seems odd that the Unionists did not grasp the mood of the majority of the settlers before they proceeded to have this matter decided by the white electorate. But, for some reason or other, they were confident of their chances and, indeed, if one were to take a completely objective and dispassionate view, they had the best arguments, particularly in the economic field. But, as we have seen in the case of the UDI dispute, white Rhodesians have the virtue of being able to ignore economic considerations when it suits them.

Strange as it may seem, it was the race issue which was the deciding factor. I refer to the anti-Boer feeling that most English-speaking Rhodesians have always had, especially at this time. If, for instance, the Union of South Africa had not become an accomplished fact and Southern Rhodesians had been asked to unite with the English-speaking Cape and Natal Colonies, there would not have been much acrimonious argument about it. I imagine that white Rhodesia would gladly have thrown in its lot with these southern neighbours. But this was no longer the case. In the impassioned arguments that the referendum caused, there was not much doubt that the Responsible Government Party understood the psychology of the white settlers. It understood that the memories of the Boer War were highly relevant to the choice before the country and that the majority of white English-speaking Rhodesians, particularly the artisans and the lower and middle ranks of the civil servants, hated the Afrikaans language, the Afrikaans culture and the very idea of being dominated by the Boers. Skilfully, the Responsible Government Party played on these emotions and, in the event, the majority of the white

162

voters opted for self-government under the aegis of the British Crown. If today the wheel has turned full circle and white Rhodesia is being mothered and fathered by South Africa, it is only because the fear of black domination has proved too great for it to do otherwise.

As everyone knows, in 1923 Southern Rhodesia achieved self-government, which gave the Europeans the right of complete self-determination and enabled them to build the strength on which their Rhodesian Front leaders declared independence in 1965.

There can be no doubt that sooner or later Southern Rhodesia was going to have the right to govern itself. That it attained such an advanced form of self-rule in only thirty-three years of white settlement testifies to the extraordinary mixture of cunning, skill and fear that the white settlers possessed. The basis of this fear and haste was the African. Without the presence of the African and particularly without the bitter memories of 1893 and 1896, I suggest that European settlers would not have been so antagonistic to the administration of the British South Africa Company. It is also debatable whether they would have demanded such an onerous and expensive form of self-government from the British Government. But because they were afraid of the Africans and suspicious of letting anyone else but themselves control African affairs, they demanded and succeeded in attaining the kind of self-government in which they were effectively the sole masters of African progress. From now on, the fate of the Africans was not going to be decided by the cool judgement of the appointed representatives of the business-orientated Board of Directors of the British South Africa Company. It was to be placed in the hands of the white members of the country's Legislative Assembly whose mandate came from the votes of the white artisans, shop-keepers, farmers and miners, whose horizons were entirely limited by their racial prejudices. Not many of them would have been able to hold their own even in South Africa, let alone in England. But in the view of the British Government, these little men, with all their human inadequacies and twisted sense of their racial superiority, could be trusted with the future of the African people.

On paper, however, the 1923 Southern Rhodesian constitution sounded plausible and respectable. It pledged equality and the vote to everyone who was suitably qualified, irrespective of race or colour. To get the vote, all that was required was the ability to fill up the voting application unaided, to own property or to be in receipt of a certain amount of income. It was a 'colour-blind' franchise and in theory could in due course have led to a democratic system of government and a non-racial society in Southern Rhodesia. Some educated Africans were so pleased with it that they voted for self-government. Having the vote as stipulated by this constitution, they believed they would have first-class citienship, which would in effect make them black Europeans. In this way, they hoped that they would be emancipated from their unfavourab'e tribal environment and obtain good jobs with good salaries, and a host of other privileges. In other words they were led to believe that Rhodes' famous dictum of 'equal rights for every civilized man' was going to be implemented by white Rhodesia. Whatever suspicions and misgivings some of these Africans might have had, were minimized by the knowledge that the British Government retained in the constitution the final authority to approve or disapprove of any measure affecting black peop'e.

Strange as it may seem, although up to now Britain had done nothing obvious to protect their interests, the Africans seemed to trust her implicitly. Having been brain-washed into belief in the might and justice of the British Empire, they were prepared to believe that its Parliament and Government at Westminster would keep their pledges in the Rhodesian constitution. The only constitutional provisions about which they were disappointed were those relating to European liquor and firearms which were not to be supplied to Africans. But these restrictions were inserted in obedience to the terms of the Berlin Congress agreement, whose European signatories, knowing the harm liquor and guns had done to the American Red Indians, had banned the supply of these commodities to the African natives. Until the Morris Carter Land Commission reported its findings in 1925, many Africans thought the 1923 constitution held out the chance of emancipation by peaceful, constitutional means.

But these optimistic Africans were to be disillusioned. They were to learn that neither the British Government nor the white settlers had any intention of keeping their promises and sticking to the spirit of the constitution. They were to experience the bitter reality of a white-controlled form of government which could change the franchise system and make laws of discrimination without interference from the British Government. Too late the Africans discovered that in spite of what it said, the 1923 constitution had made Britain's power in Southern Rhodesia non-existent and abandoned them entirely to the tender mercies of the local Europeans who both feared and despised them.

Most of the VaShawasha people remained ignorant of these developments. They did, of course, receive garbled and distorted versions of what was going on or was to happen. They heard, for instance, that even white men were fed up with the Chartered Company's government, the taxes it imposed and its arrogant policemen, who illegally continued to use the sjambok, though not so openly and frequently as before the rebellion. From such scraps of information, they concluded, though not without reservation, that a change of government was undoubtedly a good thing. Apart from these superficial incursions into the complicated arena of Rhodesian politics, they were mainly preoccupied with their day-to-day affairs and, of course, with the past from which their national problems stemmed.

* * *

At this time I was slowly growing up. As yet I could hardly be expected to have a proper appreciation of the unlucky past, present and future of my people. This came only with the slow process of growth and with my corresponding ability to assimilate the ugly facts of a situation which, even in the 1920s, was bad enough for my people. The full realization that we were condemned to an almost hopeless future did not come until I left Chishawasha. I finally reached this sad conclusion not only because I had witnessed the disintegration of the tribe, but I had also seen how the Mission's religious influence was being swept aside by the forces of white power and could no longer give my people the physical, psychological and spiritual protection it once had offered them.

165

Only now in retrospect do I realize that people are not usually moved by events in which they are not personally involved, least of all by the historical misfortunes that overtook those who lived in a different age. In the day-to-day course of events in Mashonganyika village, life was too full of ordinary human experiences for me, a child, to feel that any part of my personality was connected with the past or to be obsessed by its mishaps and its mismanagement. The repeated efforts of my elders to make me feel emotionally identified with the past seemed far-fetched and irrelevant. Their accounts were interesting, absorbing and, perhaps, moving; but because they were not part of my personal experience and because, anyway, I was more interested in the present and, of course, the future, I soon grew bored with past history. Like the modern young generation of British people, who do not feel nostalgia for the forgotten splendours of the British Empire and who do not get emotionally disturbed by accounts of the horrors of the Second World War in which their fathers fought in the cause of freedom, I could not see the past as my grandparents saw it. Nor could I take too seriously the vaunted glory and subsequent downfall of the VaShawasha tribe as told by those who had experienced both, and demanded that their offspring should share their attitudes. Admittedly, as I grew older I had flashes of pride or pity, but I did not feel anything like the obsessive regrets and recriminations which my grandparents and people of their generation succumbed to as a result of their misfortunes and deprivations.

But there came a time when I could not divorce the past from the present. The system that the older people resented, often with so much venom, spoke against itself so often that in time I came to realize I belonged to a conquered race. Certainly it did not take me long to understand the implications of the fact that the tribe was living in Chishawasha entirely at the pleasure of our missionary landlords. Had I been a white boy living in the isolated rural environment of Chishawasha, I imagine that I would have had little cause to be interested in the Government of the country. But being an African, a member of a despised and conquered race, I soon came to know of its existence, its relationship with us and the harsh judgement of my people against it. Although it was impersonal and distant, from time to

166

time its long arm was liable to stretch into our tribal society. I have already described the occasion when a white trooper came into our village and arrested my grandfather for failure to pay the dog-tax. Incidents such as these only served to make white rule more unpopular in our thinking. We did not make any distinction between the policeman as an individual, who could abuse his office, and the institution which vested him with power. How could we, when we were totally unrepresented in the Government which these men served and of which they proudly claimed they were the eyes, ears and voice? As far as we were concerned, they were instruments of white rule and therefore against us; more than that, their conduct caused individual and family strains in the tribe where none had existed before nor need have arisen had we been left entirely to ourselves.

Nevertheless, the young, hopeful tribespeople, who were unencumbered with what seemed to be the sterile memories of the past, did not judge white civilization and their own future in the same way as their parents and grandparents. They had more confidence in themselves and in life generally. This was mainly because, like me, they were ignorant of the essential truths of white rule and white attitudes towards black men, whereas the old had lived long enough to know better. What in effect white enterprise in Southern Rhodesia had done, particularly at this period of rapid economic change, was to divide African society psychologically into the old and the young. The old people had despaired, and thought that white civilization could not and never would prove itself because it had failed them completely on all fundamental questions such as land, justice, truth and human relationships. Thus they saw the Western system as essentially selfish, rapacious and inward-looking. They had found out the hard way and now fully realized that where black and white interests clashed, and even where they were complementary, the manipulators of the system saw to it that the blacks always lost out. On the other hand, the younger generation held a more favourable view. Stated simply, the African tribal structure, particularly in Chishawasha and other areas near white centres such as Salisbury, was disintegrating. Naturally, without political power or influence, my people could do nothing to avert this danger, if danger it was.

167

As we have already seen, the VaShawasha people were more fortunate than the other Shona in facing the difficult conditions following the 1896 rebellion and they had every reason to be grateful to the Jesuit Fathers who helped them to make the necessary adjustment and overcome their problems. But there were disadvantages in this otherwise privileged position. If it was a good thing for a people to preserve their tribal identity and maintain their tribal traditions within the limited scope allowed by their conquerors, these people were being forced to relinquish their way of life more quickly than most other tribes in Mashonaland. In the Native Reserves, the African people were generally allowed by the Government as much freedom as possible to practise their customs and traditions. I do not doubt that the Government thought that by preserving the Africans in their natural state of conservatism it would succeed in subjugating them, and so did not interfere with their beliefs or coerce them into accepting education and other alien values. But this view was not shared by the Jesuit Fathers, who were committed, both in theory and in practice, to the task of educating and raising the Chishawasha men and women from what must have seemed to them a physically and psychologically hostile environment. But such a gigantic undertaking could not be accomplished overnight. It would take a great deal of time, as well as patience.

The years between the end of the rebellion and that of the First World War were those of real partnership and fruitful co-operation between the VaShawasha people and the Jesuit Fathers at Chishawasha Mission. The defeat that my people had suffered and the care that they had enjoyed from the missionaries at such a difficult time obviously had much to do with this happy relationship. But from the oral evidence that was given by everybody, including my grandparents, there is no doubt that the one man who made this understanding possible was the Rev. Father Richartz. They described him as a unique personality, in fact a saint, if ever there could be one in a white community composed mainly of reckless land-grabbers and spoilers in every sense of these words. He gave the tribe the stamina and the will to rise from the ashes of defeat and to live in hope once again. By his devotion to their welfare and by his personal integrity, he convinced many of the VaShawasha people that the Church would liberate them from their own darkness and the injustice of white rule. He achieved this trust and child-like reverence possibly because he himself sincerely believed in the good faith and the ability of the white man in Southern Rhodesia to carry out his civilizing mission in this part of the world. In a way, he seemed to have had something like David Livingstone's idealistic view of Western civilization as the one system that could and would give the African true emancipation. But while he believed in this objective, Father Richartz appears to have realized at the same time that the process would be a gradual one. And so he did not try to force the pace of progress on his Chishawasha wards. Only the young were compelled to attend school. His was a policy of persuasion and conviction, especially in the conversion of men and women to Christianity. Out of sheer common sense and, no doubt, for tactical reasons, he accepted the way of life of the tribe for what it was, and left it to time and gentle persuasion to bring the Catholic faith into the otherwise tradition-bound hearts and minds of these people. In other words, he left the old people alone to make up their own minds as regards the salvation of their souls in the world to come. As a result of this tolerant attitude, a very happy relationship was built up all round.

But some time during or after the war Richartz was transferred from this Mission and with his departure, the old VaShawasha were forced to realize that even the Church set limits to their freedom. The man who came after him saw things differently; he saw no reason why the captive Chishawasha Africans should continue to be treated with velvet gloves. Seeing that matters of the soul were not matters of fancy, the successors of Richartz decided that the Church could do very well with a great deal more aggressiveness against heathenism.

One of the most awkward and sensitive questions that Richartz had tactfully avoided during his long reign was that of polygamy, a practice and an indulgence which was as common among the Shona as cars in today's consumer societies. A man who could afford to do so acquired as many wives as pleasurably, honestly and proudly as he acquired cattle, and he grew proportionately in social stature and tribal influence. Polygamy was as old an institution as chieftainship or the *Mhondoro* spirit cult. And it was perfectly sensible in the African society of that day, however critical we might be today. Under this system, prostitution was completely unknown and adultery a rare exception. More than this, polygamy effectively ruled out the problems of insecurity and loneliness as well as most crimes of sexual passion. Indeed it was an African panacea for most of the social and psychological ills that are associated with monogamous societies in the Western world. When the missionaries arrived, almost every man with self-esteem and means had several wives. Some had acquired them in the ordinary way of love and marriage, while others inherited them from deceased brothers, cousins or nephews. In the latter case it was an inescapable tribal duty.

Imagine then the indignation of the VaShawasha polygamists when, for the first time in their recorded history, a foreign Church institution and culture arrived and expressed its vehement and dogmatic opposition to this practice, and threatened that there were no places for them in Heaven unless they discarded all but one of their many wives and received the holy water of baptism. If the VaShawasha and their Shona compatriots were sure of anything, it was their inalienable right to enter the Kingdom of God after they had been released from the toil and tribulations of this world. That is why whenever anyone died they always said that the person had gone to 'rest' —*kuno zorora*—for ever, unless he or she had committed an act of murder, incest or stolen somebody else's marital partner. But then it was unusual to find people who sinned to this dreadful extent, and they could always, if they wished, be cleansed of these misdeeds by special and elaborate ceremonies, before they left this world to face their judge in the next. Thus, unlike the white men, the Shona people did not choke their path to Heaven with complex dogmas, commandments, theology and moral strictures which were impossible to obey. To say that the way to Heaven depended on the sprinkling of font water on one's forehead was not only incredible, it made God seem like a monstrosity of contradiction and cruelty. If true, it implied that the millions of black people who had lived and died before the white man came to Zimbabwe with this particular key to

170

Heaven were lost. The sheer awfulness of it all, if true, made the old VaShawasha bristle with resentment and they were not slow in thinking that perhaps the Church, for all its generosity and work of mercy, was a wolf in sheep's clothing, pursuing the same ignoble ends against black men as the Government. It was bad enough to subdue a people, to take their land and freedom and to reduce them to non-persons. But on top of all this to tell them that there was no place for them in the next world unless they embraced the white man's religion was like telling them that they had no right to live. Why then had they been created? They asked this again and again.

I heard these matters discussed openly, especially by the menfolk, who watched the political and Church affairs which impinged on their lives. Of course, the threat had not been made that unless polygamists got rid of their wives and were baptized they would be thrown out of the Mission farm. The Fathers were not so stern. But since the departure of Father Richartz, the Church had become increasingly intolerant towards those of their African tenants who stuck to their own beliefs. This was particularly the case when the Superior of the Mission was the man they called 'Baba Mataramanga', mentioned earlier, who seemed to have had a distinct sense of urgency all his own in fighting heathenism. While he had some conspicuous virtues, he certainly created an atmosphere at the Mission which made polygamists and other unbaptized Africans feel like lepers, and they reacted by talking about the Church as if it was a conspiratorial agent of the wicked white Government. They felt all the more disenchanted as they remembered that, under Father Richartz, the Church had been almost the only haven of physical and spiritual peace left to them. Under Father Richartz, they said, they had not been interfered with in their way of life, they had not been told to give up their wives, nor had they been told that Chishawasha was no longer their land from which families or individuals could be expelled. These and other grievances hurt them deeply, so much so that some began to say that Father Richartz had deliberately deceived them.

There was a conflict of outlook between the Church and the State on the African right to choose what kind of religion and

171

mode of living he desired. The Native Commissioner did not share the missionary view that the African should embrace Christianity. The Native Commissioner at Goromonzi had nothing against the VaShawasha marrying as many wives as they wished and practising their own customs, provided, of course, they did not break the laws of the country. It was said that he did not think it was a good thing for black people to follow all the ideas of the missionaries as some of them were liable to lead them astray. He made the point again and again: ultimately the African people would be better off to remain as they were and to rely on the guidance of the Government he represented rather than on the missionaries whom he found just as peculiar as the tribe did. This kind of advice, given privately, not only added fuel to the fires of the tribal resentment and confusion. It made the tribe feel that white men were an even greater puzzle than they had originally thought.

Seen from the African point of view, there was a conspiracy in the general role of the Church in Southern Rhodesia. For the Church, like the rest of the white society of which it was an appendage, did not recognize nor care to understand many of the values in the traditional institutions of the VaShawasha. It took the attitude that it knew what was best for the African people and in all spiritual matters expected them to follow like sheep without giving so much as a hint that it understood their difficult position. Thus the old traditionalists were roundly condemned as children of darkness because they clung to their own beliefs and practices. In turn these people wondered why it was so difficult for the priests to appreciate the simple fact that if, for instance, they gave up their wives the tribe would be landed with insecure women, particularly the old ones, who had passed the stage at which they could raise their own crops and fend for themselves.

The Shona social system did not, of course, have such things as pensions or insurance schemes. Therefore, any wholesale break-up of these tribal marriages, however justified on doctrinal grounds, would have been highly irresponsible. But it had, in my opinion, a much more sensitive regard for the individual human condition than the white system. This virtue was something that the VaShawasha were not willing to give up

172

whatever the Church said on the point. Accordingly, these old traditionalists made their attitude known by silent defiance. This unfortunate state of affairs had the effect of pushing them and the Church farther and farther apart. This was a tragedy because in spiritual life and mysticism my people were a great deal closer to the inspiration of the Church than the average white man was, with his consuming passion for material wealth, power and the domination of his environment. If you eliminated the rich ritual of the Catholic Church, with its complex world of canon law, theology and all the other ecclesiastical details, thus reducing it to its basic elements, it did not require much imagination to grasp the simple fact that the Church was preaching to the converted; the VaShawasha could teach Western theologians and moralists a thing or two, especially as regards human relationships, whatever the race, colour or creed.

But the arid, cruel background of Southern Rhodesia did not provide conditions in which wisdom and foresight in both the Church and the State might develop. The whole organization of the country rather engendered a spirit of arrogance and blindness in those who held power, be they of the Church or the State. The results of this unfortunate situation are evident in the present-day Rhodesia, where the Church has not been able to do anything more effective than denounce the system in angry pastoral letters. That this kind of episcopal protest has had no visible influence on the bulk of the Catholic and Protestant European supporters of the Rhodesian Front regime is so apparent that it needs no elaboration. So debased have our European fellow men in Southern Rhodesia become that some of them have even stooped to denouncing the bishops for siding with the Africans. So corrupted are they that some of them are even reported to have found a Christian justification for racial segregation.

I am not questioning the motives of the Church, nor saying that it deliberately set out to destroy the freedom and dignity of the African people. As a product of Church education, I know better than to deny that on the whole the Christian Churches had the best intentions in carrying out their joint mission among the African people in Southern Rhodesia. But because the Church is an institution organized and represented

173

by white men, it was, unhappily, inevitable that it reflected the interests of the white system within which it operated.

A Catholic priest and professor of politics in Brazil, commenting on the injustice and the revolutionary atmosphere in Latin America today, is reported as having said recently that the Church was 'the biggest whore in the world. She opens her legs before the biggest power there is'.

I find this analogy very applicable to the Church in Southern Rhodesia. Only in the past ten years or so have we seen signs that the Church in that very race-conscious society is concerned with questions of political, social, economic and racial justice. But this is much too complex a topic to discuss fully in this book.

13

*Analysis of VaShawasha customs and
traditions; the new Nehanda; the
ceremonies of* Mashave *dances and of the
threshing of 'rukweza'; the role of the*
nganga, *the African healer, and his
inward-looking turn of mind,
characteristic of the African personality.*

As this account has shown, ours was a highly religious tribal
system. It was based on the belief that man was made of
both flesh and spirit and that he lived on after death. Thus,
if you wished people to recognize you as the good, normal and
well-bred individual you thought you were, then you did not
dare question the beliefs and religious practices of the tribe. We
might question, ridicule or better still refuse to accept the white
man's religion. But our own was above human curiosity, particularly the curiosity of the young, who, in these matters, were
essentially observers of the highly guarded secrets of the adult
spirit world. Consequently, I found that many of our rituals and
taboos and the reasons for them were wrapped in the impenetrable fog of adult silence. Any attempt to break this mystery by
talking about it was considered gross impudence, if not a sign
of mental imbalance.

Yet certain things could be talked about and were explained
to the younger generation, even if the logic of these explanations
was at times very strange. But now I understand and appreciate,
though I do not necessarily accept, the justification of the system
that did not encourage criticism and open doubt of the customs
upon which it was based. For instance, one day in the week,
Wednesday, no one was allowed to work in the fields. We were
told that this Wednesday observance was in honour of one illustrious Chief Nzwere who had died on that day many years

before. I could see that this seemingly arbitrary tradition was a practical necessity. In the rainy season the tribe as a whole worked like bees, utilizing every hour of daylight to get the work done in the fields. This was particularly the case during the ploughing, weeding and harvesting periods. Now that my people were under foreign rule, they believed even more firmly than they had before that self-sufficiency in their own food supplies was essential to their limited freedom. As long as they grew enough food for themselves they were spared the humiliation of working for white men, especially for the farming and mining types who were harsher than most. And so, we toiled from early dawn to late sunset, on only the customary two meals per day. It was a back-breaking task and under the circumstances the days of rest on Wednesday and Sunday were a physical necessity for everyone and did not need any other explanation. But such a simple, rational excuse was not considered good or binding enough. As it was, the Wednesday was regarded as being holier than Sunday and the most awful consequences awaited any individual who did not refrain from labouring in the fields on this day. It was held that if you ignored this sacred custom one of several evils might descend upon you. For example, you might be chased or eaten by a lion, or struck by lightning. Like all the dead ancestors, the much revered as well as feared Chief Nzwere was supposed to have extraordinary powers over the living and would punish anyone who had the temerity to disobey his wishes, which, of course, had the blessing of the Supreme *Mwari*. Under the threat of these binding spiritual forces, no one in his right tribal mind would ever allow it to be said that he had disobeyed this law and that a lion had as much as roared or lurked in the nearest bush or that he had had a near-miss from the bolt of a lightning flash. All men, women and young people, Christian or non-Christian, did exactly as they were told to do, no matter how strong the temptation might be to carry on with their work in the fields.

We young people were forbidden to eat eggs and certain other parts of the chicken such as the heart. The reason for the ban came under the general excuse that it was not done, *zwino shura*, meaning that some sort of unknown power, did not permit it under pain of bad luck. This induced such fear and obedience

176

that, although we suspected we were missing something rather special and tasty, we did not dare eat eggs and other forbidden parts of the chicken on the sly. *Zwino shura,* let me add, covered an extraordinarily wide range of objects and actions and even words. Some of these taboos applied to one particular sex, many were applicable to all, irrespective of age.

In the 1920s the new Nehanda medium was very popular. But unlike her predecessor, she did not seem to have any political role to play. Her power and influence were largely confined to the religious affairs of the Zezuru-speaking Shona people. I suppose that the only sense in which she could be considered to have played a political role was that of standing as the foremost representative and champion of the ancient beliefs of her people. At this time these beliefs were being particularly fiercely assailed and undermined by the forces of white materialism and the combined strength of the Protestant and Roman Catholic missionary organizations. Though speaking with conflicting tongues about their God and how to attain His Kingdom, these denominations were nevertheless united in the destruction of African heathenism. It is understandable, therefore, that Nehanda should have been preoccupied with the religious life of her conquered people.

I never saw the Nehanda in person, since she lived outside Chishawasha and she had to avoid the missionaries who were as odious to her as she would have been to them. Yet it made very little difference whether one saw her with one's naked eye or not. Being the living fountain-head of the tribe's spiritual heritage, she was ubiquitous and her reputation was constantly in the minds and on the lips of all men and women in Chishawasha. Seldom was she directly referred to as Nehanda. Like all her predecessors, she was called *Ambuya,* grandmother, and was always spoken of in reverential and affectionate tones, as if she was next to God. All the elders of the tribe, men and women, had an unquestioning faith in whatever she said. So much so that I had the impression that she only had to tell her followers to rebel once more and they would have done so as bravely as they had done in 1896. But clearly she and her adherents did not feel that their problems could be solved in this way.

In everyday matters, however, her guidance and her decisions seemed to dominate and to influence everyone. And there can be no doubt that the patience and caution that the VaShawasha and other Shona tribes of the 1920s showed in their relationships with both the Church and the State were as much due to her restraining hand as to the bitter lesson they had learnt in the *Chimurenga.* I remember clearly the secret trips that Chief Mashonganyika and other elders of the tribe made repeatedly to consult with Nehanda at her headquarters. Some of them may well have been of a political nature. Two of them, however, were to do with rain. On the first occasion there was a serious drought which threatened famine. This event caused the Chief and the privileged few he always took with him to disappear for about a week on a mission to *Ambuya,* for they still believed that she could solve problems of this kind. When they returned, they set out, with an air of great solemnity, to do as they were told by Nehanda. Certain chosen families were to brew large quantities of beer, while the Chief was to kill a number of cattle according to the prescribed tribal rites. These were to be consumed at a subsequent ceremony of propitiation, consisting of tribal prayers and of songs and dances.

If I remember correctly, the clouds gathered and darkened and rain came down in torrents even before the dancing and feasting were over. This positive answer to their prayers brought ecstatic joy to everyone present.

On the second occasion, which I believe was in 1925, the rains were so heavy and persistent that the tribe thought it was faced with the grim prospect of ruined crops and therefore starvation. This would have made the much-disliked employment on white farms inevitable for many. Again the Chief and his men betook themselves to the Nehanda oracle. Again when they came back, beer, meat, dancing, singing and feasting appropriate to this particular problem were featured at the ensuing ceremony. The result was that in due course the rains subsided and everyone was greatly relieved.

Both results might have been coincidences, but as far as the tribe was concerned, this was what they had done in the past and this was how their prayers had always been answered. They would have felt very offended, or would have laughed in derision, at any suggestion that the coming of the rain or its abatement after their propitiations was a natural phenomenon. I believed them because the evidence was overwhelmingly in their favour, until a few years later when I went to school and discovered that the Christians too prayed for rain. At this point I could not but wonder which prayers God answered. It was a great puzzle. But it was of course only one of very many other puzzles which were to cross my youthful horizon as I became more and more aware of the battle of religious claims and counter-claims being waged between the tribe and the Church.

From the great many accounts I heard about her, Nehanda was of the same mould as the famous holy men and women about whom we read in Christian literature. She was reportedly simple, ascetic and averse to public acclaim. And yet she had an influence over her followers that, in its own Shona way, would have been comparable to that of Mahatma Gandhi. Before her Shona men and women of every rank humbled themselves as if they were of no consequence whatever because in their eyes she was God's lieutenant and the intermediary between God and his people and also the intermediary between them and their ancestors. Indeed, they felt that she was above everyone throughout the country, black and white, above the Church as well as the Government. Little wonder that she was so exalted and her person was shrouded in such deep mysteries and secrets, open only to the very few Shona men representing the tribes whose allegiance she enjoyed.

In her household, I was told, she was prevented from coming into contact with a married woman or any woman who was not a virgin, the state of such persons being considered unclean, for, it was added, uncleanliness, in the sense of sexual impurity, was supposed to have the effect of diminishing her spiritual gifts. To ensure that no such misfortune took place, a number of young girls were selected from time to time to live with her and serve her and they were asked to accept this position as one of special honour and responsibility. Before they were actually chosen, however, each and every one of the aspiring candidates had to submit herself to a proper and thorough inspection to prove her virginity and her purity of thought and deed. This function was carried out by an elderly woman, truly experienced and wise in such delicate matters. The successful maidens then

179

took up their duties and lived with Nehanda for as long as their state of mind and body remained untarnished. But the moment they were suspected, either individually or as a group, of being victims of impure thoughts and sexual urges, which would have been at the age of puberty, they were variously, severally or all at once, relieved of this privilege and replaced by other virgins who had passed the stiff physiological and psychological examination.

It would seem that Nehanda herself was not married, for no mention was ever made of her husband. If she was married, then it was to a man who was reduced to complete anonymity by the dazzling fame of his wife.

The rain and other tribal ceremonies of a similar nature came under the general title of *Kutamba Mashave,* to perform spirit dances. They were mainly of two kinds: those for thanksgiving, such as after a good harvest, and those intended to placate the souls of the departed in moments of national crises, such as the shortage of rain or too much of it. For all these ceremonies, the prerequisites were good weather, plenty of grain for food and beer, meat and drums of every description; and to them came a great number of the representatives of the VaShawasha society, including those outside the Mission.

The preparation for and anticipation of such an event caused a great amount of hustle and bustle and an atmosphere that alternated between moments of extreme joyful excitement and tension. Everyone was seen to be doing something; women rushed back and forth as they prepared beer and food; the principal male and female organizers went about their duties with a great air of secrecy, while the musical experts attended to their drums, of all shapes and sizes, which they dusted, oiled and tuned in readiness for the great occasion.

When the great day at last arrived, the excitement was electric. The revelries usually began in the late afternoon. They were ushered in by a sudden burst of drums, which boomed on for several minutes and put everyone on tenterhooks. The drums were later reinforced by a *crescendo* of high-pitched female voices, which in turn were blended with a chorus of deep, rolling chants from the men. Later, trumpet-like, ululating women's cries exploded and added to the richness of the musical ensemble. As

180

the rising tide of drum resonances and the lusty voices of the gathering rent the whole air of Mashonganyika village, the flood of human emotions was let loose. Men and women, at various times and as their individual moods dictated, rose and stamped their feet on the ground in a medley of song and dance. Initially, the drum beats and human voices went up and down, in short, sharp, *staccato* sounds and now and then in a continuous and extravagant combination of musical harmony. The effect of all this was to excite some of the deepest emotions in the human bosom, even in us young people who did not have the vaguest notion of what these rites symbolized or achieved for the tribe.

As the evening wore on and as everyone became thoroughly soaked with beer and the spirit of the occasion, various men and women went into trances. Purporting to be possessed by *Mashave* and *Mhondoro* spirits, they began a display of muscular paroxysms; their twitching and writhing were like acrobatic feats, and while possessed, they spoke in strange tongues. They imitated the sounds and the language of animals and some drank the raw blood of chickens, so that the effect was to chill one's spine. The terror which I felt was heightened when stories went about that some of the animals that the *Mashave* people were mimicking, such as lions, baboons and monkeys, were actually lurking in the surrounding bush and somehow participating in these revelries. At this stage, however sceptical one might have been in the beginning, one felt now that somehow the whole adult world around had entered into a common realm with their dead wherein they had direct communication with the ancestors. For while they were in this state, their tense, sweaty faces, fiery, glazed eyes, twitching muscles and writhing movements, seemed no longer controlled by material or natural forces, but instead by unseen, intangible presences. But whether or not this was so, the fact remains that this extravaganza of song and dance was enough to excite mass hysteria and to produce a great variety of physical and psychological emotions which must have had the cathartic result of relieving individual as well as group tensions. Certainly while they were reliving their past in this way, the white man and his crazy, oppressive world might well have been on the moon for all they cared.

Another form of entertainment that must have had the same

181

therapeutic effect was connected with the threshing of rukweza, the very small round grain, usually dark brown, which looks like sago and is still used by the Shona for making porridge or beer. The quickest way of separating the grain from the chaff of this otherwise very difficult crop was to work in large groups; each family, after harvest, took it in turns to brew beer of an appropriate amount and to invite the neighbours to give a hand in threshing some or all of its rukweza. The services of those who came to do this work were paid for in free beer and food. It therefore meant that during each reaping and threshing season most people in Mashonganyika and the other Chishawasha villages went on daily or weekly rounds of *nhimbe,* as they called these gatherings. If a particular housewife had a reputation for making good beer—and some of it was as intoxicating as spirits, if made in the proper Shona way—then everybody turned up. Many people invited themselves and they were welcomed as long as they were prepared to work.

To my recollection there was no direct religious significance in this task. But the strange thing about it was that when the actual threshing began, the people threw every shred of shame and modesty to the winds. To start with, everybody approached everyone else with the proper tribal decorum and social correctness. They were duly served with mugs of beer, which had the effect of loosening tongues and ridding them of their inhibitions. The occasion demanded that when the work started, all forms of social restraints, deference, shyness and introversion be cast aside. Apart from this being a time for practical co-operation, it was intended to afford every individual the fullest opportunity to feel free to express himself. In the normal course of village human contacts, a person's behaviour was strictly regulated by a multiplicity of taboos and other rigid social conventions. But on this occasion, men and women could let themselves go and rid themselves of their pent-up emotions. Goodwill, good conversation and sparkling wit came very easily and everyone exuded charm. People talked about ordinary things in tones that painted life in rosy colours. They exchanged views about the harvest, the finer points of good, tasty beer, about the rain, hunting and other blessings. Morbid thoughts or any form of human unpleasantness had no room here and not even the tightening tentacles of white civilization were allowed to spoil the atmosphere. People pretended that such things did not exist.

After a while, a signal was given and all downed their drinks and picked up their *mhuro* (wooden sticks like golf-clubs, about six to seven feet long and thick at one end). They rose to their feet and formed themselves into a circle, in the centre of which was the heap of rukweza to be threshed. Work like this was always done with singing. And so someone began a solo, which was followed by a recurring chorus, while the *mhuro*-wielding participants beat the grain in strict, rhythmic timing and moved slowly round and round the rukweza heap. All the words of whatever song they chose to sing were improvised, thus giving the imagination full rein, particularly as the singers were in a competitive spirit and were, by custom, compelled to shout out the bawdiest and most obscene words imaginable. For just this once, sexual modesty in any shape or form was completely discarded; men and women stood shoulder to shoulder. Fathers and mothers-in-law and everyone else, however closely or remotely related, were given and accepted complete and full licence to scream and hurl at one another all the otherwise unmentionable and indecent words and thoughts that they could think of. They concentrated their singing on their respective sexual organs. Each organ had several synonyms and these were recited with obvious relish by both sexes, who tried to outshout one another in an orgy of verbal abuse of the human body. Very naturally, with the increasing flow of beer in their veins, the imagination became more and more vivid, and this public outpouring of salaciousness omitted nothing. No one touched anyone with hand or lip, no one made any suggestive movements, but everyone recited all the dirty words and phrases they could think of relating to the sexual organs of the other sex; their shape, size, ugliness, where they were situated in the human anatomy and such descriptive embellishments as flashed into the mind of each man or woman were loudly shouted out in song. No one was ashamed or embarrassed. On the contrary, each person in this strange carousal was delighted, accepting the entire procedure as good fun and a challenge to their verbal prowess. No one cared in the least about the presence of young people. As far as the men were concerned, the point was to impress on the other sex that they knew all about them and that therefore there was no point in their making a great mystery about themselves. On the other hand, the womenfolk, perhaps with more pungency and earthiness, described the man's private parts in all their details and as the biggest menace and ugliest things in creation.

This oral licentiousness was confined only to the actual moments when the group was singing and threshing the grain, but never during the pauses when they retired for drinking. Indeed, outside these scenes, swearing in public, particularly in the presence of both sexes, was one of the strongest of the many taboos imposed on everyone in the tribe. In anger the odd individual naturally swore, but he caused embarrassment to all around and had to apologize. Well-bred people would never dream of letting their tempers get the better of them to this extent. But it is evident that in their wisdom and understanding of human nature, the Shona evolved this custom, so that men and women might unburden themselves of all their filthy words and thoughts in a moment rather than leaving them to do so individually under stress.

At the time, however, I never ceased to wonder why the tribal adults who were normally so puritanical went berserk on these occasions. But such thoughts did not stop us young people from holding our own mock *nhimbe* in the bush and imitating, almost exactly, the example which they set in this respect.

Neither the Church nor the law of the land showed any signs of being aware of this custom or, if aware, of trying to interfere, let alone put a stop to it. Christians as well as non-Christians participated with equal enthusiasm, which suggested that whatever else white influence might change, this particular custom would endure for as long as the tribe continued to enjoy the tenuous freedom of residence that it still had in Chishawasha Mission.

There was no doubt that certain institutions in Shawasha society would resist and survive the onslaught of the Church and Western civilization for the foreseeable future. One of these was the *nganga* and his secret, semi-spiritual art of healing. The *nganga* is variously called today herbalist, witchdoctor or medicineman. At this time, he was everywhere and he was master of his rural African environment. Like Nehanda, he was a timeless institution, albeit a less exalted one. He alone possessed the power to heal mental and bodily sickness and to enable people to understand something of the mysteries of life and the working of the minds of dead ancestors. He was all things to all men. He was a medical doctor, psychiatrist, psychoanalyst, horoscopist, in fact jack of all mystic trades to do with body and mind. He had to be, even at this stage, for the services of his white counterparts were still denied to the majority of my people. While every able-bodied man of age paid tax and while some of the African men were often called upon to do certain duties for the Government, such as the notorious *kutakura mangwanda,* to carry heavy loads, our health did not seem to concern our rulers. No one felt that there was a pressing need for a hospital or clinic, let alone a visiting doctor to care for the requirements of the Chishawasha community. The nearest white doctor and hospital were in Salisbury, more than fifteen miles away and to reach them took a whole day by ox-wagon and five to six hours on foot. In any case, at this stage the white doctor was as much a grotesque figure of devilry and crookedness to many people in my tribe as the African medicineman was to the European. Unable to make any distinction between a surgeon and a medical practitioner, the VaShawasha image of a white *nganga* was a luridly macabre one. Having heard that the white doctor carved people up, three quarters of the people in Chishawasha of that period were more than happy to have nothing whatsoever to do with him. Little wonder that they associated the whole science of medical operation on the human anatomy with the dark arts of witchcraft and sorcery. I was not treated by a European-trained doctor until I had left Chishawasha several years later. Under the circumstances, we were in no position to refuse to eat out of the palm of the hallowed hand of the *nganga.* And he certainly made the most of his privileged status in all the areas which were as yet un-touched by white values. When he came into any household, he was given the best of everything, especially food, free of charge, no matter however long he chose to stay with those who had invited him for his services. In most cases, his hosts clung on to every word he said and tried to satisfy all his unpredictable, if sometimes unreasonable, whims.

185

Yet when taken individually, there were signs that these monopolists of the tribe's physical and psychological power were, like the tribe as a whole, far from feeling secure. It was already noticeable that the element of commercialism was operating very strongly among them. Year by year the number of claimants to the art of healing and fortune-telling increased with the result that the reputation of the African doctor diminished considerably. As more and more of them climbed onto the bandwagon of the profession, competition became fiercer and more and more of them resorted to self-advertising stunts, like commercial salesmen, and followed a plundering mode of life which made their intended victims more and more wary, so that people began to refer to the more obvious charlatans as men with the cunning, crookedness and rapacity of white men. In fact it became a common opinion that these men should be taken with a pinch of salt until they had proved themselves.

From my own experience of being present at a witchdoctor's consultation with some of my relations, these people could be divided into two broad classifications. There was the experienced psychoanalyst-cum-healer with genuine knowledge of his profession, and the unscrupulous amateur and quack who was in the business largely for what he could get out of it materially, regardless of his own reputation and, often, the ill-effects on his victims. The first was more convincing because he asked to be paid by results, whereas the latter insisted on a down-payment first, did whatever he had to do and cleared out, probably never to be seen again. Unfortunately, it was not customary to criticize or contradict any *nganga* in his presence nor to withhold his fees for any reason at all. As this was a world into which neither the Church nor the State could be admitted, the victims of medical malpractices had no way of getting legal protection or restitution. Moreover, these medicinemen did not belong to any professional organization. They were probably the most individualistic and secretive group of Africans and there was no method of enforcing certain standards of professional conduct or of protecting the public they served. The individual was wide open to exploitation.

My people believed that every form of sickness and suffering in the world, except perhaps the common cold, was caused by sin and man's failure to live strictly in accordance with God's will. And they believed that God, when he chose to, allowed the ancestors to get angry with their living relations, who in turn would be exposed to the evil of witchcraft, which brought about physical and mental suffering. For these reasons, the *nganga* could not proceed with his cures without first of all exploring the tribal and spiritual background of his patient to find out the basic cause of the illness. And if only to impress his clients, he did this in a most ingenious and often dramatic style. In fact, the typical Shona *nganga* was something of a clown, an eccentric and a showman all in one. His clothes attracted the greatest amount of attention and created the necessary atmosphere of awe and credibility. Unlike the modern doctor, he had unlimited time for his patient and he might take a whole day or week setting the stage for his undertaking. He arrived with a bulky bag of medicinal supplies and lived and ate with the family of the sick, thus creating an atmosphere in which people could regain their peace of mind and in which confidence in his abilities could grow.

The medicineman's first serious task was *kukandira hakata,* to cast bones. *Hakata* were four to five, short pieces of wood or bone, about three to five inches long and one inch thick. Each was marked with characters and from these symbols and their juxtaposition as the pieces rested on the ground, he could read various meanings and messages. During a consultation which was usually in the form of an unequal dialogue with a senior member of the family in the presence of others, the *nganga* held his audience spellbound with his incantations. When he began, he held one or two *hakata* in each hand, chanted certain poetic phrases, banged the pieces together and then let them drop to the ground. Then he made a fairly long pause, during which he stared at his *hakata*, as if in a trance. If necessary, he then proclaimed loudly whatever message each or all of the pieces spelled out. With a quick, sweep of his eyes, he looked to the sky and then to the person consulting him and asked him a question or two. Working himself up to a greater intensity of concentration, the doctor picked the same *hakata* from the ground and mixed them together with the remainder; he looked up and down as he mumbled many words; he banged all the pieces together with both his hands as before, and threw them to the ground. He picked them up again, banged them together and let them drop to the floor, whereupon he picked them up once more, and repeated the process as often as he thought fit. Finally and with greater force, he bashed them onto the floor or dusty ground, whereupon his brow darkened and knitted as he gave each *hakata* a lingering and inquisitive look. He capped this process with a series of quick, shrewd questions, some of which he did not even wait to be answered.

This kind of interview could last anything from thirty minutes to an hour or more and the clients were usually greatly relieved when it was all over. Each session could be gruelling and often rose to moments of drama during which the doctor behaved like a hostile prosecuting counsel, who bullies and twists the emotions of the accused to cause confusion, shame and frustration. It was conducted essentially as a public confession of sins. The healer spared no effort in badgering and goading the senior member of the family into bringing out all its sinful secrets. Pain, suffering and trouble, he would say, were the wages of evil actions or evil intentions. If the family hoped for a cure of the sick relation, then he had to know all they had been up to, what the patient, his father and his mother had done wrong or what sort of relationship they had, not only with the neighbours, but also and more important still with their dead ancestors. He threatened and pleaded as he tried to probe into the darkest regions of the physical, mental and spiritual life of the entire family. He would say: 'I see here signs of *ngozi* (retribution, particularly for the murder of an innocent person)... Will you deny that there is *ngozi* in your house? Come on, tell the truth! What is this I see?...'

If the answer was yes, then the rest was easy and often, after ascertaining certain facts about the admitted act of sin, the *nganga* terminated the interview, and settled down to dispensing the appropriate medicines and deciding upon the steps that should be taken to cleanse the rest of the family.

If the answer was in the negative or so non-committal as to give no clue by which he could make a sensible diagnosis, he prolonged the proceedings. He poured out questions that were even more like a criminal inquisition, heavily interspersed with

188

threats and intimidations that gave one the impression that the doctor felt his professional reputation was at stake. 'Who is this very sad man or woman I see here?' he would say, his face and eyes looking like those of a man in a fiery rage, his finger pointing accusingly at his *hakata,* which according to him could not possibly lie.

'When this man died, what happened to his property? . . . What about his *guva* (grave) . . . was it *rowa* (literally 'beaten', but this means 'consecrated')? . . . Now, now, there is real trouble for you! Is it not true that out of shame you are hiding something from me, some horrible and terrible family deed? Don't deny it! This *hakata* says so. . . . Why is it that your late uncle is in a rage? . . . his fury might destroy this entire household unless you confess and atone. . .'

By building up such an atmosphere of panic and by frequently throwing his bones, talking to and deciphering them, his fast-talking voice alternating between anger and kindness, and occasionally pleading with the dead for mercy and compassion as Portia does in Shakespeare's *The Merchant of Venice,* the wise man or charlatan, as the case might be, eventually won the day. Having dwarfed and terrified his clients in this way, this seemingly infallible man elicited enough information for him to make his prognostications and track down the basic cause of the sickness. Who, indeed, could outsmart a man who seemed able to commune with the very angels and saints of the Shona people? Understandably, many of his clients were so mesmerized and frightened, that they said yes to any form of accusation that he levelled at them out of his *hakata.* And it was then up to him to sift out the wheat from the chaff of the conflicting and often improbable evidence he had extorted.

But when all this had come to an end, he was as gentle as a lamb, exuding charm and confidence, all of which had the happy effect of reassuring both the patient and his family that their problem was not beyond solution. He then spent hours explaining his findings and what was to be done to restore the sick man to normal health. Undoubtedly, one of the most difficult aspects of this exercise was to ensure that his instructions were well understood and that the various medicines which he had concocted would be taken in the right quantities and at the right time.

189

Most *nganga* were like mobile clinics or chemists as they trudged the countryside with their stock of herbs and mixtures. This medicinal paraphernalia took quite some time to sort out and to mix as well as to explain how the remedies were to be administered. Where necessary, he would make short trips into the bush to dig up certain roots that he did not have. Strange as it may sound, some of his medicinal discoveries were supposed to come to him in dreams. This kind of claim greatly enhanced his standing, if only by reassuring the clients that they were in the hands of a very special expert.

And yet when he had turned his back, it was not unusual for him to be the butt of criticism and disbelief, if not vilification, from the very family who, in his presence, had behaved like mutes. If his efforts did not have the desired results, then he was denounced all the more. But, of course, if he had reason to come back and to explain why he had not achieved a cure, he was not lost for excuses. He could always say that his prescription and his instructions had not been interpreted and carried out precisely as he had given them. He could say he had not been told the whole truth during his *hakata* consultation. And so nobody was any the wiser.

It would be wrong to conclude from this account that there was nothing good to be said about these men and women who embodied one of the most important aspects of Shona life and culture. A great many of them were people of great learning within the context of their own environment. They possessed a stock of medical knowledge and skill and cured certain cases which baffled white doctors. This was particularly so in cases of a schizophrenic nature. I think that they still work in many of the areas where modern doctors are few and far between.

Unfortunately, they were so jealous of their secrets that most of their knowledge died with them, and future generations were thereby denied their learning and art. Here is one of the failings in the African ethos which might explain the relative backwardness of the black races and the African continent. Although we are on the surface a loquacious and a gregarious people, we are essentially a secretive, inordinately jealous and individualistic race. It sounds an outrageous thing to say, but it is nevertheless basically true. Unhappily, jealousy and secretiveness do not go with co-operation and progress. Until fairly recent times, it was inconceivable to think of black Africans as a united and go-ahead people. But that did not mean to say that we were less intelligent and less ambitious than other people were. As I see it, it was because we lacked an open mind, a national conscious-ness and foresight to build for the future rather than for the present. Thus anyone discovering something new, particularly in the field of curative medicine, was not inclined to let others know about it. The view common to inventors and discoverers in the Western World, that humanity should profit by their know-ledge, was not generally entertained by their African equivalents. The most they did was to pass on what they knew to one person in the family; he too would then use his art for the benefit of himself and of his patients, but most certainly not for society as a whole. Consequently, until the aggressive white man arrived on the African scene, the peoples of Africa as a whole had not reached a stage where they were involved in a conscious and deliberate effort to amass and preserve their knowledge for the benefit of posterity in all Africa. Colonialism, like all adver-sities in the life of any people, forced Africans to recognize their common interests, especially in the political field.

Yet it is still true to say that this inward-looking tradition holds the black people in shackles today. Admittedly, African countries are showing a greater sense of awareness of the need for unity and co-operation. But their attempts in this direction are fraught with suspicion and qualifications that make progress painfully slow. Indeed, outside the circle of the very small number of politicians and the educated Africans who have a cosmo-politan outlook, you cannot avoid observing that tribalism and narrow nationalism have become much stronger forces in inde-pendent Africa than they were under colonial rule. In the struggle against colonialism many African leaders used to boast that when freedom was achieved a man's black skin would be an adequate passport for him to move, live and work in any African-governed country. But in many African countries, 'foreign' Africans find it harder to be admitted, let alone to live and work, than white persons. To the arbitrary boundaries made by the colonial powers have been added passport and visa regulations, residence and work permits and other requirements which are enforced so inflexibly that the concept of African 'brotherhood' sounds more mythical than real. Black Africa is one of the areas of the world which have suffered most from 'brain-drain'. Thousands of expensively trained and educated Africans are living and working in Europe and America because outside their actual places of birth they are regarded as 'foreigners' in another African country. Nobody in responsible African circles is seriously concerned with this phenomenon because it is not regarded as a problem. But to me it is a tragedy so great that I am often overcome by despair at the apparent inability of my people to pinpoint their priorities and so make their continent one of the greatest areas of human creativity and unity in the world.

Apart from humanitarian considerations, Africa cannot in the long run develop substantially without giving its people maximum freedom and making full use of all its trained brains, regardless of tribal, national and geographical boundaries. America—in fact all industrially prosperous Western countries were developed on the basis of four principles: private enterprise, mobility of labour, shared knowledge and experience, and, of course, maximum use of human intelligence, regardless of its souce. Surely something of this recipe might be of advantage to my people, who have shown an astonishing, if at times juvenile, fascination for Mercedes Benz cars, jet planes, and other flashy trappings of civilization. There is, of course, an understandable anti-capitalist feeling throughout political Africa despite the obvious fact that at heart most Africans are capitalsts; even some of those who openly denounce capitalism do not hesitate to live well and to keep secret fortunes. I admit that in these days of easy communication and thirst for education, intellectual intercommunication is rapidly developing between Africans. But this healthy process is more than counterbalanced by narrow nationalism and tribalism which make it difficult, if not impossible, for African skilled and experienced manpower to move freely within the continent. I am aware that my analysis may be considered over-simplified. But I maintain that behind this lack of cohesion in Africa lies a state of mind which is little different from that of the witchdoctor. He regarded open competition, the sharing of knowledge and working together with his fellow witchdoctors as a source of weakness rather than strength. But he was not alone in pursuing this isolationist line. The African blacksmith, the African chief or military general, indeed everyone was guided by the same principle. The result was that the people of a whole continent were imprisoned by a tradition which allowed little, if any, change.

But to return to the *nganga*. As was only to be expected, both the Church and white society in Southern Rhodesia made an unqualified condemnation of African medical knowledge and of any other manifestation of African culture. Few Europeans either in the Church or the State took the trouble to understand the true meaning and value of any aspect of African life. The good, but misguided Jesuit Fathers at Chishawasha, like all the other missionary bodies, pronounced dark warnings against the *Mashave, nganga* and other symbols of African civilization. In this way, tragically they threw the Shona people into confusion, particularly the young and those who took Christianity seriously. But the majority of the old VaShawasha, finding that the white man had nothing better to offer them than oppression and provocation, clung with greater tenacity to their old traditions. This generated friction between them and their missionary guardians, and as I grew up I sensed a growing spirit of rebellion among the conservative tribesmen. They expressed this feeling by staging the *Mashave* dances which were forbidden by the priests even more frequently. The sounds of the *Mashave* drums could be heard for many miles outside Mashonganyika village. The priests reacted with angry church sermons. They admonished everyone to avoid the *nganga* because they felt that they were messengers of the devil. But the tribal traditionalists continued to patronize these 'devils' they knew, rather than those they did not know. Incidentally, the *nganga* were not permitted to tread the Christian grounds of Chishawasha Mission; but they did so nevertheless, with the connivance and protection of the lawful residents whose spirit of defiance increased in direct proportion to the degree of regimentation and oppression imposed on them by white rule in general. Except for minor mediums, most professional *nganga* came from outside and the more distant and exotic they were the more highly they were rated. Some VaShawasha people, finding that

193

this missionary control was becoming too irksome for their pride and peace of mind, left the Mission. There is no doubt that many would have done likewise and quite of their own volition, had they not been ejected for breaches of the numerous rules and regulations imposed by the white landlords. But these people were intense loyalists and were restrained by the desire to be near their paramount chief, who was now a very old man, tottering to his grave, for his great remaining wish was to die and be buried in Chishawasha, the land of his illustrious fathers.

14

The beginnings of tribal disintegration in
Chishawasha under white rule; alarm and
despondency among the old as the young are
corrupted by Western civilization;
the first prostitute in Chishawasha;
the Arcturus mines and white farms;
visitors to Mashonganyika village,
white prospectors and tramps.

My last look at Chishawasha Mission was in 1964 shortly before
I left for the United Kingdom where I was going to take up a
new appointment. I had only five days during which I could
call on friends and relations both in Salisbury and at
Chishawasha before I boarded my plane. But after this patriotic
gesture was over, I blamed myself for having made it. Of course
I was glad to have met and talked to my various cousins,
nephews and nieces, yet I carried away with me very sad, if not
bitter impressions of Chishawasha; I could not help seeing the
abject conditions and the hopeless future that confronted the
remnant of the African community still eking out a living in my
place of birth. Chishawasha seemed to reflect the conditions of
Southern Rhodesia as a whole at that time.

I had just come to the end of my eighteen-month stay in
Zambia. There I had witnessed what was to me the most moving
political change in central Africa and one which had made me
happier than any other event in Africa had ever done. In those
eighteen months I had seen Zambia's political revolution take
place. It was a smooth, bloodless revolution, an extraordinary
triumph of the good sense and wisdom of all the people of that
country and, of course, of the politicians at Westminster. I had
seen some of my fellow Africans in Zambia ascend into the once
unattainable realms of political responsibility. I had met and

talked to some of these personalities and in doing so I had grasped the meaning of African freedom. In Lusaka where I was based and on the once tough and mentally-backward Copperbelt where my business commitments used to take me I had watched, often with incredulity, the toppling of the barriers of racial discrimination which had been one of the main distinguishing features of colonial rule in Northern Rhodesia. I had also heard and seen Zambian Africans practise as well as preach the spirit of brotherhood and humanity towards the white people who once had hated and despised them. This was a profound experience and although I was not a Zambian myself, I had rejoiced at this miraculous process, which held out the hope that one day all black people in this continent of human folly and misfortune would be free.

Perhaps I should have been content to fly straight from Zambia to London without first looking to the south. But the temptation to see the land where I was born was too strong to resist. In that very brief stay at Chishawasha, the conditions that I saw represented the exact antithesis of the process that I had witnessed just north of the Zambezi. Having been born and bred in Chishawasha, I could not fail to see what had happened in my absence, which included the three years spent in London as a Federal civil servant trying to promote the concept of racial partnership. As I surveyed the scene where I had lived until the age of sixteen I could see that the system of apartheid seemed to be approaching at a quickening pace from all sides. True to pattern, while the white man's 'grabbing' civilization was spreading in its blindly ruthless way, the area within which the missionaries and the Africans could live and work was shrinking almost to vanishing-point. By 1964 a great deal of Chishawasha had quietly, but irrevocably passed into white hands and was no longer open to African occupation or cattle grazing. The only redeeming features were the old junior and senior primary schools, the Seminary of St John Fisher and St Thomas More and the new secondary school which were still going concerns. Otherwise there was a feeling of insecurity and the threat of the total erosion of my people's right to occupy a piece of land which was once part of the kingdom of their forebears. My people by now knew that what little freedom and dignity they still had would sooner or later be offered as sacrifice on the altar of separate development, which, in Southern Rhodesia, is always synonymous with force, oppression and plunder against the African people. As one of them said to me, they feared all the time the almost certain prospect of being told one day that this whole area was European and that they must quit. This is a fate that thousands of other Africans have experienced since the Pioneer Column burst into Zimbabwe in 1890. It is a weapon that white Rhodesia, so fully committed to its sheep-and-goats philosophy, has never hesitated to use where and when its rulers have thought it necessary. And so, after talking to many of my relations and other Chishawasha Africans, I was left with the impression that they were without hope or any sense of purpose. All I could say to them as a source of comfort, if comfort it was, was that their lot was essentially no different from that of any other black person who had the misfortune to be born in Southern Rhodesia.

But we only have to go back to the 1920s to see an entirely different picture of this place and its people. Though conquered, though decimated by the quick-firing guns against which they had fought for their freedom in 1896 and by the scourge of the influenza of 1918, though circumscribed and controlled, the Chishawasha community of that day throbbed with vitality. Any stranger visiting the area at that time would have dismissed as morbid fantasy the suggestion that fifty years hence my tribes-men would have been reduced to less than one third of their number, that Chishawasha would drift into decay, that its inhabit-ants would be further degraded into a state of hopeless resignation.

Yet looking back with the benefit of hindsight, it was in the 1920s that the process of tribal disintegration began when the fate of the Africans of Southern Rhodesia was sealed almost beyond hope of redemption. Up to the end of the First World War there was still a chance that the Imperial Government would recognize its duty to the black people. But it allowed the white settlers to have everything their way by granting them self-government. And for the VaShawasha, living, as they did, so near the centre of the settlers' political and economic power, the effects of those winds of change were more dramatic than they were in other areas of the country. But for the fact that

197

we were under the benevolent tutelage of the missionaries, we should have been in a highly vulnerable position from the very beginning of European economic enterprise. By the beginning of the 1920s this part of the country was already the chief magnet towards which black people, white people and all kinds of development projects were being attracted. As a result we were as subject to many of the effects, good and bad, of the country's rapid social, economic and political changes as were the Africans living in the towns and mining compounds. By this time many of the VaShawasha men were regular wage-earners who worked in Salisbury, less than two hours from any Chishawasha village by bicycle. We were surrounded almost completely by a European area in which we could clearly see evidence of much economic activity. Moreover the education and the discipline which were instilled into us by the Jesuit Fathers at Chishawasha Mission were all geared towards the European order of existence. Therefore ours was a society which was forced to change as rapidly as possible.

Although the old people tried stoutly and desperately to preserve their old world which was being imperilled by the new order, they realized that their people did not have sufficient reserves of moral and physical stamina to resist the corrupting influence of the white men. The corruption became more and more real as time went by and it demonstrated that their bitterness and resistance were futile in contemporary white-ruled Southern Rhodesia. What they thought and said in a country run by a Government which neither represented nor cared about African opinion made no difference whatsoever to the situation. The stage was set for the country's political, social and economic revolution and its price would be exacted from the VaShawasha and any other African people who were in its path. Their only choice was to retreat in sorrow and uncompromising opposition to all the things they abhorred and feared.

Yet the majority of the young people were more than willing to be sucked into the materialistic machine of the white men. In fact they hurled themselves into the new order with an enthusiasm that made the bitterness and despair of their elders seem all the more hopeless. They were lured from their tribal environment by the promises of education and economic enterprise, which, with their emphasis on individual fulfilment, were now clearly the main motivating forces in materialistic man in Southern Rhodesia. In this way the old bonds of tribal and family cohesion, loyalty, discipline and other things which had kept the VaShawasha people together in the past were torn asunder.

One of the first signs of moral corruption in Mashonganyika village was the case of a woman called Misi, who took up prostitution, which the Africans of that day regarded as the worst possible form of human degradation. As far as I know, she was the first African woman in Chishawasha to fall from the state of tribal grace and to succumb to this vice, which was among the first and most loathsome importations of European civilization into Africa. Of course, as white industry expanded and uprooted more and more Africans from the safety of their highly moral tribal environment, prostitution became more common and less shocking, particularly among the Ndebele and the Manyika peoples. But at this stage, the otherwise innocent and puritanical people of Mashonganyika were scandalized and angered when they discovered that one of their own womenfolk had fallen in this way. The conservative VaShawasha seized on Misi's case as one of the best pieces of evidence they would have against the bad influence of the white man. And they not only made Misi a tribal issue, but also regarded her as a special kind of traitor to the good name and traditions of their tribe. They tried to banish her altogether from Mashonganyika, but the chief subsequently discovered that he had no power to deprive any one of his subjects of the right to live and move wherever they chose, and to earn their living by prostitution or by any other non-criminal means if they so wished. Confronted with such a hard fact of white Rhodesia, they could do nothing physically to solve this particular social problem, serious as it was. As I remember only too well, they were not only horrified by Misi's moral depravity, her obvious lack of shame and her defiance, which was shared by her mother. They were also afraid that Misi would lead astray some of the other women in Mashonganyika. They had visions of their hitherto clean-living tribal settlement turning into a hot-bed of immorality which they believed was the hallmark of European civiliza-

199

tion. However, fear and moral indignation were one thing, and they indulged in both to their hearts' content, but stopping the process of licence and its bad effects was quite another. Power was in the hands of the white man and he certainly did not use it with any apparent concern for the moral sensibilities of the conquered VaShawasha. Thus, in time Misi made unimpeded progress towards the profession of prostitution. She had all the necessary natural ingredients for making a success of her calling and she did. She had great beauty. She had brains and charm and ruthless craftiness. Starting in the neighbouring farm and mining compounds, which employed large numbers of unattached migrant labourers from Nyasaland and Portuguese East Africa, she eventually spread her activities farther afield. She went to Salisbury, then Gatooma, Que Que, Selukwe, Gwelo, Shabani and, of course, Bulawayo, the city of pleasure, where white men and black men were reputed to have more money than brains.

As a young boy I used to see her from time to time when she returned from her travels. From these far-flung outposts of white economic enterprise she came to her parents' home loaded with gifts and the impression she gave to everybody was that she was doing a very lucrative trade. On these periodic holidays at her home, Misi also brought other women, mostly Ndebele, who were supposed to be more experienced than herself in this trade. Exactly as the village sages had anticipated and feared, these emancipated ladies greatly excited local men of the younger set whose simple, work-worn wives and sweethearts were not as alluring nor as well washed, sweetly scented and finely dressed as their arrogant rivals from the towns.

Strange as it may seem, Misi had been a respectable woman. She was married and had three sons. Sometimes in the early 1920s our village became a centre of attraction for weekend visitors from the working African population in and around the Arcturus mining township. She was an instant attraction to some of these men. When her husband heard about her lack of morals he came all the way from Salisbury where he worked and tried to settle his domestic problem by attempting to kill his wife. He nearly succeeded, and was nearly killed himself. As we did not live far from them, I witnessed part of this bloody scene, which was fortunately stopped just in time by a white police trooper who happened to be passing on horseback on patrol duty. Had he arrived a few minutes later, Misi's husband would have died from his wounds, particularly from one through his abdomen. During this life-and-death struggle in which both parties had used knives and spears, the husband had lost his balance, giving Misi a chance to wrench away the spear that he was holding and hurl it deep into his stomach. This had turned the tables in favour of Misi, for the would-be killer collapsed to the ground through loss of blood which rushed from his wound like water from a tap. It was at this very moment that the policeman arrived, thus preventing Misi from killing her husband, if she had intended to do so. The white man took control of the situation and attended to the wounds of both husband and wife, who herself had been stabbed in several places and had lost one thumb. The husband was arrested and taken to the Goromonzi Native Commissioner's office, which this time met with the entire approval of the people of Mashonganyika, who had not been able to separate this couple in a fight that was obviously leading to the murder of one or the other, if not of both. Surprisingly, the husband survived his seemingly fatal wounds, thanks to the medical treatment which he received at the Salisbury hospital. And that, of course, put an end to the marriage of this most incompatible couple and provided Misi with an excuse to become a professional prostitute.

There were other symptoms of the stresses and strains that crept into the social structure of the VaShawasha people as a result of the political and economic transformation of our environment. But the case of Misi was, in my recollection, the worst and the most dramatic in its psychological impact on a people who were desperately trying to preserve their social and spiritual values.

As for Misi herself and the family to which she belonged, they typified the adaptability of the Shona people. They were an extraordinarily intelligent people. Her father had seen something of the Rhodesian world because he had worked in different parts of the country. Although he was getting on in age and was regarded as one of the elder statesmen of the tribe, he was a liberal and progressive man who accepted the inevitability of social changes. Misi's two brothers were tradesmen, one being a builder, while her two sisters were trend-setters in the world of dress fashions. As for her mother, who went by the name of Dzapasi, translated 'earthly', she worshipped everything implied in the term *chirungu*—Europeanism. There was no doubt that, given full opportunity, most of the members of this family would have distinguished themselves wherever they chose to apply their brains and physical energies. Unfortunately, prostitution happened to be the only profitable enterprise open to an emancipated African woman of that day.

Dzapasi was notorious for, among other things, her ingrained fear of witches and wizards, who were supposed to go about at night digging up dead bodies and casting evil spells on sleeping people. She had a large permanent scar on her right knee which was self-inflicted as a result of her over-reaction to the fear of being attacked by one of these nightly visitors. The story was as follows:

When her husband, Chipere, was away on one occasion, Dzapasi, as usual, took the most elaborate precautions to prevent any witch or.wizard having the remotest chance of gaining entry into her bedroom. Apart from putting heavy objects against the door, she also slept with a sharp axe beside her. Feeling quite certain that all was in good order, she eventually went to sleep. But her witch-ridden brain soon went into a dream. In this vision she saw the evil human objects which she had always dreaded. They were slowly but surely closing in on her, and, like all such nightmares, it woke her up in sweaty fear. She was trembling and telling herself that at long last her 'enemies' had come. When her hazy, sleep-glazed eyes peered into the darkness, she indeed saw what looked like a shadowy human figure, poised for an act of rape or strangulation against her person. As she had practised many times, Dzapasi cautiously and noiselessly reached for her axe and raised it. Then, with all the strength it was possible for her to command from her position, she brought it down on her assailant. But he or she turned out to be her right knee, for she had gone to sleep with her knees up and they had cast the dark form which she attacked. Her screams of agony brought neighbours to her rescue, but only to find that Dzapasi's home-made witches and wizards had finally come home to roost. However, this tragi-comic incident became a good

202

example of why no one should take their beliefs in witches and wizards too seriously.

Until the depression set in and that was not for some time, the strongest blasts of change came to Chishawasha, particularly to Mashonganyika village, from the Arcturus mines and the neighbouring white farms. The Salisbury-Arcturus road was barely a quarter of a mile away from our village and in a way served as a barometer by which we could measure the extent of the incursion of European civilization into our rural life. We could see and hear almost every form of traffic that passed through by day and night in both directions, especially ox-wagons and, of course, motor cars as well, when they became more and more fashionable. Indeed, to our simple minds these were fascinating indicators of the increasing prosperity of the white world. As the 1920s rolled on we understood that we were being hemmed in by the forces of economic enterprise. The wagons made their presence known by the sound of the human voices and the great creaking and squeaking of their wooden frame-work and iron-tyred wheels as well as by the enormous clouds of red dust they threw up from the road. Initially, much of this traffic was composed of ox and donkey vehicles which lumbered through agonizingly slowly, with their drivers cursing and swearing at their animals and cracking their whips in the air and upon the hides of the beasts. Each season, each week and each day their numbers increased, reflecting the affluence of white Rhodesia and its tightening strangle-hold on our tribal world. On the way to Salisbury after harvest, they were loaded to the very top, mostly with bags of maize, and on the way back with bags of sugar, tinned foodstuffs, whisky and other necessities of the white farmers. The trek would take several days each way, its duration depending on the distance, the size of the load as well as the judgement and sense of responsibility of the driver, *muchkairi*. Each span consisted of sixteen oxen, so that they and the wagon formed a long, winding trail, moving forward at a snail's pace, especially when they were carrying maize. The men in charge, all Africans, except in only one case, included the driver, the man who walked in front of the span and one or two general helpers. *Muchkairi* was very much the boss and was usually envied for having attained one of the best

203

jobs open to Africans in European employment at that time. This kind of position mostly went to men from South Africa, especially Cape 'boys', because they were considered to be more responsible and willing to work. I also imagine that it was a small consideration for coming up with the white Pioneers and fighting on their side against their fellow Rhodesian Africans.

Although this increasing traffic and its human appendages were visible manifestations of European encroachment which the elders feared and resented, they, like most other symbols and novelties of white power, brought a sense of excitement and colour to our surroundings. Because of the good beer, which was always available at weekends in Mashonganyika and, naturally enough, the lure of local girls, most drivers made it a habit to outspan their wagons close by and spend Saturdays and part of Sundays taking part in local activities. Provided they behaved themselves, and most of them did, they were treated with the natural, traditional hospitality of the VaShawasha people and enjoyed themselves, drinking and dancing, dispensing wit and worldly wisdom as easily as they dispensed gifts from the resources of their employers, such as sugar, tobacco and snuff, which was very fashionable in those days. In some cases they brought whisky, no doubt taken from their employers' supplies. They would find ways and means of explaining to the lawful owners why and how certain things were short. Interestingly, neither the VaShawasha nor the visitors thought it wrong to rob the white man in this way. He was considered to be fabulously rich and anyway he was himself the biggest and most brazen thief in creation, he even stole countries.

Being so young, my fascination with these men, particularly the drivers, was in their bravado and worldly wisdom, derived from working for and living in close proximity to white people. Taking advantage of our rural ignorance and gullibility, they made a great impression not only on me, but also on most grown-ups, for they claimed to be experts on the subjects of the true character, the mind and ways of the Rhodesian European. Little of what they said in this respect was to the credit of the white man. His thirst for whisky, his spoilt women, his cunning, his worship of money and more especially his utter disregard for the black man as a human being were thoroughly analysed and

204

dissected by these men who had the unquestionable authority of firsthand experience. This information became fuel for the fires of prejudices of people like my own grandmother whose attitude towards the white race in general would hardly have been different from that of any member of the Rhodesian Front or the Fascist Movement towards the negro race. Yet, while stressing the cunning of their white masters, they would in the next breath say that these people were also easy to fool, especially by flattery. Also, while complaining that Europeans treated Africans like 'things', they generally spoke of *murungu* as though a white person was a 'thing' or an animal, but one which was full of 'dirty tricks', instinctively ready to hurt and oppress the African without any qualms.

In due course, the amusing strangers became such an important part of the local social colour that their visits were very much looked forward to. Privately, of course, the VaShawasha continued to regard them as *imbga dza vasungate*, that is to say, literally, 'the dogs of white men', who were not only detribalized, but who had been used by Europeans to rob the Africans of their freedom in this part of Africa. Curiously enough, while my people were prepared to ignore the criminal past of these individuals, they were not similarly disposed to forgive any MuShawasha or member of any other Shona tribe known to have been a traitor in the 1896 rebellion. Such people were permanently branded and would never dare to show their faces among any of the VaShawasha, either in the Mission or elsewhere.

Once a *muchkairi* arrived on the scene who immediately aroused more than usual interest. He was a white man, who surprisingly soon broke the ice of embarrassment and broke down the wall of tribal resentment, prejudice and suspicion and in time made himself one of the most popular of this strange, amusing and fun-loving body of wagon-drivers.

This man, whose name was Turi, Shona for Tully or Tooly (there being no letter L in Shona), had a farm of his own just beyond the Arcturus mines on the eastern side of the (Baboon) Mapfeni River. Instead of following the firmly established convention of employing African labour to drive his wagon, he did it himself and was proud of it.

That he became accepted by the tribe, even by such racial bigots as my grandmother, at a time when the general run of white society, except missionaries, had very little to commend themselves to VaShawasha hardliners, was a measure of his forceful and colourful character. But he had to be accepted because there was so much in his favour. Turi had chosen to go 'native', as white Rhodesians would say, and, but for his pigmentation, he was a most convincing African in so far as any white person could attain such a distinction or sink so low, depending on whether the person judging him was black or white. He spoke ChiZezuru as fluently as any one of us and had such a command of its vocabulary, accent and wit, that if one heard only his voice without actually seeing him one could not tell that he was non-Shona. But perhaps the strongest point in Turi's favour was that he had married an African woman, a MuShawasha from Chikwaka, whom he made a great fuss of, just as she made a great fuss of him whenever the two of them were together, which they always were.

At first there was disgust and criticism against this odd pair, which caused grandmother, in a bout of horror, to look up to the heavens and exclaim, 'God of our Fathers, what have we done to deserve this?' I thought she was going to faint, so deep was her revulsion and she made the sign of the Cross, as if this gesture could ease the pain and sorrow she was experiencing. This was the first and last time I saw her making the sign of the Cross, a Christian symbol, to aid her in steadying her emotions. She was not alone of course in this emotional distress. But she happened to be the person I was nearest to and, as in most things, she was more forthright than others in expressing her feelings. She said again and again that she would never accept this couple. And to prove her point, on at least the first three occasions that Turi and Rhoda came to the village of Mashonganyika, she maintained a conspicuous and disdainful distance. She declared to everyone that she would not change her attitude, and hinted strongly that everyone else should do the same so that the pair would stop coming to the village.

It is odd that people, black and white, with strong racial phobias, often try to bully others into their line of thinking. Each time Turi and Rhoda were gone, grandmother had a lot to say against them. How very wrong it all was for black and white to contract marriages, she would say. These marriages were unnatural; they were against the law of God and an offence to the tribe and the ancestors. Why upset the sensible, natural order of creation as between black and white? What about the children of such marriages! They were not white, they were not black either, but *mabastera* (bastards), like those she had seen at Chishawasha Mission Convent orphanage.

Madzidza was particularly vitriolic against Rhoda who, she said, should have had the good sense to say a firm No to Turi and thus prevent the union that deeply offended the prejudices of grandmother and her kind. Madzidza disliked the white smell and she wondered how Rhoda could bear to touch, live and sleep with her white husband every day of her life. In short, she conjured up all sorts of indescribable nightmares which were the inevitable consequences of black and white sexual relationship, as if a white person was some kind of a horrible, creepy animal.

However, Turi and Rhoda continued to come and each time they visited us good reports about them reached Madzidza's ears. As a result, she became more and more curious, so that in the end the temptation to get closer to this amusing couple got the better of her and she gave in. To cut a long story short, Madzidza and Turi ultimately became very good friends. It could not have been otherwise. Turi and Rhoda were the sort of people who would have been accepted anywhere there was fair play and by anybody who was prepared to judge human beings as individuals rather than as representatives of a particular race or creed. Turi struck me as a brilliant, witty man, but one without any sign of condescension. Need one add that he was also a reckless rebel against his own people. Rhoda too had an extremely active mind, was just as witty, if not wittier than Turi and she was so beautiful that the local men and women said it was understandable that the white man had lost his senses over her.

At first Turi suffered the inevitable humiliation of being referred to as *murungu,* white man, in an impersonal way. But he strongly objected again and again to this practice. When his protestations failed to achieve the response he desired, he

207

appealed to Chief Mashonganyika for his intervention, explaining that the use of *murungu* in reference to himself made him feel unwanted and a stranger, whereas in his heart and mind he was a member of the tribe and not of the white race which he despised and disliked as much as the VaShawasha did. At this stage, we young people, being the chief culprits, were forbidden to use the offending appellation. But it was easier said than done and even grown-ups persisted for some time in the use of the word.

One day Turi and my cousin Francis Kaseke clashed dangerously over a woman at a beer drink, of which both were very fond. They nearly came to blows but other people intervened and kept them apart. Up to this point they had been the closest of friends, both being about the same age, handsome to almost the same degree and just as gallant towards the opposite sex. On this occasion, while most people present were dancing, singing and drinking, Francis observed Turi having a tête-à-tête with a woman whom he happened to fancy himself and concluded that a romance was just about to blossom, if it had not done so already. So annoyed did Francis become that he shouted to Turi, saying: 'You, *zirungu**, you are going too far, watch your step . . .'

Turi, predictably, reacted angrily and not, it turned out, because his motives had been misunderstood, but, more important, because he had discovered racialism where he least expected it. When their respective tempers had cooled, I heard Turi lecturing Francis, saying among other things, '. . . If you cut your arm and I cut mine, do you think our blood would look different? If not, then you of all people should not try to set me apart from the tribe . . . I am not and I don't wish to be a *murungu*. . . .' Francis apologized profusively and I never heard them quarrel ever again.

Turi and Rhoda became very well known all over Chishawasha and beyond; he was a white man, and defied his own kind and so became something of a legendary figure around whom many a story, rumour or anecdote was woven. Some people said he was not genuine in the position he had taken, but was only being led by the nose by his rather forceful wife,

*Contemptuous form of murungu.

while others said he had been married to a white woman before but had gone through such a bitter experience with her that, in desperation and out of sheer spite against spoilt, unruly and neurotic white womanhood, he had decided to take a black wife. Others said that he had become so tribalized that he fully believed in all African customs, *nganga* and ancestral worship, and, to cap it all, that he had his own *shave*, medium. They said that whenever there was sickness or any other kind of suffering on his farm, such as need of rain, he did exactly what the VaShawasha elders did. This might well have been true, because Turi did not seem to draw any line when participating in the social life of Mashonganyika.

As for his relationship with his own people, we heard that he was extremely unpopular, being accused of letting the white man down. We heard that Government officials had time and again tried to persuade him, often with veiled threats, not to associate with Africans to the extent that he did, even if he kept his black wife. But he had turned a deaf ear to these pressures. Since then certain white farmers in the Arcturus district had begun dropping strong hints among their native servants that *Baas* Turi was not quite right in the head. But he was so deeply respected by most Africans that they used to tell him what his fellow men were saying about him. His answer to this malice was that it was they, not himself, who were sick in the head. He kept guns and dogs at his farm and generally made it known that if any of his white enemies dared come to interfere with him and his wife he would not hesitate to use both on them. As far as I know, Turi never changed his character. The old people often said that if all the Rhodesian Europeans had his common sense and humanity there would be some prospect of a lasting understanding between black men and white men.

Meanwhile the traffic between Salisbury and Arcturus kept increasing and as the years went by, more and more cars of all shapes and sizes appeared and overtook the number of animal-drawn wagons and carriages, emphasizing the growing prosperity and technical progress of white Rhodesia. To our unsophisticated eyes, all cars seemed the ultimate in luxury and speed. They were to us also the most convincing proof of the extraordinary intelligence of the white man. Yet when it rained, some of them lost something of their magic, for in those days of untarred roads, the Salisbury-Arcturus highway turned miry in places. They got stuck in the thick, fast-gripping mud, so much so that the only way to get them out was either to use chains and stones or to ask Mashonganyika men to pull them out with their yoked oxen. In this way, we were able to judge the character of white people more objectively and realistically, that is to say, as individuals rather than as an impersonal race as we had done before. After helping them out some said 'thank you' sincerely and politely gave money or food. Others said nothing, but threw us such things as biscuits or sandwiches. Some neither said nor gave anything, but drove off as if we did not exist. At first we did not expect anything at all, except the thrill of pushing or pulling these strange, petrol-smelling vehicles, which we called *ndundundu*. But in due course greed took its inevitable hold, so that we were furious when no concrete sign of gratitude was proffered. We soon learned that most of the wealthy Europeans were well-bred and had manners and a feeling of appreciation for services rendered. But the poor ones were hard, coarse and foul-mouthed. From these experiences and also from the opinions of town and farm workers, we divided white people into two broad classifications. The good ones were the proper English and the ill-bred, bad ones were *MaBunu*, Boers from South Africa, which, of course, was not strictly true, as I was to find out many years later. There is no doubt that the impression, which the African still has, that the Afrikaner from South Africa is the most uncouth white person in Africa, especially in his attitude towards black people, was encouraged by all sections of English Rhodesia. To us at that time, *MaBunu* were like human beings with horns.

But not all white people who passed through Mashonganyika possessed means of transport. In this great and largely meaningless movement of men, animals and machines, a certain section of white men was as underprivileged as ourselves, if not more so. These were the foot-slogging, poor, pathetic-looking and, to us, aimless vagabonds. At first they were a very small element. But towards the 'thirties more and more of them appeared and brought home to us the realization that the white man's world was not all paved with gold and that in its operation even the white man himself was not immune to the ravages of greed and inhumanity. Of course, it was the existence of gold or rather the belief in its existence which accounted for their wanderlust. Chishawasha was in the same geological belt as the Arcturus mines, where white and black men had been swarming like locusts and sweating themselves dry for gold and silver ever since these minerals had been discovered. We called these white tramps *makwachka,* probably from the sound of their heavy boots which, to the Shona ear, made *kwachka, kwachka* noises on the ground. Unwashed, unshaven, unkempt and often, by white Rhodesian standards, ill-clothed, they strayed into our village to ask for directions, occasionally for food, water or beer and also let it be known that the object of their bush peregrinations was to look for *mali,* money, in the ground. Did any man or woman, young or old, know of any old workings or shining rocks in the neighbourhood? What about the mediums or *nganga,* could they help in the matter and cast *hakata* for the precious metals that would put an end to their harsh existence and enable them to live in prosperity like other more fortunate white men? No one in Mashonganyika offered to render services of this kind, for all the people in the tribe knew only too well that it was the dream of gold which had lured the white settlers from across the seas to rob and make slaves of the Africans in Southern Rhodesia.

Yet while we despised them for their condition and particularly for their gold-mania, we could not help feeling sorry for some of them. We especially pitied the old ones, who looked as if they might die in the bush all on their own. One man easily looked in his seventies and could hardly walk without dragging his feet and leaning heavily on his walking-stick. But he had an African servant, as some of them did, who carried his tin trunk. When he rested close to our village and opened his tin for a bite of his sandwich, the trunk was seen to contain little more than a few tools, two whisky or brandy bottles and a few odds and ends, including a kettle. The African servant explained that once his master was well-to-do somewhere in the Gatooma-Que Que area, but suddenly his mine had stopped yielding any more gold. Other white men bought up his tools and machinery and he went to live in a Salisbury club or hotel

211

where he drank and gambled away all his money. In the end other white men did not wish to be his friends any more. Now, like a great many others, he was roughing it in the bush, confident that one day he would make a rich strike and be able to regain his wealth and importance in the white community which did not care for individuals without money. We asked the servant what he was getting paid by this pauper of a man. 'Nothing,' he said and we asked why he worked for him. He said that he knew the white man was mad. But they were all mad really, rich or poor. 'But when he was rich he was all right to me. Why should I leave him when he has fallen on bad times? I am not a white man and cannot do a thing like that,' said the African servant. Further more, he observed, if he left his boss for a different employer, how would he know that the new boss would not treat him like a dog? After all there were many bad white men, who thought that black men were nothing. No, his master might be mad, but his heart was good, he said.

It did not escape our notice that the gold-seekers never travelled in the company of other white men, but alone or with African servants. Grandmother thought that the reason was that where gold was concerned, white people did not trust one another. If two men found it, it was more than probable that one would murder the other so that he would not have to share it with his companion. In the white man's world, which she feared and despised, and painted in garishly ugly colours, the individual cared for no one but himself. A worrying thought, she would say repeatedly. And she worried that there must be a great many white people where these came from and she feared that they would keep on coming until black people lost all their lands and what little else we had at the time. She would say, 'You know what a swarm of locusts does. It keeps coming and it keeps eating whatever it can get at. Perhaps I shall not see what is coming, thank the Good Man above. But you will see more white human locusts. . . .'

15

The VaShawasha people and their
relationship with white farmers; the traders
and the hordes of migrant workers in
Chishawasha; their hard conditions and
their dreams of reaching South Africa.

Grandmother's forebodings could no longer be ignored. White people *were* increasing in numbers. Now we had white farmers as neighbours. In the good old days, the old people remembered, any member of the tribe could walk or travel over any distance to Chikwaka, Goromonzi, Makumbe, Mrewa and beyond, without let or hindrance, knowing that this was tribal property, any part of which he could use and share with his fellow men. But now every European who bought a part of this land put a stop to this freedom, for sooner or later he made it clear that his particular farm was his and his alone, and erected barriers, such as fencing wire, gates and regulations to deter African or animal trespassers, in some cases employing power-drunk native patrolmen to keep out intruders.

It meant then that, unlike in the past, there were to be no short-cuts from Chishawasha to neighbouring districts and vice versa and travellers were expected to stick to roads, which made journeys longer and more tiring, unless one was prepared to hazard treading on the forbidden territories of white men. Many farmers promised that they would shoot anyone found wandering on their property, except if they were on legitimate business, such as looking for work. Some fired shots into the air in order to frighten off would-be or actual trespassers. But the more common form of punishment, particularly among farmers of South African origin, was sjambok-flogging or forced labour in their fields for as long as it pleased them, without pay. Although these practices were illegal, the culprits often got away with it.

213

Most Africans knew from bitter experience that it was one thing to accuse a white man for doing wrong, but that it was quite another to stand up in a court of law and prove to a European magistrate that a European had done you an injustice. The chances were that the police and the magistrate would be more interested in convicting Africans of trespassing than convicting Europeans of flogging, for where black and white interests clashed white men were still as much above the law as the members of the Pioneer Column had been.

But traditional habits did not die that easily. The practice of taking short-cuts, however risky, continued and became, like smuggling, something of a relished undertaking because it was full of adventure, requiring skilful planning; it offered bold men the thrills they needed now that hunting dangerous big game was no longer possible. Some men travelled under cover of darkness, others used special routes; some offered the excuse that they were visiting relatives or selling chickens and eggs on the farm in question, while the more daring characters, like my uncle Marimo, armed themselves with axes which they were prepared to use, especially on native patrolmen who were so misguided as to challenge them.

This growing menace of private tenure of land and the restrictions on freedom of movement among local Africans naturally became a great source of tribal rancour. But like everything else, it was obvious that no amount of fiery political tub-thumping in the village could stop the grasping, grinding wheels of white progress. Nor could it make much difference to the compulsive way that most white farmers took advantage of their privileged positions. And so the tribe watched helplessly as the masters of Southern Rhodesia spread themselves out at will, each creating his own kingdom and his rule in what was once the realm of the VaShawasha people.

But not all our white neighbours were hated. Once one had accepted their presence and newly-established order, there was no choice but to take each man as he came. There were good employers, there were bad employers, each had his own individual sense of justice for the black man, each his own irksome peculiarities, apart, of course, from the universal attitude of paternalism with which they confronted all Africans. Accord-

214

ingly, we gave each a name which we thought summed up the man's character and temperament, by means of which any African could tell immediately what kind of a person the farmer in question was likely to be. I thought at first that this was an oddity of the VaShawasha only, but later discovered that it was common to most colonized Africans. The remarkable thing was that not only was it humorous, but it also showed a high degree of perspicacity: my people sized up these farmers very quickly. Inevitably, each name turned out to be accurate. At least I thought so.

One farmer was called *Mandebvu,* translated simply 'the bearded one'. But it also meant that he was of a benevolent, placid and paternalistic nature and therefore relatively easy to get on with. But his opposite was given the unflattering name of *Kamhiripiri,* 'very strong red pepper', which indicated that he was an abnormally hot-tempered, thoroughly anti-black and inhuman individual, whom one had to watch for bouts of violence. Indeed, *Kamhiripiri's* reputation stank like foul air in Mashonganyika; he was easily the most hated white farmer in the vicinity. Those who knew him well said that he raved and ranted, particularly if he had had a quarrel with his missus. He sjamboked not only trespassers, but also his own workers. For this reason he was always short of native labour, those he employed being almost exclusively men from Nyasaland and even they did not stay long with him unless they were indentured. Yet in spite of everything, he displayed some practical generosity. He gave easy credit to his workers. As many Nyasa people regarded the acquisition of a new bicycle the highest fulfilment of their material aspirations, he made extended loans and so managed to retain their services for the duration of the credit. One of his alleged peculiarities was having a false eye; it was said that if his workmen were in the fields and he had to go to the big house for his meals, he left his slouch hat and false eye on a tree stump, saying that if they slacked, the hat and the eye would tell him about it. The poor Africans, who had never heard of nor seen false eyes before and any way generally believed that white men had stronger magic than themselves, believed him. They therefore worked even harder in his absence than when he was present. Again, emphasizing his generosity, they said that on feast days such as Christmas he gave them large portions of meat and had ample quantities of beer brewed by their wives or concubines. He also allowed prostitutes into the compound of his labourers as long as they did not cause jealousies and fights. Those who pried into his private life a little more deeply passed rumours that when his missus was away in Salisbury, *Kamhiripiri* took the nanny in his employ for his pleasure. The first time it happened, Jessica, the nanny in question, resisted very strongly, but *Kamhiripiri* took his gun and said that if she did not submit to his wishes he would shoot her, whereupon the frightened girl said he could do as he pleased. Later Jessica told one of her male relations what the white man had done to her and he advised her to do whatever the white man would ask her, provided she was careful that the missus did not find out, for then she might be shot all the same. Now Jessica found the whole experience not only acceptable, but also rather exciting, because it gave her a superior social position among her fellow Africans who, in turn, privately called her *hosikadzi,* 'the governor's mistress', which made her somewhat cocky. But being a woman endowed with good sense, she was always willing to be used by them to extract little concessions from the employer they otherwise feared.

Yet another farmer was called *Kambanje,* marijuana or Indian hemp, implying that he was bad-tempered, but also frivolous and forgiving. One moment he would curse and tell his workers what miserable, stupid savages they were and the next moment he would say, 'We are men, let us be friends again.' *Kambanje* was reported to have several dislikes, one of them being the Shona generally, because he thought they were proud and lazy, seeing that they did not readily offer themselves for farm work except for positions of authority such as foremen or as cooks, waiters and bedroom boys. Another and stronger dislike of his was that of 'educated boys', especially mission-educated ones. Nyasa workers who came to our village informed us that he advanced the theory that the real enemy of the black man was the white missionary with his religion and education, both of which were 'bad poison' to Africans. They said he stated that if he were the Government he would close places like Chishawasha Mission and all the other black schools and send white missionaries back to Europe because they were doing harm by their educational efforts which made black people confused, dissatisfied and useless. He himself did not believe in religion, but if the 'boys' had to have one, said *Kambanje,* it was better for them to stick to their own rather than to accept that of the white man. Anyway, Jesus was not a black man, but a Jew and Jews were a bad lot because they did not become farmers, policemen or anything like that, but preferred to stand behind counters for easy money. For these reasons, Christian Africans or those who had a smattering of education and who worked for him kept these offending facts secret from this particular man. But apart from these prejudices and faults, they said, *Kambanje* was a fair man who paid his wages promptly and didn't much like policemen interfering with his workers on the farm.

To the east of our village was a farm which belonged to a man we called *Muskwatadzi.* The road to his homestead branched off the main Arcturus road scarcely a mile away from Mashonganyika and passed through our fields, so that occasionally we saw him going either to or from Salisbury. His big house, which we could see from our fields, looked like a castle built of stone or cement blocks and stood on the opposite bank of the Mapfeni River. While the countryside was very beautiful, with many trees, rocky hills and streams of clear, clean water, the soil was generally sandy and unlike that of the other farms where the rich red soil was the envy of the Africans because it was fertile and easy to cultivate. It was obvious that there was something wrong with *Muskwatadzi's* farm, for the owner seldom lived there or cultivated it much. The elders put it about that his big house was haunted by a ghost which did not like white human beings and that, despite the efforts of priests who had performed several ceremonies of exorcism, it persisted in making life intolerable for the owner or any other white person. Some said a white man or an African servant had been murdered in it, and hence the angry ghost. The fact that the farm was in a state of semi-dereliction made this story credible.

One day, my grandmother, Aunt Catherine and I were just about to finish field work, the time being near sunset, when we heard someone shouting. Looking in the direction of the noise, we saw a white man dressed in full khaki uniform, helmet, belt, red and gold lapels and brown boots, so that he looked like a police officer or soldier of considerable rank. He was alone, walking towards Salisbury and shouting all the time. I was at some distance away from my grandmother and Aunt Catherine. Having been brought up on the belief that any *murungu* was a potential danger and was liable to use violence against black people, at first I froze in sheer terror; here I was standing not very far from one of them and he was obviously out of his mind. After a little while, however, I recovered and ran to the protection of my grandmother and aunt. Yet the man did not seem to take any notice of us, being too wrapped up in his own business; he evidently imagined he was in command of some troops, fighting some battle. He was barking out orders, marching forward, turning right and left, saluting and pointing his walking-stick like a gun at some invisible enemy.

Collecting our hoes and other impedimenta, we made a hasty departure for home and when we told others of our experience, several of them said that they had seen him that week, at about the same time of day, dressed in the same way and shouting. It was *Muskwatadzi* himself, an elderly gentleman and, no doubt, an old campaigner either in the wars that had led to the conquest of Southern Rhodesia, the Boer War or the First World War. There was no doubt that his nerves were in pieces and his brain was tormented. We felt very sorry for him, but at the same time some of the old people came to the conclusion that his condition was *ngozi*, a sign that God was punishing him for stealing their country. We never saw him again after this incident.

There was also farmer *Chitsiru*, so called because the Africans thought he was foolish, short-sighted and clumsy. He never ceased telling his workers that they should be eternally grateful that they had the white man to look after them, as without him they would be the slaves of the savage Ndebele or the heartless Arabs; and for this protection he expected them to serve and obey the white man without asking questions. *Chitsiru* was so full of himself that he insisted on always being addressed as *Ngosi** and his wife *Ngosikadzi,* terms which the VaShawasha and other Shona people usually reserved for the Native Commissioner and his wife respectively. His workers accepted these instructions, but behind him called him 'the foolish one' and worse.

There were several others, but these were probably the most famous, or infamous. The main point about all this is that even at this early stage of minority-ruled Southern Rhodesia and at the early stage of my own understanding of its affairs, the white Rhodesian farmer was already remarkable for his reactionary attitudes towards black men. In our eyes, he represented the worst in European racial feelings, both in the role of employer and as an individual. He was harsh, domineering, unfair, inhuman and took the law into his own hands when dealing with Africans, some of whom felt that they were placed in the same class as the cattle or even lower. In Mashonganyika, the grown-ups used to say that white farmers had hearts of stone and *mbongoro* (donkeys') heads; that is to say, they had no kindly feelings and were as stubborn as asses. As our own answer to these unpleasant characteristics, we developed an almost universal anti-farmer mentality, which considered that a Shona, especially one from Chishawasha, had sunk very low, socially and economically, if he worked for a white farmer, unless of course he was given a superior job, such as a foreman, or a driver when cars came into fashion. For the same reasons, we felt both sorry for and contemptuous of our fellow Africans from Nyasaland and Mozambique who were almost exclusively the farmers' source of labour and suffered conditions which we regarded as only fit for cattle. Yet even they complained loudly about their lot under this type of employer; for, supported by the laws of the country and its administrators, as well as by their own ignorance and greed, an employer could do just about anything he liked with them. They were often very confused and frustrated as a result of encountering this type of white man. He did not exist in their own countries where the Africans mostly came into contact with white missionaries and Government officials whose attitudes were more Christian and benign than those of the less God-fearing, more prejudiced Rhodesian Europeans. In

*Term of respect

219

short, the moment they arrived, they realized that Southern Rhodesia was indeed a white man's country.

The Europeans at the Arcturus mines were somewhat different, and it was difficult to give them such distinctive and disparaging labels. But we noticed that they fell broadly into two categories: those who were in the mining business proper, and the traders, *maJuta*, Jews who ran shops and other non-mining commercial ventures. We were by now effectively, but erroneously, indoctrinated with the idea that all white men who owned shops were *maJuta*. But these traders turned out to be the most friendly and, as their business interests dictated, were closer to the African people. They were more human and humane. Friendliness and humanity to us meant smiles, chats and jokes as the occasion arose and we responded in equal measure. They always endeavoured to put us at our ease, to make us feel that we were human beings and the result was entirely satisfactory, in both human and commercial terms. They tried hard to learn our language, idioms and customs, which was in itself a good sales-gimmick, for with their atrocious foreign accents and broken grammar they provoked in us plenty of laughter and amusement, particularly among the womenfolk. In turn they were given rather flattering names, usually characteristic of their manners of speech and business techniques. For instance, one man was called *Makokisi*, a large ebullient-looking man, with a big head, so-called because he was in the habit of offering his African customers sweet buns which were as hard as toasted bread and were called *Makokisi*. Another was called *Chumachangu*, 'my money', for he would almost cry if a customer refused point-blank to spend anything in his shop. Still another was named *Pfumandiwe*, 'O.K. you win, I lose', a phrase he used whenever he wanted a buyer to feel that he had been successfully argued down to a lower price than the one originally asked.

Men like these, however, brought into very sharp focus the acquisitive, often ruthless instincts of the European to gain wealth, which we did not have, and we therefore had cause to despise as well as to fear him. The shopkeepers used every trick known to them to make Africans spend their money. They never marked the prices of any of their articles. Instead they preferred haggling and cajoling, starting from the highest price; on the whole this was very effective as we Africans liked to think we were getting wonderful bargains if, for example, we paid fifteen shillings for an article that the trader had priced at twenty-five shillings when the bargaining started. Some, by the sheer power of their persuasion, succeeded in making their customers reveal the amount of money they had in their wallets and then relentlessly subjected them to every form of sales-talk until their victim had spent the very last penny of what they had declared. *Pfumandiwe* used a trick which usually worked very successfully with men from Nyasaland. When they came into his shop, he treated them as guests of honour. He took them to a special room, fed them with plenty of white bread and sugared water (as tea) and inquired about their health, jobs and relations first before any talk of business. Thus physically and psychologically well cared for by this benevolent and friendly *Pfumandiwe* whose behaviour contrasted so favourably with the often high-handed and tyrannical attitudes of their farming employers, they literally opened their wallets in a spending spree. These men bought any rubbish which crafty *Pfumandiwe* dangled before their faces. Not having had any specific plan in mind beforehand, they let the trader decide for them and they spent all the money they had. Nevertheless they went away very pleased with themselves and thinking highly of this white man who, let me add, always claimed that everything he stocked was of the very best and made in England, which in those days was the best guarantee for quality and reliability. But some of us got to know that what he claimed was not necessarily true and that a lot of his stuff was junk, probably from Japan, at that time just about the most inferior type of goods one could buy. Yet, like all the others in the 'native' or 'kaffir truck trade', who had as many ideas as things to sell, he seemed to thrive on overt dishonesty and on the general gullibility of the Africans, especially those from outside the country.

We from Chishawasha, on the other hand, were more circumspect because we traded mainly in grain and we could not be as free-spending as the others. In any case, as a result of our history since the white man's arrival, we were not inclined to trust every white person who claimed to be doing us so much good. But it was from these early experiences that I formed the impression that we Africans more than any other people I know of are the easiest to flatter and to charm and to exploit, whatever our degree of sophistication. In those days, a simple smile or a cigarette from a white person had such a disarming effect that some Africans would part with almost anything. With this in mind, I suggest that it is conceivable that had the majority of Europeans in Southern Rhodesia been able to exercise elementary patience and civility towards their fellow African citizens, we might have been able to learn to know and trust one another as human beings, surely the first and most vital step on the difficult road to the democratic building of a nation, especially in a country composed of two distinctly separate races and cultures.

Other white traders actually came into Chishawasha and Mashonganyika village itself in order to get at some of the African cash lying about. They believed, with good reason, that the older men and women in the tribe preferred to keep their money in tins, clay pots and under the mud floors of their homes, and that they would part with some of it if the titbits of the white man's civilization were actually brought to their doorsteps. Indeed, people like my grandfather and grandmother saw little value in money, except as a means of appeasing the insatiable desire of the white man for it. They neither worked hard for it nor rushed to spend it when they made it. On the contrary, they held on to their money like misers for as long as possible, until real necessity arose. Thus when grandmother opened her tin it was usually full of glittering pieces of gold and silver: pounds, half-crowns, florins, shillings, sixpences and tickeys that had been accumulated over months, if not years, for lack of the desire to spend it, until some white man twisted her arm. Somehow they did not trust paper money and would always insist on being paid in silver or gold.

When the travelling traders sailed into the village, with their gaudy wares and sleek ways, the hoarded coins were reluctantly fished out in exchange for such things as beads, bangles and edibles. But in every case there would be haggling and bargaining and a contest of wit. A very regular visitor of this kind to Mashonganyika was one called *Pondo, Mr 'One Pound'*, because whatever he offered for sale, however big or small, started at the standard price of £1 until you beat him down to a lower figure. He travelled on a very old, rusty bicycle, with a large wicker basket attached to the handlebars, a leather bag tied by straps to the three pieces of the bicycle frame, some kind of a container on the carrier at the back and two haversacks, one on his back and the other over his chest, all bulging with an assortment of goods, including *makokisi* and sweets to give away as tokens of friendship and goodwill. He knew that women could not resist salt, sugar and syrup and, of course, beads and bangles. Almost the first remarks he made were a summary of his general philosophy of life, or what he felt his black fellow men should do for his benefit. He said that money was something to spend and not to keep under mud floors. However, in spite of his charm, Pondo showed plenty of signs that he did not trust his customers, for he always kept a sharp eye on his goods, believing, no doubt, that they might be stolen, a thought that would never have entered the head of any Mashonganyika resident, young or old, because such an act would have been a breach of one of the strongest of our customs regarding the treatment of friendly visitors. *Pondo,* like most others, came from the Arcturus mines, which were so near that one could cycle to the village in the morning, do all the business in hand and get back in the afternoon of the same day.

Mashonganyika, the biggest village in Chishawasha, was most certainly the nearest to the Arcturus mines, the sound of whose mills and time steam-whistle we could hear by day and night. Being so situated, it was the best possible place by which to assess realistically the rolling tide of the events that had been unleashed by European economic enterprise. It was obviously a hive of industrial activity, which, to us, served as a reflection of the general economic progress the rest of the country was making under the control of the Europeans. It made the whole area, stretching for many miles, throb and vibrate at all levels of human endeavour. The effect was most noticeable in human communication, which expanded everywhere in direct proportion to the European economic development. Because of its location and hospitality, Mashonganyika became one of the centres of attraction in Chishawasha, not only for the wagon men, but also for the Arcturus farm and mine labourers whose work-worn bodies and harassed minds sought relief in week-end beer-drinking. Chishawasha beer, made of maize and rukweza, was a real work of art in terms of its quality and alcoholic strength. It was in itself a sufficiently potent attraction for the hard-working, hard-living men to come and drown their cares. But there were other reasons for their visits. Not the least of these was their natural desire to escape, if only for a time, the drudgery and boredom of a controlled existence and the inhibiting discipline which their white masters imposed; they could find relaxation and excitement among the Mashonganyika people, with their friendliness, their relatively care-free surroundings and, of course, the presence of their women, whose charm and honesty far surpassed the baser attractions of the largely degraded, rootless and rapacious women at the mines and on the farms.

Nyamapanda was one of the few places that had justified Cecil Rhodes' dream about the land of Ophir and its gold. There someone had struck this much sought-after mineral together with silver, and had called this hilly piece of Shawasha country Arcturus before I was born. Since then it had mushroomed into a bust-ling mining township, attracting all manner of white men and black men for the prosperity it generated and the good life it offered to those able to pay for it. In the 'thirties, however, it creaked and ground to a horrible halt, refusing to yield anything like the amount of gold that the settlers had originally expected. However, in the 'twenties it seemed to us to be going from strength to strength. From the moment that mining operations began there, its African workers had drifted to Mashonganyika during their free time and now that the mines and their ancillary industries, the shops and farms, were employing more and more people, the current of human movement into Chishawasha swelled accordingly. Indeed, so much so that at the peak period of its prosperity the number of African working people from this place in and around our village at weekends ran to several score, if not hundreds. They came, young and old, men from all parts of Nyasaland and Mozambique, men who had left their relatively poor countries in search of the proverbial wealth, bright lights and beautiful women of Southern Rhodesia. Travelling in big or small groups and out for a good time, they created a new atmosphere and transformed our surroundings into a kind of weekend fair, with much drinking, animated conversation and, of course, that very African habit of dancing and singing, right through Saturday until late Sunday afternoon when they had to get back to their jobs. As they had money and, by virtue of their numbers, could not have all the food and beer free, they introduced an element of commercial consciousness among the local tribesmen and women. The people of Mashonganyika made good money out of the food and beer they sold, the prices they charged fluctuating according to the time of the year and the conditions of supply and demand, as well as personal relationships. As in the shops, these largely unattached men did not particularly care how much money they spent as long as they thought that they were having a good time, and the local people were encouraged to brew more and more beer, thereby causing some of them to deplete their supplies of grain. But this ready-made market also had the effect of introducing to many of the VaShawasha the concept of a purely commercial existence, which they had hitherto despised and loathed. As their piles of gold and silver coins swelled, their commercial horizons and acquisitive instincts grew, so that it wasn't just the Government tax they now had to think of, but also bicycles, sewing-machines, ploughs and the wonder of wonders in those days, the gramophone. Indeed, the men and women of Mashonganyika and other Chishawasha villages became more industrious on the agricultural front in order to grow enough for themselves as well as to sell to their wage-earning friends from the farms and the mines of Nyamapanda.

And so, for the young and the ambitious, these times were described as *kunze kwa chena*, 'there is light', an expression which summed up their hopes and dreams of the new materialistic era that had burst over their horizon. But the traditionalists were not in the least charmed or amused. They described these times as *zuva riri kudoka*, 'the sun is setting', thus burying in the shadows the good old days when life was free and untarnished by greed and individual selfishness, which to them spelled aimlessness. However, they took the invasion of their village in its stride and did not hesitate to accord their visitors the hospitality required of them by African tradition.

Certainly, for everyone there was plenty to live for, if one took a strictly materialistic view of things. The alien workers, apart from their money, brought with them a colourful, invigorating spirit of conviviality, which, for the optimists, made life more interesting, purposeful and rewarding, if more complicated than it would have been normally. Against the background of easy communication, beer and a relaxed atmosphere, these visitors widened our outlook on life. They talked about their bosses, in whose virtues and vices they seemed to be fully knowledgeable. They talked about the hazards and rewards of their lives in a country controlled by largely hostile, mercenary and conscienceless Europeans such as Southern Rhodesia was, and among black people whose social customs and habits were different from their own. They talked about their countries of origin, where life was controlled by a more spiritually-developed type of white man, particularly the missionaries and in the case of Nyasaland even Colonial Office administrators; they talked of their wives, children and their restless search for a more satisfying form of existence. Almost without exception, the goal for this search was Johannesburg or Cape Town.

Our visitors had the village rocking with songs, dances and rhythms which were fascinating, being so different from our own. They seemed to be more expert in harmony and dancing than ourselves, allowing for the fact that they did and said things on a slightly exaggerated scale, both to get rid of their pent-up emotions and to impress the local people, especially the women whom they fell for heavily. Not unnaturally their desire was to be fully accepted, which was not always easy because of tribal and language differences. Nevertheless, word had come from the Native Commissioner to say that while foreign Africans were to be allowed freedom of movement, they were otherwise to be regarded as having no common interests with us. Furthermore, they were to be reported at once, if, in the opinion of Chief Mashonganyika, their presence was not conducive to the peace and the good government which we enjoyed. Such a general directive covered every type of misdemeanour, from politics down to brawls or interfering with local women against their wishes. And so, while they formed genuine friendships with the local people, their social intercourse was to a certain extent

226

circumscribed. They could not, for instance, quit employment and settle among us without official permission. Nor could they receive impartial justice if, for example, they became carelessly involved in disputes with local inhabitants, particularly in marital matters. They were at the very bottom of the already caste-ridden Rhodesian society, with its differing scales of administrative, social, economic and political justice.

For these reasons, most of these men left no one in any doubt that they were in Southern Rhodesia for what they could get out of it, and when something went wrong, the individual or individuals concerned either left the country or turned to crime. The type of criminal who now emerged in the country from the ranks of the alien workers was called *gandanga*, highway man, who lived in the bush, robbed wherever and whenever he could, and raped and murdered women in the process. The area between Arcturus and Chishawasha, which was hilly and thickly-wooded, provided the ideal terrain for this type of out-law. It was infested with *Magandanga* whose activities for a time caused wide-spread panic in Mashonganyika and its environs and inevitably and unfortunately encouraged an atti-tude which branded any foreign African as a potential robber, rapist and murderer. In the neighbouring village of Chi-Gomo, which was about one mile away from Mashonganyika, and where my father's elder brother, Gukwe, so called after his father, was headman, at least two or three daylight robberies were commit-ted within such a short space of time that in the spine-chilling scare that ensued, foreign workers were forbidden to enter our area for several weeks. Only when the culprit had been appre-hended and it was established that he had been responsible for all three burglaries, was the ban removed. When interviewed by a local man called Chakamanga who caught him after a life-and-death struggle, the man said that all he had tried to do was to steal some food to keep body and soul together. He had lived in the forest for several weeks after running away from one of the nearby farms, where working conditions were not to his liking. Because he could not terminate his contract legally, being heavily in debt to his employer and knowing that he could not get a job elsewhere without being discovered by the police, who would return him to his slave-driving master or charge him with desertion, he had chosen to live the way he did and trust to luck.

Against such a background we were taught to believe that immigrant Africans were all right in the safety of the village or the company of local people, but certainly not in isolated spots. If you were alone and met one of these strangers, you ran for your life. In retrospect, however, I think that, considering their insecurity and the harsh nature of their circumstances, they were a remarkably law-abiding and patient people, whose contribution to the development of Southern Rhodesia was almost as great as that of the indigenous Africans and, of course, the Europeans. Yet we used to despise them for their patience and submissiveness. We held them partially responsible for the insufferable conditions on white farms and in the mines, and also for white prejudices against Africans in general. We imagined that without them we could make things difficult for the arrogant white settlers by refusing to do their dirty jobs and refusing the kind of wages they offered, and by somehow driving into their stubborn heads that we were as human as they were.

We never ceased to wonder how so many men could leave their countries, walk two or three hundred miles and more through lion-infested bush and at the end of it all submit to a form of life that was little better than slavery. It appeared that most of them had been misled, and regretted afterwards the adventure that had lifted them from the frying-pan of a barren existence in rural, poverty-stricken Nyasaland and Mozambique into the fire of exploitation and regimentation in the white south. They were misled by their own people and by their tax-greedy governments, whose officials seemed to be chiefly concerned with trying to satiate the ceaseless labour hunger of white Southern Rhodesia and South Africa. And they were misled too by their own dreams of wealth, women and other pleasures of Salisbury, Bulawayo, Johannesburg and ultimately Cape Town, which most ambitious men aspired to reach; once there they rarely came back to the dusty villages of far-away Nyasaland and Mozambique and, if they did they became total misfits and strangers because they had been transformed into new human beings. But in spite of this common disillusionment with Southern Rhodesia's mirage of the good life, once they were

228

in the country, Nyasaland and Portuguese East Africa became little more than accidents in their lives and their romantic search for the El Dorado and the fleshpots of white-controlled southern Africa went on. When their lusty, rough voices were raised in song and poetry, they did not recall their distant homes, wives and children, but such places as Gatooma, Que Que, Selukwe and Bulawayo in Southern Rhodesia and the supposedly 'heaven-on-earth' cities of South Africa. The Arcturus mines and dreary farms and *Herrenvolk*-type employers were mere stepping-stones to the greater splendour of the Union of South Africa. As the Crusaders of old were drawn to the Holy Sepulchre in Palestine, these men were irresistibly drawn to the south, and with such a compelling urge that the hazards of the trail seemed not to matter. They related how some of their companions had died on the way to Southern Rhodesia from snake bites, fevers and smallpox; how others had been snatched away in the bush by man-eating lions or swept away to their deaths in the fast-running currents of flooded rivers and how others, perhaps still alive, had fallen into the hands of the much-feared cruel Portuguese authorities and been thrown into the inhuman prisons of Mozambique where they languished for long periods without trial. They knew also that the same dangers awaited them before they finally reached Johannesburg, including arrests and beatings from the harassed Rhodesian and South African border police, to say nothing of the violence of the Johannesburg *amalaita* gangsters. But each man, as though under the influence of opium or a *Mashave* spirit, was undeterred from striving for the good fortune that he believed awaited him just beyond the southern horizon. Each one felt that misfortunes were for the other fellow and that by hook or by crook, he would get there in the end and having arrived would become wealthier, wiser and surer of his place in the African sun.

But being Africans, without much, if any, education or skill, their dreams for the future went hand in hand with submission to fate and belief in the protective powers of their medicines and spiritual ancestors. They claimed that they had medicines to turn themselves into wild animals, that they could temporarily raise people from the dead and even fly in the form of bats at night to visit their relations in distant Nyasaland, all of which

229

sounded complete nonsense, but was claimed in dead earnestness. But true or not, I formed the impression that poverty, ignorance and lack of opportunity not only bred discontent, crime and violence, but also fertilized witchcraft and superstition by which men and women can do terrible mental and physical harm to themselves and each other. Many of them had deep cuts on their bodies, frightfully filed teeth and other disfiguring marks and they wore charms on their persons, all signifying that they were protected against bad luck, sickness, accidents, even ill-will from other people, including white people, and were at the same time guaranteed success in money, jobs and love. Such fantastic claims tended to widen the gulf between them and us and naturally increased the social problems of the foreign worker.

Although the local men did not on the whole necessarily live up to their Church marriage vows, Chishawasha women of the younger generation were now completely converted to the concept of monogamy and therefore did not easily accept foreign men, many of whom were married before setting out to seek their fortunes in Southern Rhodesia. By their own admission, most of these immigrants had been given wives at as early an age as twelve, a fact which horrified the VaShawasha people. About this strange custom, Madzidza often remarked that of all women in the world those of Nyasaland and Mozambique were the most unfortunate, not only because they were married young, but because a disproportionate number of them must live for years and years without their husbands, many of whom would never return to their domestic fireside. There were youths of about fifteen years of age who said that they had left wives and children at home and who themselves had never seen their fathers. Yet these very same people, who had experienced the insecurity of broken homes, had no intention of ever returning to their wives and brides themselves. To us it all seemed tragic and we blamed both the white man and these immigrants who did not seem to have the same sense of responsibility as we had. We did not, of course, have a real understanding of the poverty in Nyasaland and Mozambique. Nor did we have a grasp of the complicated economic system of Southern Africa. But its effects were all too clear, particularly in respect of the Nyasas and the Portuguese Africans, who were drawn into the system on such a vast scale and with no apparent resistance. All the evidence showed that these men were willing parties in this process of exploitation, which resulted in countless broken homes and grass-widows in their homelands.

This made most Mashonganyika women doubly suspicious of strange men, fearing, with just cause, that if they married them, they too might eventually be deserted by these rootless, restless people whose final goal, almost without exception, was South Africa. As a result, most attachments that developed between the men and women of this divided community were regarded by conservative tribal elders as sordid and mercenary, and indirectly the white man's fault. But this understandable caution or bigotry could not altogether withstand the new economic forces against which Chishawasha tribal society, like a tiny fishing-boat in a stormy sea, was labouring. Women, who became emancipated and found the tribal environment too constricting for their liking, left Chishawasha and, like Misi, threw themselves bodily and mentally into the melting-pot of compound life at the Arcturus mines, on the farms, and, more especially, in Salisbury. There they swelled the ranks of the hordes of indigenous and foreign women who had succumbed to the temptations of professional prostitution, that most obvious importation of Western Christian civilization, as the elders were now saying with great bitterness.

But it should not be supposed that too many of our women fell immediately for the good life—if one can so call it—that was now so easy to find in the towns. On the contrary, if one wished to estimate the resilience of the VaShawasha tribal values at this time, the best example was the average woman in Chishawasha Mission who proved herself a great deal more level-headed than the average man in the face of strongly disruptive conditions. I remember that for many years the number of fallen Shona women in Central Mashonaland, where European economic and social influence had started and made the most impact from the very beginning, was tiny compared with their Ndebele and Manyika sisters. In Chishawasha itself, the influence of the Church, of course, helped a great deal in strengthening the moral fibre of the VaShawasha tribe. The

231

Church deserves no small praise for its share in mitigating some of the evil effects of an economic, social and political order that took little, if any, account of the human and especially family interests of the working Africans. But the VaShawasha people themselves deserve the main credit for being able to withstand the destructive effects of the white system for as long as they did. Without their tribal tradition, their spiritual ethics and their special kind of pride, they would almost immediately have been overwhelmed, physically and morally, and it would not have been necessary for white employers to turn to Nyasaland and Mozambique for the bulk of their black labour. Here again, as in everything else, Southern Rhodesian white society was following the traditions of South Africa which valued black labour, but disregarded its social and spiritual needs. Thousands of men were being imported into the country without regard for their physical and psychological health, let alone that of the indigenous people. They were subjected to bad conditions, including bad housing, paltry wages and were discriminated against in a great many spheres on a scale far worse than we local Africans were.

But the lot of the immigrant Africans differed from that of the local people only in degree and not in kind. Fundamentally we were all locked in the same system—except that the people of Nyasaland would eventually gain independence, freedom and dignity in their own country, whereas we were fated for what seems endless subjugation in present Rhodesia. But looking back on what I saw then and subsequently, I believe that the African people have remarkable physical, psychological and moral stamina which I think Mr Smith and the ideology he espouses in Rhodesia will find indestructible, however hard he and his supporters try to perpetuate racialism and white supremacy.

But to Chief Mashonganyika and his councillors the accumulation of evidence of the creeping white civilization was most disturbing. They understood that its ultimate end was the destruction of the tribe. They could see the writing on the wall; they could appreciate the chain-reactions of a ravenous industrial organization, hungry for black brawn, creating in the young of the tribe new appetites, restlessness and rebellion against what the elders held to be sacred. The rumbling wagons, honking cars and smoke-belching lorries on the nearby road, the seemingly aimless white tramps, the visiting drivers, beer-thirsty miners and farm labourers did not bring the message of progress, but that of the advent of darkness. And prostitution, which they had never known before white culture had burst into the country and built the towns, mines and farms that sucked the men and women of Central and East Africa into their innards and transformed them into unnatural, irresponsible members of the human race, somehow epitomized this engulfing darkness.

16

Has the Christian Church had any
positive influence in Rhodesia?
The education of the African people and its
influence on the people of Chishawasha;
the young are liberated from tribal bonds
and leave to be faced with new values in the
towns; the tribe is torn apart.

Has the Christian Church had any positive influence in Southern
Rhodesia? I think that every honest African will say that the
Christian Church has failed as a symbol of peace, understanding and brotherhood among men and needs to re-examine its
position very seriously. It has failed because it has not been able
to influence the heart and the mind of the European in that
unfortunate country into accepting his fellow African citizen
as a full human being, a child of the same God that the white
Rhodesian believes in and prays to in his churches. It has not
been able to change the structure of our system which rests firmly
and unashamedly on race and colour and therefore consigns the
African to a permanent position of inferiority, a man who is discriminated against because he cannot change his colour. With all
its fine dogma and message of brotherly love which is the central
theme of Christianity, the Church has failed to make the white
man in Southern Rhodesia see the terrible wrongs and injustices he
is imposing on the black Rhodesian. If a society has to depend
for its survival solely on machine-guns, rather than on its attractions of freedom, justice and the enduring foundations of respect
and loyalty between its people then it is clear that its architects
have failed to subscribe to the values on which Western Christian
civilization was founded. Until this record of overt and covert
injustice and discrimination on the grounds of race is effaced

from Rhodesia, it is too much to expect the African to think that the Church has done its full duty.

But it must also be said that no fair-minded African under-estimates the role that the Church has played in the education of his people. It was largely through Mission education that we became aware of ourselves as part of the family of man and acquired the political sophistication necessary for our struggle, which we were beginning even before self-government was granted to the white settlers in 1923. The first political move-ment in Mashonaland, the Southern Rhodesia Native Associa-tion, was led by Church-educated men. This was followed in the late 'twenties by others, particularly the more militant Industrial and Commercial Workers' Union, which had been founded in South Africa by Mr Clement Kadalie from Nyasa-land and was brought to Matabeleland by men like Masocha Ndhlovu, Thomas Sikaleni Mazula and Job Dumbutshena, who in turn sent a young man by the name of Charles Mzingeli to Mashonaland after the granting of self-government. Other African political movements began to emerge. And all, without exception, were led by individuals who had been wholly or partly trained at missionary academic institutions which, perhaps unwittingly, had lit the fires of their nascent political awareness.

A significant aspect of Southern Rhodesian life is that, until perhaps the 1950s, the few Government schools that had been grudgingly established for the benefit of Africans, such as Domboshawa in Mashonaland and Tjolotjo in Matabeleland, tended to produce, in the main, men whose ambitions were restric-ted to becoming policemen, government office messengers, inter-preters and agricultural demonstrators. But schools run by missionary denominations have turned out a much more inde-pendent type of person, who has provided the nucleus of what political leadership has emerged in the country so far. Admit-tedly, most educated black men now see the whole educational system in the country as the product of a deliberate process of brain-washing, designed to make Rhodesian Africans conform to their allotted position. We tend to accuse the Church, both Roman Catholic and Protestant, as having been a willing party to this conspiracy which seems to have succeeded in destroying both the past and the future of five million people in their own country. But I believe that without the efforts of the Missions, which have from the beginning accepted the responsibility of educating the African as a *sine qua non* of their religious enterprise in Southern Rhodesia, we should have been left to languish in illiteracy and ignorance altogether; and had that happened we should have been incapable of seeing through the clever political frauds that successive Rhodesian Governments have contrived in order to gain minority independence. The white settlers are not highly educated themselves, and while they have been ready to use black labour in most of their economic endeavours, they have always baulked at spending money on the education of the Africans. This is because they believe that an illiterate African is less liable to threaten their position of privilege. Thus, most of what has been achieved in African education has been possible only through the dogged perseverance of missionary bodies who have pressed on with African education in the teeth of white fear and penny-pinching; and, even this has, unfortunately, often been misdirected and is, as a result, unsatisfactory. The tragedy is that in a country so completely buried in the mire of race discrimination most educated Africans find little, if any, recognition once they have entered the economic, political and racial jungle that has been created in the so-called Rhodesian 'democracy'.

But since any education is better than none, the people of Chishawasha were most fortunate in having a community of Jesuit Fathers and Dominican nuns dedicated to educating them to the extent permitted by the people in power. It was not an easy task to carry out against the barriers of white ignorance and all the ugly emotions that had been engendered by the costly, bloody rebellion of 1896. They also had to contend with the Africans' own limitations: fear, suspicion and unwillingness to give up the life they had known for a culture that was not only imposed, but also alien in its accent on individualism and materialism. Nevertheless, their work had a profound influence on the whole character and future of the VaShawasha tribe.

Having introduced compulsory school attendance from about the age of ten, Chishawasha Mission was assured of a steady supply of boys and girls, who were to stay for at least six years

236

during which time they learnt to read and write, as well as the catechism and, later, trades, for which Chishawasha became famous until other institutions followed suit. Unfortunately, technical training petered out in the 'thirties when the Government assumed greater control of native education and let it be known that skilled jobs were for whites and not for the blacks. But until then Chishawasha turned out well-trained carpenters, builders, shoe-makers, plumbers and other artisans. As it happened, these people not only worked in Salisbury. They also worked and built many a homestead on white farms in the vicinity and earned wages which were far in advance of those of most other Africans who were without literary and technical training. Thus my first impression of working Africans who were getting on in the white world were those of the VaShawasha people who had had this kind of education. Unlike their less privileged fellow men, they were more alert, sophisticated, and ambitious and as a result more prosperous. Even those who entered Government service seemed to find some sort of promotion, as police sergeants, chief messengers, clerks and interpreters —all fabulous jobs in those days. The more intelligent and inspired of these men chose to work for the benefit of their own people and were trained as teachers at Chishawasha and then sent out as pioneer lay-missionaries to various parts of the country. The most famous names are those of Mr Joseph Dambaza, the father of Robert Chikerema, Vice-President of the Zimbabwe African People's Union, who, together with Father Loubière, founded Kutama Mission, today one of the leading African secondary schools in the country; also Mr Britto Mhembere who went to St Triashill, Rusape, and Mr Lawrence Sawada, who was sent out to Empandeni Mission in Plumtree. But for their colour, these and other famous individuals would have received public recognition for their pioneering work and their contribution to the development of Southern Rhodesia, especially in the field of African education.

Perhaps the most distinctive feature of Chishawasha education lay not so much in its defiance of the white opposition to African training, and its numerous innovations (which were later discarded because officialdom thought they were too dangerously similar to the syllabus in white schools), but in its discipline, which was more Prussian than English. For this Father Biehler deserves the credit or notoriety, whichever way one looks at it. There is no doubt that this was intended to make the African tough and resilient so that he could stand on his own two feet in a ruthless society. Many of these Chishawasha-educated men proved the value of their training when they went into the competitive world of commerce and industry. Had they not come up against indestructible colour barriers, they would have attained great distinction in their various professions and earned the gratitude of their country. Many of them appreciated the discipline, the teaching and training which they had had from Father Biehler and all the other Jesuit Fathers who had had a share in the development of the African in Chishawasha.

When I started school, the authoritarian standards that Biehler had laid down were still being followed. Most boys considered this kind of regime too harsh and quite unnecessary. I thought it was cruel. Had attending school been voluntary rather than compulsory, I do not think I would have gone anywhere near the Mission, for long before I had reached school-age I knew what Chishawasha education entailed. I saw evidence of it in my own family on the numerous occasions that the school authorities tried to force my reluctant uncle, Marimo, to attend school. To start with, Marimo had no objection to education. The first two years were pleasant enough for him because he went to the girls' section of the Mission, as everybody had to, presumably in order to get a proper foundation from the Dominican nuns. These nuns were kind, generous and sympathetic and were all good teachers, whose training and delicate femininity made learning a truly pleasant experience. Whatever rebellious leanings Marimo had in him, he never gave a hint of them while he was under these able and warm-hearted teachers. But two years later he had to transfer to the boys' school nearby. Here the atmosphere, the teaching, the discipline and everything else were different. Here he discovered that learning was a penal experience, made all the harsher by the frequent beatings he had to take from both senior boys and teachers. It was at this stage that his nascent streak of rebellion, his pride and anti-European feelings came to the surface. Marimo vowed to have nothing whatever to do with the school or anything else connected with the white man's way of life. But the school authorities were not prepared to countenance such defiance from any boy or girl whose parents were tenants in their Mission farm and they took action as soon as they were informed of Marimo's truancy.

One night six strong-looking boys knocked at our door; as soon as it was opened, they rushed in and pounced on Marimo, tied him up with ropes, hand and foot, and spirited him away before he or anyone else in the family had time to recover their breath. It was all very quick and dramatic and no questions were asked nor explanation given. A week or so later, Marimo came back, and told everybody that he had been beaten and tortured for his misdeeds. But being the stubborn, bellicose boy he was, he cheerfully promised that next time they would never be able to take him away. He meant every word he said, for whenever this gang of boys came, by day or by night, Marimo was thoroughly prepared and put up all the courage and fight he had in him. He used knobkerries, knives, spears and axes, anything near to hand, to defend his right to remain uneducated. A small, lean and tense-looking man, once his freedom was in danger he staked everything, even his life, and sent the much bigger boys who came to apprehend him packing. This went on for some considerable time until it dawned on the school authorities that if they continued competing with the iron will of this young man they might soon have a death on their hands. And so the forays into our village for Marimo were discontinued and he won his freedom. On the other hand, my two elder brothers who had tried the same game, easily gave up the struggle; later, however, they ran off to Salisbury, where it was virtually impossible to trace resourceful truant schoolboys.

These incidents reflect the unpopularity of the harsh Chishawasha school discipline among a great many boys who did not see the point of it, nor indeed the value of school in their lives as a whole. This attitude was actively encouraged by most grandparents, who viewed education as part of the European grand design to undermine Shona tribal society and dehumanize their young people. Despite my grandmother's avowals to the teachers and senior boys that she did not support Marimo's recalcitrance, she was one hundred per cent behind him in his struggle and said so within the family circle. 'You are the only one with any sense in this household,' she would tell him. 'What good can anyone get out of the white man's education?' She felt convinced that education was a process for turning unfortunate Africans into clever liars, thieves and other social misfits after the pattern of the white man, who was a degenerate, warped member of the human race himself, all because he knew more than was good for him. Thus, to grandmother, to be a respectable, sane and wholesome person, you had to be not only black, but also untainted in any way by white education, thinking and language. Madzidza held the view that not only was the white man the lowest human creature. He was 'mad' and 'dangerous' as well. He was a congenital liar and a brazen thief, and he was dangerous because he used every means to achieve his objective, force and blood-shed being his ultimate weapons, if subterfuge and mendacity failed. Why did he have to know so much, to cross the natural boundaries between black and white which God had purposely created to keep the two races apart so that the earth should be a just and equitable place for all men? Why did the white man come into the black man's country and cause so much trouble and unhappiness?

Grandmother and most of her generation in Chishawasha speculated as to what possible good God could have intended when he created the white race, excepting, of course, individuals like Turi. Deeply proud of her Africanness, Madzidza thought it unfortunate that any individual should be born white or, for that matter, Indian or Chinese and be proud of it, when they should be feeling sorry for themselves. Like white racists who refuse to see any value or dignity in people of African descent, Madzidza found it very difficult to see any virtues in Europeans.

In Rhodesia or South Africa today I have little doubt that Madzidza and all those whose thinking was like hers on the question of racial exclusiveness would be hailed as the proper representatives of African opinion. But there was a fundamental difference between their view and that of the white Southern Rhodesian or South African. These African racial puritans stood for a total, not a diluted form of apartheid, so that they could be left entirely alone to determine their own destiny. But white

240

Rhodesia and South Africa are committed to what Lord Malvern called 'the horse and rider' partnership, in which the riding white man controls and decides what is good or bad for the horse, the African. In supporting her son's rebellion against the school, for instance, grandmother was making the widest possible interpretation of his freedom. In her eyes, Marimo's refusal to be educated was not essentially different from the struggle of the Shona people as a whole in 1896. He was fighting for the preservation of his sanity and dignity, which disappeared once an African was sucked into the European system of education which taught him to despise his black origin and idolize white values and their material symbols. And Marimo's frame of mind remained that of his mother's. He stayed at home all the time, except on the rare occasions when he was compelled to go to the Arcturus mines to buy himself clothing from the proceeds of his crops. But, of course, not every young man thought and acted like Marimo.

I am always amused as well as saddened when I read that in some African countries a group of people, usually young party-organizers who tend to be easily carried away by the fervour of patriotism, have issued a directive, asking all their supporters to go back to their African culture. I feel this way because these no doubt well-meaning advocates of negritude remind me of my tribal elders who undertook the same cultural crusade. I cannot help thinking that, like the VaShawasha Africanists, these people are running away from reality, for the collective will of their followers, simply stated, is to catch up with the rest of the world, economically, politically, educationally and culturally. To stem this silent, but nevertheless raging human emotional current, which is quite consistent with the African national wish for self-fulfilment, is something that nobody who respects the right of any people to evolve as they wish should attempt to do. My experience in Chishawasha and later on in other parts of Southern Rhodesia and elsewhere in Africa has taught me to realize that few Africans are prepared to live by ideals alone. For while a few Marimos accepted and lived by the philosophy of Africanness in the narrow sense propounded by the elders, the majority of the younger people went the opposite way, which had been shown them by their Chishawasha education. They rejected their age-old African world and took this new path because it led to wider vistas. For instance, the influx of foreign workers into our part of Chishawasha stimulated trade and the profit-motive sufficiently to create an active community of Mashonganyika women who went regularly to the Arturus mines and neighbouring farms to sell finely ground maize meal, chickens, eggs and other home products. In return they brought home European foods such as bacon and tea, which in due course created a wider taste for good food and good living, with its inevitable demand for continuous and sustained rather than seasonal industry, which had been the pattern of Shona traditional society. Tribal opposition to this development on the grounds that it put the women traders in moral danger fell on deaf ears, and commercial awareness grew and prospered as time went by.

By far the most significant movement among young educated Chishawasha was that away from the traditional environment in which men and women had once lived practically all their lives, to Salisbury and beyond. Once the average boy had done his stint at school, inevitably the tribe was too narrow and sterile for him; it was as if he had been deliberately poisoned against it. He left for the richer, wider horizons of the outer world, abandoning his unhappy, anxious parents and grandparents to the loneliness and the barrenness of the village life he no longer considered part of him. The eldest son of my father's elder brother, for instance, made what at the time seemed a sacrilegious break with his people; it was unprecedentedly bold and complete, and quite unexpected of him or of anyone else as well-bred as he was. Edward Nhawu, as his name was, on coming of age and finishing his education, in 1923, left Chishawasha, the tribe and Rhodesia by pitchforking himself into the industrial maelstrom of South Africa. That he should embark on this adventure even before he had given his parents the elementary satisfaction of seeing him get himself a wife and beget children was a matter of such grave importance that it was talked about in Mashonganyika over a long period. The reason for the fear and despondency at Nhawu's departure was the possibility that it could trigger off an exodus of their educated young men for the El Dorado of the distant South Africa. They were afraid of the

242

development of a Nyasaland-type situation, with its deserted wives and children, frustrated virgins and neglected fields. Until Edward Nhawu made this break, they had thought that only inadequate, unpatriotic and deprived Africans from abroad could be attracted to this extreme form of vagabondage for the sake of material wealth. They had believed that the Shona, with their strong pride and love of family life, sense of tribal belonging and rural domesticity, were much too solid a people to sacrifice their allegiances for the illusory dream of a better life in South Africa. Nhawu shattered this belief. And they interpreted his emigration as an ominous event, proving, as it did, that the forces of change were stronger than their tribal idealism. Indeed, as time went on other daring souls followed Nhawu's example and left for South Africa. Not even the occasional rumour or letter from these 'lost' adventurers brought any real comfort to the relations at home who looked upon South Africa, particularly the sin city of Johannesburg, as a place of doom. As a matter of fact, such information as filtered through from Johannesburg tended to confirm the worst fears of those in Mashonganyika, whose image of this gold-mining centre was that of a white man's city gone mad because of its reportedly unequalled incidence of thuggery, murder, and other forms of human depravity. We could not understand why any of our people should wish to live in a place run by lawless gangsters and policemen. But these men seemed to think that these dangers were more than compensated for by high wages, beautiful women and civilized Europeans. In short, the attractions of South Africa, they said in their letters, made Southern Rhodesia look like a God-forsaken country, which they now despised as intensely as they were resolved not to be a part of it in their future lives.

However, the majority of the Chishawasha 'evalués' preferred the less distant towns of Salisbury, Umtali, Gatooma, Gwelo and Bulawayo. There they became post office messengers, drivers, clerks, foremen, waiters, cooks, policemen and anything else, other than menial tasks, which gave them a sense of identification with the magic and prestige of the white man's civilization. Disregarding the prejudices of their elders, the young people of Chishawasha allowed themselves to be swept off their feet by this dream of personal identification with the white man's world because it promised them a freedom which tribal Chishawasha did not allow; it offered them the chance to realize their unfulfilled hopes. And so they went to the towns, where money, shops, merry beer halls, lively smoky dance clubs and liberal and wider intertribal social intercourse obscured the problems of the serious-minded, stoical village society in Chishawasha.

It was inevitable that only very ardent tribalists and employment-shy rebels like my uncle Marimo and cousin Francis Kaseke would not join the fashionable trek to Salisbury where one saved up for a brand new bicycle before one thought of buying a decent pair of shoes or suit of clothes. As early as 1925, my two brothers, John and Joseph, both scarcely of age, were already proud town-fellows, while the husbands of my three aunts were by now among the affluent, dashing young men about town in Salisbury; when they came home at weekends, which they did almost without fail, if only to reassure their parents and wives that they had not lost their sense of proportion, they brought piles of parcels and the latest tantalizing gossip about urban life and its fast-moving tempo.

There is no doubt that every open human society goes through the conflict of thought, attitudes and loyalties between the old and the young. But in most cases there are areas where basic trust and tolerance remain and make it possible for society to move forward as a whole, rather than being driven to rigid positions leading to psychological disintegration. But the old and the young in Chishawasha, like Africans in other parts of the country, were not able to find points of agreement.

And so ours was to be one of the first Shona tribes to succumb, through our educated young men and women, to the idolatry of what is proudly described by leading Rhodesian politicians as 'the European way of life'. Thinking Africans today regard the process with misgivings, even downright distaste, because it has turned sour. But up to the tragic drama of UDI this was the goal which the ordinary educated African strove through hard work, self-discipline, savings and unremitting study, to attain. The majority of the literate VaShawasha whom I knew and was influenced by in Mashonganyika village and Chishawasha were

244

an extremely adaptable, ambitious people. They went all out for what they could glean of Salisbury white society to which they belonged, on the side-lines, as household, office or factory servants and artisans. They were having what, in retrospect, I consider to have been the best of both worlds. Most of these men kept their families and retained their agricultural rights in the Mission and so either commuted daily between Salisbury and Chishawasha or came to spend their weekends at home. On Sundays they put on their best clothes, and they could have held their own in any fashionable society anywhere. Either at Sunday Mass or at the indispensable weekend *bafudee*—birthday parties —most of these people, particularly the men, were dressed flaw-lessly, according to the latest fashions. They put on well-cut suits as well as such things as spats, coloured waist-coats, watches with gold or silver chains, gold rings and white gloves, while others wore tweed jackets and knickerbockers and carried walk-ing-sticks and indeed, in some cases wore pince-nez. These were things they had seen worn by Europeans and had set out to save hard for and acquire, despite their small incomes. In many of the exhilarating *bafudee* parties they held, there was little to suggest that African traditions mattered in any way to these avant-garde town-fellows, who slavishly imitated the airs and graces of European social gatherings which they had seen in the hotels and the homes of their masters in Salisbury. Ridiculous as it may seem, they aped such habits as the singing of 'He's a jolly good fellow', 'Auld Lang Syne' and 'Rule Britannia'.

The old people, naturally, looked upon such slavish admira-tion of European ways with contemptuous despair, expressed not infrequently by calling their errant sons and grandsons *majoki*—that is to say, 'a reckless, confused and unreliable lot'. Judged by the simple standards of the tribe, this assessment was not far-fetched. For our townsmen, like most urban dwellers, were a pretty sharp set of people. The example of some of the more openly dishonest Europeans for or with whom they worked, plus the fact that they were not particularly well paid, led them to supplement their incomes by racketeering in stolen goods, especially foodstuffs, such as butter, sugar, tea, meat and flour and, of course, European liquor of every kind, including beer, all of which, under the Southern Rhodesian Constitution and the agreement of the Berlin Congress, was strictly barred to Africans, except on very rare medical grounds. The result of this hypocritical concern for the moral welfare of the African by the white man was that the forbidden liquor became an irresistible temptation to black men and a lucrative sideline for people who worked in bottle stores and whose thirsty African customers were prepared to pay any price for the white man's *kango-pisa,* 'fire water'. In the view of these traffickers in stolen goods, most Europeans were much bigger thieves than they themselves could ever be and so they had no compunction whatever in helping themselves, like the ox-wagon drivers, to the possessions of their white employers. Indeed, it gave them a sense of satisfaction because it was one way of expressing their animosity towards the economic exploitation and political oppression of which they were victims. They said that it was quite easy to rob their masters because white men thought Africans were stupid and, so, of course, they encouraged their employers to go on thinking that way. Obviously, our townsmen were doing very well.

How some of the Salisbury meat, grocery and particularly liquor-dealers managed to stay in business in the face of this large-scale pilfering was a puzzle to me. But it added substance to the widely-held belief that most Europeans had more wealth than they knew what to do with and did not much care that some of it was stolen. At the same time it brought home to me very forcefully the message that life in the towns was not only very tough, but also very wicked. These men, who in Chishawasha were honest, decent and respectable, took on a totally different character when they went back to Salisbury, where they pilfered and behaved dishonestly, as if it was the most natural thing to do. Here, indeed, was a practical example of a people keeping double standards according to the prevailing environment and the circumstances of their lives. At home, behaving dishonestly or stealing from anyone would never have entered into the head of any one of these people. But fifteen miles away in Salisbury, many of our working relatives threw all their tribal restraints and Christian scruples to the winds and regarded anyone who did not live on his wits as a fool or someone who was not 'civilized', as if the essence of Western civilization was dishonesty and deviousness in dealing with your fellow men. This view is perhaps to be expected, in an environment where the white man set the standards of conduct by which every individual was out for himself, for they were acutely aware of exploitation and discrimination by the European settlers. It was clear to them that the settlers' conduct was guided by material considerations rather than by impartial justice and moral values, especially where their interests clashed with those of the Africans. In those days any African who earned more than five pounds per month was a rarity and would almost have been rated a millionaire, considering what five pounds could buy then. The vast majority of 'boys' in so-called good jobs rarely earned above two to three pounds per month and that did not satisfy their grandiose notions of attaining a 'European style' of life, let alone meet their basic needs. Consequently, Chishawasha tribal and Church codes of behaviour easily melted away in the jungle of the towns.

I can remember very clearly how Mashonganyika society was scandalized when evidence filtered through various sources that some of their people were taking up the fashion of keeping mistresses, namely *mapoto* ('cooking-pot') wives. This was greeted with a special horror because it was sordidly underhand. It lacked taste and propriety and anyway town women were little better than vermin. Polygamy was open, customary and clean and carried a permanent bond in which all the parties concerned accepted full responsibility. But this new-style instant concubinage had nothing to commend it. So everyone agreed without trying to understand that up to a point the tribe had brought this social problem upon itself inasmuch as it had built up a rock-like public opinion against the right of married women to live with their husbands in the towns where they worked. In one breath they said that the best way for respectable wives to protect themselves from the rottenness of Salisbury was to stay away from it as much as possible, but in the next they were shocked by the knowledge that their working husbands had given way to temptation; they made no allowance for the frailty of human nature in a situation they knew reeked of vice and moral laxity.

Most concerned were naturally the wives of these *majoki* men. Emancipated by education and Christianity, they were like Western wives and fought on all fronts for their marital rights.

They fought through pressure groups and the Church, but without getting very far because most of the evidence was hearsay; it was as big and as intangible a problem as politics, white rule and white civilization itself. It was something they had to live with. The nub of the problem was that it undermined the once stable edifice of Shawasha family life, the very foundation-stone of the tribe, and thus contributed to its eventual disintegration. Perhaps disintegration is too strong a word to describe a process by which men and women no longer counted tribal or Church marriage as a life-long contract, but, unlike in the past, something that could be broken if circumstances warranted it. Most certainly it created an atmosphere in which women generally, especially wives, felt emotionally insecure, and, because of this, became less and less satisfied with their traditional position of subservience. The women of Chishawasha abandoned their simple obedience and self-abnegation and became instead more aggressive, more demanding and more unfeminine. And as insecure, suspicious wives resort to nagging, this whole development introduced a note of social discord into the Shawasha domestic life which had hitherto been largely confined to a few luckless polygamous families. In a rural setting such as this, where social gossiping and trivial tit-bits of scandal add spice and flavour to the business of living, rumours about mistresses were plenty; no one was free of suspicion. The upshot was that when the *majoki* men came home, their wives, if they had any imagination, would have scores to settle and explanations to demand from their husbands who couldn't possibly be innocent of the vile practice of keeping *vakadzi ve mapoto*—'women of the pots'.

My three aunts, all married, were very good at this and I remember any number of occasions when they provoked some of the most futile and time-wasting husband-and-wife rows it is possible to imagine, and all on hearsay evidence. Aunt Catherine in whose house I lived most of the time was perhaps more outspoken than her two sisters. Seldom did she fail to raise the subject with her husband and always from the premise that she was convinced that he kept a woman in Harare, the African township of Salisbury. His earnest denials did not seem to calm her in the slightest. Some of these quarrels were pure entertainment, especially if they were carried into the open air by the

248

more irate and indiscreet wives, who felt the need for the sympathy and admiration of their neighbours; they loudly advertised the supposed misdemeanours of their husbands. In other cases, the bolder women went as far as travelling secretly to Salisbury, just in order to catch their men red-handed. I remember the story of one woman who, on reaching Salisbury, walked into her husband's living quarters and, finding another woman there, belaboured her to within an inch of her life. In those days many Africans, married men as well as bachelors, were accommodated four or more to a hut—a round, corrugated sheet and grass-thatched arrangement that was the best housing the Salisbury municipality could provide for working Africans in Harare. Anyway, the angry wife from Chishawasha found out a few minutes afterwards that the woman she had beaten up with so much venom was the wife of her husband's room-mate. She was fined both for assault and for entering the municipal property without a visiting-pass, one of the early paper documents that the segregation system of Southern Rhodesia required to control the movement of Africans. Thus this woman learnt the hard way that her husband was innocent. At the same time her experience served as a further example to others that white society was not interested in their marital rights, a fact which is still true today. For even as I write, married life for many urban Africans in my country, in particular domestic servants, is a luxury that they can only have in secrecy and that at the risk of being punished for breaking the Land Apportionment Act and the Urban Areas Accommodation and Registration Act. In terms of these laws, wives are trespassers at the places where their husbands live and work, unless the latter have certificates to say these wives are officially 'approved' and these men have accommodation in a native township. In those days officialdom had gone only as far as requiring a visiting-pass, issued for very limited periods and without which wives and other unemployed Africans were subject to arrest and fines. This system paved the way for the rapid breakdown of family life among Africans, not only in Chishawasha, but also elsewhere. It encouraged hordes of loose women from the less resilient tribes such as the Ndebele, who had been given lands where it was difficult if not impossible to make a decent living, to flock to the towns and live alongside the working men, thus making the 'mapoto-wife' institution thrive. For such women these legal restrictions of movement were easily overcome by bribing the police, as crafty prostitutes do all over the world. Married women obviously did not behave like this and therefore were forced to live apart from their husbands, as indeed many still do today.

No sooner had the men left the sheltered environment of Chishawasha for Salisbury or any other industrial centre than they underwent a radical psychological change. But while they imitated the vices of the European, they also cultivated his virtues, and tried to improve on them, because they felt that they would thereby enhance their own lives and become richer and happier members of the new society. When they met socially, they often dwelt at length on the Africans' lack of opportunity, particularly in education, which they accepted as the key to success in the white-dominated political, economic and social life of the country. They were not satisfied with just being police sergeants, postmen or underpaid artisans. They wished to be something more elevated, to be magistrates, doctors, engineers and so on, achievements which for the African of that period, unfit to walk on the pavements of the Salisbury streets, were like man's dream to reach the moon before the year 1969. Such ambitions, discussed so openly, showed the solid confidence my people had in themselves. I have no doubt that if the Missions or the Government had established higher institutions of learning, they would have had no difficulty in finding pupils and parents ready to make sacrifices to give their children better opportunities in the new world that they knew had come to stay. Unfortunately, no African school of that period offered anything better than primary education, and industrial training was generally very limited in scope. Ambitious men in Chishawasha felt deeply disturbed, even desperate about this, concluding, quite rightly, that white Rhodesia was afraid of educated Africans.

How right they were is proved by the policies of the Rhodesian Government today. Following the example of South Africa, its source of inspiration in the philosophy of apartheid and repression, the Rhodesian Front regime is unashamedly cutting down on African education. Instead of following the path taken by

African countries which are advancing towards the greatest educational revolution in the history of the black continent, these 'guardians' of Western civilization in Rhodesia are actually reversing the process, so that they may continue to hold the reins of power indefinitely, justifying their racist policy on the grounds that the African is not yet ready. It seems that the Rhodesian African, particularly the adaptable, go-ahead Shona, is being penalized for his capacity for progress. Had we not been so quick to learn and absorb the skills which our white compatriots claim to have taken more than two thousand years to evolve, the vicious Rhodesian native policy might have been tempered with compassion and benevolent paternalism. Less than twenty years ago, especially during the short-lived era of the Federation of Rhodesia and Nyasaland when the policy of partnership was in vogue, some prominent white Rhodesian politicians used to make statements which implied that as the Africans improved in education and living standards so would the Government relax their racial system; black men would be treated more and more like their equals. But if one studies Rhodesia more closely, one finds that quite the reverse has been the case. The fact that Government policy has become more and more reactionary and savagely repressive with the spread of education and material prosperity supports my contention that theirs is essentially a policy of fear. The more progress we have made in education and, inevitably, in political consciousness, the more white fear and its corollary, oppression of the black man, have been intensified. In other words, whatever their propaganda says, white Rhodesians are terribly and deeply afraid of the consequences of giving their Africans equality of opportunity in education, in government and in all fields of the country's national life. Only in this context can Mr Ian Smith and his followers justify, explain and sustain their dream of being the only fit and proper hands to maintain the so-called bastion of 'Western Christian civilization' in Rhodesia. Had we clung on to the old world of Paramount Chief Mashonganyika who thought that Western society was rotten to the core and to be avoided like the plague, perhaps we would have been benevolently tucked away in some kind of a human zoo in the remote recesses of the Zambezi valley or the Sabi River for the curiosity of anthropologists and of

251

those whose charity and compassion are aroused only when men are actually caged and starved like animals.

But my grown-up cousins, uncles, nephews and all the other relations and friends in the tribe, who graduated from Chishawasha school, did not cherish the old world, the Zambezi Valley or the thought of being permanent hewers of wood and drawers of water. Neither were they content to be impersonal, sheepish kitchen servants. The white man himself had, through education, made them discover themselves, and they wanted everything he wanted, to be everything he wished to be, to work and sweat and toil in the interests of personal gain, to rule and to govern, to tame their circumstances to their convenience and at the end of the day to sit back and indulge in the dignity of feeling that in their own country, the only one they have, they were exactly like other people. It was this compulsion which made them work hard and invest what they had earned in good clothes, good living and in building better houses, which they equipped with the gadgets and trappings of white culture.

But events have proved that they and all those who came after them, including myself, were not only burning their boats behind them, but were also frightening the white man on whose doors they were knocking; they were providing him with additional reasons, apart from those learned in 1893 and 1896, to barricade himself within a fortification whose finishing touches were completed on 11th November 1965, and is now garrisoned by troops from South Africa.

Postscript

As the decade of the 1920s approached its closing stages, Mashonganyika village lost more and more of its character, thus giving way to the influence of the young town-dwellers, with their money and their outlandish ways—parties, dances and talk.

But most important of all, the tribal elders began to die one by one. The first one to go was my father's elder brother, Gukwe. He was an important man, almost next to Paramount Chief Mashonganyika and had his own small domain, a village called Chi-Gomo, or Che-Gomo, because it was situated on high ground and was surrounded by hills. He suffered from what at first looked like a harmless boil in his ear-drum. But as time went on this condition grew worse and worse. His wife who was a medium and regarded by most people as an expert at spotting the causes of sickness was unable to help him. It soon became obvious that Gukwe could not possibly recover. Several weeks later he died. But, like most people of his generation who refused to accept Christianity while they were still sound of body and of mind, he finally agreed to be baptized when he realized that the end was near. He was buried with a mixture of tribal and Church rites.

Several other distinguished men and women soon died. Each death was the end of an important era and this was reflected by the remaining men and women of their generation, who withdrew more and more into themselves, becoming less and less interested in the political, economic and social revolution that was going on around them.

The final passing of the old world came when Paramount Chief Mashonganyika himself died, again coming to terms with Christianity in his last moments. Practically the whole of Chishawasha African society was plunged into mourning. African mourning is something in which emotions are given full rein and literally means screaming and shedding floods of tears in a display of human feelings. It is something in which some of those very close to the dead, especially the women, throw themselves to the ground in utter and complete despair, as if death was not a common occurrence. There were *Mashave* dances in all their intricacies and richness. Everyone paid their *chimuti,* a token farewell gift of money which was laid on the body of the Chief during his lying-in-state. Towards sunset, he was borne on a stretcher amid traditional funeral songs and prayers and was buried at the Mission cemetery.

The death of Mashonganyika was the end of the Chishawasha tribe in the old sense. Certainly physically it was the end of Mashonganyika village. From the very moment of his death, everybody knew they had to break up and settle elsewhere. And within a short space of time, after the death of the Chief, everyone had done so. Many families went to the Goromonzi area, others to Chikwaka and others to Domboshawa, while Christians, including my family, moved some distance away but remained in Chishawasha itself.

It was part of the Shawasha tradition. When an illustrious Chief died, the village that was wholly identified with his rule and personality had to be abandoned.

DT 962.5   Vambe
V34
1972   An ill-fated poeple

DT 962.5   Vambe
V34
1972   An ill-fated people

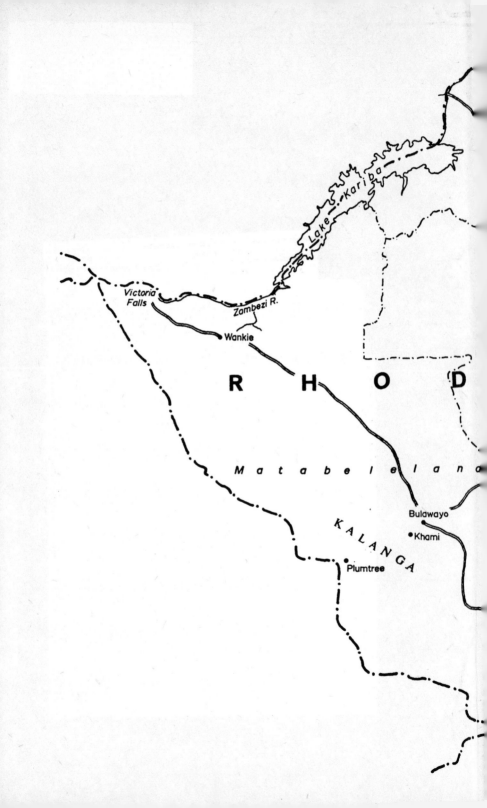